The Stylistics of Poetry

ADVANCES IN STYLISTICS

Series editor: Dan McIntyre, University of Huddersfield, UK

Editorial board: Beatrix Busse, University of Berne, Switzerland, Szilvia Csábi, Eötvös Loránd University, Hungary, Monika Fludernik, University of Freiburg, Germany, Lesley Jeffries, University of Huddersfield, UK, Jean Boase-Beier, University of East Anglia, UK, Peter Verdonk, University of Amsterdam (Emeritus), The Netherlands, Geoffrey Leech, Lancaster University, UK, Larry Stewart, College of Wooster, USA, Manuel Jobert, Jean Moulin University, Lyon 3, France

Other titles in the series:

Chick Lit: The Stylistics of Cappuccino Fiction
Rocío Montoro

Corpus Stylistics in Principles and Practice
Yufang Ho

D. H. Lawrence and Narrative Viewpoint
Violeta Sotirova

Discourse of Italian Cinema and Beyond
Roberta Piazza

I. A. Richards and the Rise of Cognitive Stylistics
David West

Oppositions and Ideology in News Discourse
Matt Davies

Opposition in Discourse
Lesley Jeffries

Pedagogical Stylistics
Michael Burke, Szilvia Csábi, Lara Week and Judit Zerkowitz

Stylistics and Shakespeare's Language
Mireille Ravassat

The Stylistics of Poetry

Context, cognition, discourse, history

PETER VERDONK

Advances in Stylistics

BLOOMSBURY

LONDON · NEW DELHI · NEW YORK · SYDNEY

Bloomsbury Academic
An imprint of Bloomsbury Publishing Plc

50 Bedford Square	1385 Broadway
London	New York
WC1B 3DP	NY 10018
UK	USA

www.bloomsbury.com

First published 2013

British Library Cataloguing-in-Publication Data
A catalogue record for this book is available from the British Library.

ISBN: HB: 978-1-4411-5878-9
PB: 978-1-4411-6790-3
ePDF: 978-1-4411-4480-5
ePub: 978-1-4411-2850-8

Library of Congress Cataloging-in-Publication Data
Verdonk, Peter, 1935–
The stylistics of poetry: context, cognition, discourse, history/Peter Verdonk.
pages cm. – (Advances in Stylistics)
Includes bibliographical references and index.
ISBN 978-1-4411-5878-9 (hardcover) – ISBN 978-1-4411-6790-3 (pbk.) –
ISBN 978-1-4411-4480-5 (pdf) – ISBN 978-1-4411-2850-8 (epub)
1. Poetry, Modern–History and criticism. 2. Style, Literary.
3. Poetry–Authorship. I. Title.
PN1271.V47 2013
809.1'04–dc23
2013007976

Typeset by Deanta Global Publishing Services, Chennai, India
Printed and bound in India

To Henry Widdowson

Contents

Acknowledgements

First of all, I would like to express my deep sense of gratitude to Dan McIntyre of the University of Huddersfield, the editor of the Bloomsbury Academic book series *Advances in Stylistics*. From the moment I had told him I was considering the possibility of publishing a selection of my papers written in the last 30 years or so, he became the driving force behind this project. His enthusiasm and commitment were boundless, culminating in writing the introductory chapter to the book in which he showed his absolute mastery of summing up and capturing the essence of what I had written. To get a better insight into my motivation and drive, Dan asked me a couple of questions about my educational and professional background as well as the early beginnings of my long-standing membership of the Poetics and Linguistics Association, otherwise known as PALA. With a great generosity of spirit, he has most delicately interwoven the professional with the personal in a way I could obviously never have done myself.

There are also numerous others, friends and colleagues inside and outside PALA, former graduate and PhD students, who wittingly or unwittingly influenced my thinking on the stylistics of poetry and therewith my criteria for making this selection. At the risk of overlooking some people, who I hope will forgive me, I acknowledge the generous support of Tony Bex, Michael Burke, Beatrix Busse, Jan Machiel Butter, Joke Bijleveld, Ron Carter, Robert Cockcroft, Jonathan Culpeper, Cathy Emmott, Joanna Gavins, Ray Gibbs, Geoff Hall, Craig Hamilton, Leo Huisman, Lesley Jeffries, Geoffrey Leech, Walter (Bill) Nash, Nina Nørgaard, Roger D. Sell, Elena Semino, Mick Short, Paul Simpson, Gerard Steen, Peter Stockwell, Michael Toolan, Katie Wales, Jean Jacques Weber, Henry Widdowson and Sonia Zyngier.

I am also grateful to those who helped me with advice or otherwise at the time when I wrote the original articles. Their names are to be found in the relevant chapter notes at the end of the book.

It seems to me that in anybody's academic career, there is always one person to whom a researcher and writer feels professionally most indebted. In my case, this is undoubtedly Henry Widdowson, whose works had a profound influence on my thinking from the very beginning I became interested in stylistics. Particularly during the time when he was my editor in the series

Oxford Introductions to Language Study, to which he had kindly invited me to contribute a volume on stylistics, he has actively shaped my ideas on fundamental concepts such as style in literature, reference and representation, the nature of text and discourse, the context of literary discourse, the relationship between stylistics and literary criticism and, last but not least, the educational relevance of stylistics. It is for these and more personal reasons that I wish to dedicate this book to Henry Widdowson.

Copyright acknowledgements

The author and publishers are grateful for permission to reproduce the following copyright material:

'Poetic artifice and literary stylistics' from Theo D'haen (ed.) *Linguistics and the Study of Literature*, 1986, pp. 42–55, by permission of Editions Rodopi, Amsterdam/New York.

'We have art in order that we may not perish from truth: The universe of discourse in Auden's "Musée des Beaux Arts"' from *Dutch Quarterly Review of Anglo-American Letters*, 17.2 (1987), pp. 78–96, by permission of Editions Rodopi, Amsterdam/New York.

'Who are the performers of Owen's "Anthem for Doomed Youth"'? from *The Journal of the Poetics and Linguistics Association*, 1.2 (1988), pp. 203–22, by permission of the editors Mick Short, Nelson Taylor and Carol Bellard-Thomson.

'The language of poetry: the application of literary stylistic theory in university teaching' from Mick Short (ed.) *Reading, Analysing and Teaching Literature*, 1989, pp. 241–66, by permission of Longman/Pearson Education, Harlow, Essex.

'Poetry as text and discourse: the poetics of Philip Larkin' from Roger D. Sell (ed.) *Literary Pragmatics*, 1991, pp. 94–109, by permission of Routledge/Taylor & Francis Books UK, London.

'Poetry and public life: a contextualized reading of Heaney's "Punishment"' from Peter Verdonk (ed.) *Twentieth-century Poetry: From Text to Context*, 1993, pp. 112–33, by permission of Routledge/Taylor & Francis Books UK, London.

'The liberation of the icon: a brief survey from classical rhetoric to cognitive stylistics', from *Journal of Literary Studies*, 15 (3/4) (1999), pp. 291–304, by permission of Andries W. Oliphant, on behalf of the editorial board.

'Painting, poetry, parallelism: ekphrasis, stylistics and cognitive poetics' from *Language and Literature*, 14.3 (2005), pp. 231–44, by permission of SAGE Publications Ltd, London.

'Style' from Brown, K. (editor-in-chief) *Encyclopedia of Language and Linguistics, Second Edition*, volume 12, pp. 196–210, by permission of Elsevier Limited, Oxford.

1

Context, cognition, discourse, history: Peter Verdonk's stylistics of poetry (Dan McIntyre)

This book is a collection of Peter Verdonk's most important and influential articles, written over a period of approximately 30 years. All of them concentrate on the stylistics of poetry and thereby represent a longitudinal view of the stylistic treatment of this most prototypical of the literary genres. Some of the chapters in this book will be familiar to readers while others may be less so; several of the earlier chapters in particular were originally published in journals and collections that are now difficult to get hold of. This is the nature of academic publishing and one of its downsides is that the concentrated thoughts of a writer can appear diluted as his or her work is disseminated across a wide variety of books and journals, each with a different range and readership. To have these articles in one place enables the readers to appreciate the depth of scholarship that each represents and to see more clearly the interrelations between them and the development of particular lines of thought. Stylistics develops so rapidly, as theories are tested and new methodologies are developed, that it is sometimes useful to stand still for a moment and take stock of where we have come from and where we are heading. This book offers such an opportunity because it is far more than a career retrospective. It is a road map of a discipline and offers detailed descriptions and evaluations of now familiar terrain as well as valuable speculations on what awaits us in new, as yet uncharted territories.

Poems as objects of study

In the early days of stylistics, poems were seen as ideal objects of study, since they tended to be short enough to be analysed in full (cf. prose fiction) while also being exemplars *par excellence* of the foregrounding that was held to be central to a literary prototype (Leech 2008: 5). This, though, can give rise to the misguided assumption that poems are somehow easier to study stylistically than other types of text. It is certainly true that prose fiction brings with it its own set of problems; novels and stories are, by their nature, long and it is difficult to manage this factor analytically. As for drama, it was not until the advent of pragmatics and its tools for the analysis of dialogue that the study of this genre was made possible (though, interestingly, prior to the availability of pragmatic tools of analysis, stylisticians were effectively limited to treating dramatic dialogue as they would verse). Nonetheless, it would be a mistake to assume that poetry is, by contrast, an easy genre to study stylistically simply because it tends not to have the complex discourse structures of other genres (Short 1996). Poems are complex texts in lots of ways. Jeffries (2008) suggests that the text worlds of particular types of poems are often not fully specified, making reader involvement in those fictional worlds difficult and comprehension of the texts themselves equally tricky, as a result of, for instance, deliberately obtuse deictic reference. It may also be the case that, in poetry, we find Grice's (1975) maxim of manner suspended almost as a matter of course, meaning that interpreting poetry can be a much more complex task than interpreting prose or drama. This brings us to what is perhaps the defining characteristic of what Leech (2008: 54) terms 'evaluative stylistics' (cf. purely descriptive stylistics), where the aim of the analyst is to understand the relationship between the linguistic form of the text and its intrinsic function, or literary effect. This has been the most widely practised kind of stylistics and is notoriously difficult to get right. If a stylistician whose aim is to produce an evaluative stylistic analysis stops short of establishing the literary functions of particular linguistic structures, his or her study will be regarded as incomplete or, worse, pedestrian and futile. Sinclair's (1966) now famous analysis of Philip Larkin's poem 'First Sight' has been criticized for exactly this, that is, being a descriptive analysis that fails to offer a full evaluation of the text under consideration (see, for instance, Vendler 1966: 461, who describes Sinclair's analysis as 'unreadable and barbaric', and Melia 1974), though it should be noted that Sinclair himself was sceptical of the ability of stylistics to deal with evaluative concerns.

So stylistics, as understood by most contemporary practitioners, involves evaluation, at least in as much as ascertaining a meaning for the text in question, if not proposing a value judgement of it. The difficulty here is ensuring that we do not succumb to what Simpson (1993) calls interpretive positivism, whereby we suppose a causal link between a particular linguistic form and a particular literary effect and assume it to be the case for all time. Language does not work like this and, over the years, research has explored how interpretive effects can vary according to the schematic knowledge of readers (Semino 1997 and Jeffries 2001), the situation of reading (McIntyre 2006), the cognitive awareness of readers (Stockwell 2009) and, indeed, the degree of reading experience that a reader has (Culler 1975). This, though, is not to suggest that, in terms of interpreting texts, anything goes. No stylistician would claim there is only ever one interpretation of a text but, equally, none would claim an infinite number of potential readings. Rather, it would seem, for any one text, there is a limited number of interpretations that are convincing. Indeed, Short et al. (2011) suggest that where differences do exist between readers' interpretations of a text, these tend to be minor variances; rather than seeing these as different interpretations, we are better considering them as different readings of a higher order interpretation.

All of the above is to say that poems encompass myriad complexities, all of which must be negotiated by the stylistician of poetry, and all of which go towards making poetry a particularly difficult genre for stylistic study. Poetry is challenging. Poems can be difficult to read, difficult to interpret and difficult to understand. For poetry lovers, this challenge is undoubtedly part of poetry's appeal. It is a texttype that demands substantial work from its readers. And for readers who are willing to invest the time and energy, it offers much in return. But the challenge of poetry can also be off-putting. Students who are new to poetry can often find the obtuseness of propositional content or the complexity of form impossible to account for. Poems can seem impenetrable and unrewarding, and after struggling to no avail to come to some understanding of a poem, it is no surprise that some readers are quickly put off poetry for good. For the stylistician, this leads to a wealth of interesting research questions. What makes (some) poetry difficult to read and interpret? How might the analysis of poetry aid interpretation? What is the relationship between form and meaning in poems? And from a pedagogical perspective, what is the best way to approach poetry in order to get the most out of it? These are all questions that Peter Verdonk has worked on, directly or indirectly, throughout his long career. This book collects together some of his answers and offers genuine practical insights into the reading, analysis and understanding of poetry.

From law to language and literature: Peter Verdonk's career in stylistics

Over the course of his career, Peter Verdonk has established a reputation as both a first-class linguist and a sensitive literary critic. His trilogy of edited books on the three main literary genres (Verdonk 1993, Verdonk and Weber

1995 and Culpeper et al. 1998) are required reading for any student of stylistics, while his textbook *Stylistics* (Verdonk 2002) is a model of conciseness and a perfect exemplar of the fusion of linguistics and literary criticism. His journal articles and book chapters are read widely by his academic peers and, as can be seen in this collection, prefigure much of what are now contemporary trends in stylistics. He was, as far as I am aware, the only professor of stylistics in the world (it is interesting to note how most stylisticians prefer an alternative designation) and although now retired from his post at the University of Amsterdam, he retains an Emeritus Professorship there and continues to produce new and insightful work and to champion stylistics internationally.

When I began writing this introduction, I asked Peter what had led him to work on poetry so much throughout his career. His answer was that this was a decision made largely for pragmatic reasons. With a heavy teaching load and numerous administrative responsibilities at department, faculty and university levels, he simply did not have the time to work on longer texts. There is an interesting parallel here with the concerns of the earliest stylisticians, namely that, for them, poems as objects of study were also chosen pragmatically, since the methodological problems associated with studying longer texts were too great to deal with. Nonetheless, it is all but impossible to study poetry without having a strong attraction to it, and so it is no surprise to find that Peter Verdonk's love for poetry is long-standing. In response to my question of what first attracted him to poetry, and why, particularly, poetry in English, he had this to say:

Since my secondary school days I have always felt attracted to poetry because of its strong appeal to my imagination, its terse and at the same time pregnant language, and of course the aesthetic enchantment of its rhythms. At the end of my schooldays I even secretly tried to translate the Dutch Romantic poets into English. Without much success of course, but it just shows that I was deeply in love with the English language. This affection only deepened when I began to study Old English and realized the close kinship between English and Dutch in its Germanic roots. My grandfather was a West-Frisian fisherman (a wonderful man!) and in his dialect I recognized lots of phonetic features which closely resembled those of Old English, which I taught for many years in extra-mural courses for prospective teachers of English in secondary education. Perhaps this accounts for my deep affection for the English language. It might also account for the attention I have often paid in my writings to the contrasting lexical make-up of Germanic Anglo-Saxon and Latinate Norman French ever since the Conquest [e.g., Verdonk 2010: 91–2].

Poetry, then, offered far more to Peter than a pragmatic solution to administrative burdens. But I was also curious to learn what it was that had led him to approach poetry from a linguistic perspective. Stylistics, of course, is well established in universities outside the United Kingdom, where it often has more of a foothold in the mainstream than it does in Britain (e.g., Chesnokova and Yakuba 2011). Part of its appeal is its potential for offering a way into literature through language, which is often a more manageable method of accessing literature than approaching it via literary theory and cultural studies (whether we are talking about literature in English or any other language). Peter Verdonk's pre-academic background is interesting here. Prior to moving into academia, he worked in international maritime law. Although he had wanted to study English Language and Literature at university, he was sent instead to a secondary school which specialized in training pupils for careers in commerce. Since, at that time, admission to Dutch universities to study languages required a background in Greek and Latin, Peter could not switch careers until he had gained the necessary qualifications in the classics. He therefore set himself to studying these in the evenings until he had sufficient experience to undertake a degree in English Language and Literature. This degree of dedication is indicative of Peter's commitment to his career in language studies. This strong background in language and linguistics was also to inform his approach to the study of literature. His experiences in law were also to prove useful. The language of communication in maritime law is English, which provided ample opportunity for Peter to develop his linguistic skills. In addition, legal language requires high degrees of precision and rhetorical skill, expertise is also required in the linguistic study of literature. So when Peter Verdonk finally made the move into academia, his background up to that point more or less prescribed the approach he was going to take in his study of literary texts.

For readers who are already familiar with Peter's work, perhaps one more piece of the biographical jigsaw remains. This concerns Peter's involvement with the international Poetics and Linguistics Association, or PALA, as it is commonly known. Although he was already using a linguistic approach in his literary research, Peter credits PALA with providing a new impetus for his work and shaping his network of colleagues in stylistics.

A long-standing and now honorary member of PALA, Peter's association with the organization began in its very early days. He recalls happening across a very small advertisement in the *Times Literary Supplement* announcing a conference at the University of East Anglia in Norwich. Seizing the opportunity it offered, Peter telephoned the organizer, the late Roger Fowler, who invited Peter to come and talk about some of the linguistic works on poetry that he had been doing with his students in Amsterdam. Peter caught a flight from Schiphol Airport in the morning and in the afternoon arrived at his first PALA conference, becoming PALA's first non-UK-based member. Following this conference, Peter notes that he thoroughly changed his approach to poetry, a move which he describes here in Chapter 5. There is something quaint in this description of how conferences were organized in the past, especially when compared with the aggressive Web- and social-media-based marketing of conferences today. But, for readers of this volume, it is fortunate indeed that the conference advertisement caught Peter's eye. Through his academic work, his administrative roles within PALA, and his support of colleagues and students, Peter Verdonk has been an ambassador for stylistics and how it should be practised.

An overview of this book

The chapters in this book are presented in the chronological order in which they were written, and thereby offer a view of Peter Verdonk's approach to poetry as it has developed over the years. The earliest chapter in this book, originally published in 1984, is representative of what I particularly appreciate about his work. 'Poetic artifice and literary stylistics' (Chapter 2) is an analysis of William Blake's poem 'London', from his 1794 collection, *Songs of Experience*. In it, Professor Verdonk considers the extent to which linguistic form can act mimetically and how the process of stylistic analysis is best carried out. What makes this a particularly valuable chapter to students of stylistics is its focus on a poem that does not obviously deviate from what Mukařovsky (1964) termed the 'standard language'. Although it is true that the Late Modern English of Blake's poem encompasses numerous syntactic and lexical differences from Present-Day English, and while it is clear that its rhymes and rhythms are common to poetry, the language of the poem is not radically different from contemporary norms in the way that, say, the poetry of E. E. Cummings is. Blake does not play with graphology, for instance, in any way that is radically different from what we would normally expect of poetry. In my experience of teaching stylistics, while students are quickly able to grasp concepts of deviation, parallelism and foregrounding in texts that exhibit these features strongly, they struggle when trying to apply the same analytical notions to texts that do not break our expectations in such drastic ways. Chapter 2, then, is an excellent example of how to deal stylistically with conventionally structured poems. His focus on what is happening at the levels of semantics, lexis, syntax, phonology and graphology clearly demonstrates how poetry works to defamiliarize the reader. The chapter is also a model of the analytical and expressive clarity that all stylisticians aim for and for which Peter Verdonk is justly renowned.

Chapter 3, 'We have art in order that we may not perish from truth': the universe of discourse in Auden's "Musée des Beaux Arts"', emphasizes the concern with context that marks all of Peter Verdonk's work. His analysis here of Auden's poem carefully locates its semantic structure within the wider context of the paintings of Pieter Brueghel the Elder, particularly his *Landscape with the Fall of Icarus*. This consideration of both the status of poetry as art and its relationship to the visual arts marks Professor Verdonk as not only a first-rate stylistician but a cultural critic of great significance. The chapter is also memorable for addressing the difficult issue of defining both style and tone. Tone, particularly, is something that students struggle with, normally because it has been introduced to them in literature classes as an abstract concept accessible only to the highly attuned reader. Peter Verdonk's definition connects tone far more closely to linguistic style, thereby making it a much less abstract concept. What is also noteworthy in this chapter is Professor Verdonk's discussion of the linguistic creation of spatio-temporal context, which to my mind prefigures later work by his Amsterdam colleague, the late Paul Werth, on text world theory (e.g., Werth 1999).

Chapter 4 tackles Wilfred Owen's famous World War I poem, 'Anthem for Doomed Youth'. Again, there is careful consideration of the poem's historical context and how this impacts on a reader's interpretation of the text, and Professor Verdonk is able to show how even the most-studied poems can reveal previously undiscovered nuances of meaning under the scalpel of stylistics. His focus is on identifying the persona in the poem and its addressees, and through consideration of both the finished text and its pre-final drafts, he identifies a distinct mind style in the way that the speaker conceptualizes his experience of war.

Chapters 2, 3 and 4, then, offer classic stylistic analyses that shed new light on the texts under consideration, as well as providing masterly demonstrations of how to go about stylistic analysis. Chapter 5 takes a different tack by focusing on the pedagogy of stylistics. This chapter, it will be recalled, is a direct outcome of Professor Verdonk's association with PALA, described earlier. In it he outlines a pedagogical experiment carried out with his own students at the University of Amsterdam, aimed at increasing students' awareness of language and its function in poetry. Using frameworks for analysis from the work of Geoffrey Leech, Henry Widdowson and Anne Cluysenaar, Professor Verdonk presents stylistic analyses of three poems – Philip Larkin's 'Going', Jon Silkin's 'Death of a Son' and Sylvia Plath's 'Ariel' – produced as a collaborative effort with his students. This chapter exemplifies the egalitarian nature of stylistics, where institutional status is irrelevant and students as well as professors are able to make authoritative claims about the function of language in literary texts if their analyses are precise enough.

The sixth chapter of this book is a reflection on 'Poetry as text and discourse', and is important as a clear indicator that stylistics long ago moved beyond its structuralist past. Poems are not simply words on a page (indeed, no texts are this alone). Instead, meaning is negotiated between writer and reader. In this chapter, Professor Verdonk builds the concept of the reader into the context in which a poem is produced and read, framing his analysis of Larkin's 'Talking in Bed' around a discussion of Larkin's own theory of poetics which sees poems as verbal devices for reproducing emotional concepts. Context and the interpersonal communicative aspects of poetry are discussed further in Chapter 7, where the focus is on an analysis of Seamus Heaney's disquieting poem 'Punishment'.

In Chapter 8, Professor Verdonk considers the connections between stylistics and the related disciplines of classical rhetoric and cognitive science. This requires the setting of stylistics in its historical context; consequently, this chapter is a useful survey of the maturation of stylistics as a discipline, showing its magpie tendencies and constant revitalizing of itself. Here again the focus is on Larkin, this time through an analysis of his poem 'The Trees', which is used to explain the role of schemata in the process of interpretation. This interest in the cognitive aspects of text comprehension is continued in Chapter 9, on 'Painting, poetry, parallelism: ekphrasis, stylistics and cognitive poetics'. This chapter demonstrates the increasing complexity of Peter Verdonk's analyses of poetry, as he interweaves stylistics, cognitive poetics and classical rhetoric in a multimodal analysis that relates William Carlos Williams's poem, 'The Dance', to another painting by Peter Brueghel the Elder, this time 'The Kermess'. This interest in the relationship between poetry and the visual arts demonstrates Professor Verdonk's position at the cutting-edge of stylistics and at the forefront of current research into multimodal texts.

As indicated in the later chapters of this book, stylistics is a diverse discipline, encompassing everything from intrinsic textual meaning to the cognitive actions involved in comprehending texts. At its core though, stylistics is concerned with style, and the aforementioned aspects of stylistics form part of this. In Chapter 10, Professor Verdonk tackles the issue of style head on, exploring its background in classical rhetoric, demonstrating its status in relation to speech act theory and cognitive poetics, and explaining the notion of style as motivated choice, a concept which is the driver of all stylistic analysis.

Fittingly, although it may not have been intended to do this, the final chapter of the book draws together the variety of methods and analytical frameworks dealt with in the preceding chapters. Professor Verdonk incorporates a whole range of analytical approaches in an analysis of Ted Hughes's 'Hawk Roosting'. Drawing on his knowledge of the historical background to the development of English, he contrasts the Latinate and Anglo-Saxon lexis in the poem, connecting this to the two sides of the titular hawk's character. He examines metre, phonetics and syntactic structure, demonstrating the tension caused by the instances of enjambement in the poem. He considers the cognitive theory of figure and ground, relating this not only to the foregrounded features of the text but also to our schematic picture of the hawk in flight, and even, indirectly, to the reading process itself. His statement that 'The meaning of style does not primarily reside in its linguistic form' may seem an unusual stance for a linguist and stylistician to take. But once the reader has absorbed the previous chapters of this book, this seems a perfectly sensible conclusion to come to. Language exists within a context; and context, through its propensity to shape a reader's schematic experiences, is as much the locus of style as language itself. Ultimately, the chapter offers clear evidence of the power and value of stylistics for facilitating our understanding of literary texts. Although stylistics can never offer a definitive answer to a literary critical question, it can provide insights that we may not otherwise have reached. Professor Verdonk himself puts it best: 'Stylistics brings literary critical appreciation into clearer focus'.

Context, cognition, discourse, history

I have appropriated Peter Verdonk's subtitle for this book as my title for this introductory chapter. I have done this because I think it neatly summarizes Professor Verdonk's key contributions to stylistics. In all his work on stylistics (not just his work on poetry), Peter has been careful to take full account of the context in which texts are produced and read. Context is sometimes used by critics as a get-out-of-jail-free card, whereby it is possible to dismiss criticism with the statement that 'of course other critics might analyse this text differently; context is key'. But where Peter Verdonk differs from such critics is in tackling the issue of context head on, exploring what it is and exactly how it impacts on texts and readers. This, of course, involves a careful understanding of the historical circumstances in which texts were produced or in which particular critical remarks were made. It involves considering texts as discourse rather than simply as marks on a page; and, of course, to do this necessitates careful consideration of the ways in which readers interact with texts and construct meanings from what a text projects. Over the course of his career, Peter Verdonk has been at the forefront of all of these activities. *The Stylistics of Poetry: Context, Cognition, Discourse, History* presents a clear, consistent and accessible approach to the stylistic analysis of a complex and endlessly fascinating literary genre.

2

Poetic artifice and literary stylistics[1]

Stylistics as an interdiscipline

At the annual PALA[2] Conference of 1983 organized by Sheffield University, I felt the need to adopt a somewhat conciliatory tone when talking about the ongoing but sometimes strained relation between literary criticism and stylistics. As a matter of fact, I said on that occasion that I was going to play the role of matchmaker between the two disciplines. I had been inspired to use this image by Geoffrey Leech, who had written earlier that 'the literary critic is still typically cast in the role of the coy bride-to-be, who rejects the advances of the linguistic bridegroom, and his promise of a fruitful union between the two disciplines' (Leech 1977: 2)[3]. So I was not the first go-between. After the sometimes overrated claims of linguists in the 1950s and early 1960s, which was the initial phase of what Roger Fowler conveniently labelled as 'the new stylistics'[4], it was only natural that for a number of years several linguists tried to improve public relations by emphasizing the interdisciplinary nature of stylistics (Fowler 1975: 3–4).

Though I know that one swallow does not make a summer, two recent publications from unsuspected sources have encouraged me not to pursue the defensive tone that I have tended to adopt so far. In a letter to *PN Review* about Donald C. Freeman's *Essays in Modern Stylistics* (1981), Christopher Norris observes that the quarrel between literary criticism and modern stylistics has subsided to a point where linguists no longer need to be on the defensive (Norris 1983: 61–2). The other publication is Geoffrey Thurley's *Counter-Modernism in Current Critical Theory* (1983), which presents a serious critique of the principal attitudes and beliefs of the major schools of twentieth-century literary criticism, among which he also reckons stylistics. On the latter, he observes that it is not so much the literary-critical wing of linguistics as the linguistic wing of literary criticism (Thurley 1983: 33–42), which goes a long way towards calling it an interdiscipline.

Poetic artifice from the poet's and the reader's perspective

Another effect these publications had on me was that they both forcefully reminded me of the perennial problem of formal mimesis: does linguistic form imitate or enact content? It seems to me that the best way to define my position on this issue is to elaborate on the title of this paper 'Poetic Artifice and Literary Stylistics'. The term 'poetic artifice' has been taken from the title of a book by Veronica Forrest-Thomson (1978), entitled *Poetic Artifice: A Theory of Twentieth-Century Poetry*. It is a blanket term, in that it includes all those special formal features which make poetry different from prose. It is these distinctive yet elusive poetic features that require me to take a closer look at their possible genesis.

Although the model has its limitations, for the purpose of this paper, it is assumed that we can distinguish five levels of organization in language: semantics, lexis, syntax, phonology and graphology. It is also assumed that, prompted by their artistic talent, poets consciously or intuitively let themselves be guided by certain principles of selection and arrangement, while operating on these levels of linguistic organization. So if we look upon language as the sum total of structures available to the poet, the artistically motivated choices they make on any of these levels of language together constitute the poem's artifice.

So far we have been looking at the use of language from the poet's point of view. Now, in trying to retrace the poet's motives for choosing certain structures over others available in their language, we must shift our attention to the reader's point of view. It is here that the second technical term in the title of my paper needs explanation. As for the kind of activity in which I wish to engage, 'literary stylistics' is defined as the interdisciplinary study of language as used in literary texts. It is interdisciplinary, in that linguistics provides the techniques to describe those formal features of which it is assumed that they contribute to some literary or aesthetic effect, in brief the poem's artifice. I subscribe to the view expressed by Leech and Short in their book *Style in Fiction* (1981: 13) that the aim of literary stylistics is to relate the literary interest in evaluation and interpretation with the linguistic interest in language description or, to put it differently, literary stylistics investigates the relation between linguistic usage and artistic function.

The question which often arises about this relational aspect of literary stylistics is 'Which of the two interests comes first when examining a literary text, the linguistic or the literary?' The answer is that means and ends, language and literary function, must receive our equal attention and it must be shown that they are interdependent. In other words, a given prominent feature in the text that appeals to first impression may be either literary or linguistic. If this observation is literary, stylisticians will seek linguistic evidence, and if it is linguistic, they will attempt to suggest its potential literary effect. In this connection, it may also be worth considering Jonathan Culler's suggestion that one should begin with the literary effects of a poem and then attempt to see how particular linguistic features contribute to and help to account for these effects. Culler holds this view on the assumption that poems contain, by their very nature, deviant linguistic structures, and that the way in which these structures operate in the poetic text may give them a function different from what the linguist expects (Culler 1975: 73).

To avoid any misunderstanding, the assumption that literary stylistics, which makes use of linguistic tools, and literary studies, in a wider sense, have (at least in part) a common function is primarily based on the fact that the medium of any literary work of art is language. It is, however, by no means claimed that the particular status of a literary work of art is due exclusively to linguistic factors.

I have now come to a crucial point in my discussion of the aims and strategies of literary stylistics, that is, the point where the problem of the relationship between form and content, which I touched on earlier, presents itself in its full magnitude. Though I am not in a position to offer any ultimate solution, I think it is at least useful to take stock of the situation in stylistic criticism.

When I assumed that in a cyclic motion of literary and linguistic observations, stylistics investigates the relation between literary effects and linguistic means, I should have added two restrictions.

Foregrounding is not an objective criterion

First, for the selection of the linguistic features which are potentially the exponents of particular literary workings, stylistic critics have to rely mainly on their intuition and alertness to such signals in the text. It is true, that for the identification of these conspicuous features, the theory of foregrounding[5] can be very helpful. This important concept in stylistics provides formal criteria for locating style markers such as deviation from normal usage, repetitive patterning or clustering, etc., and since such salient features may be relevant to literary effects, foregrounding has been rightly called the meeting point of linguistic and literary concerns (Leech and Short 1981: 69). However, it is not an objective criterion because the question of what is and what is not foregrounded against the background of language can only be answered on the basis of subjective impressions.

Second, it has to be admitted that literary stylistics does not offer a theoretical framework validating a statement that a given foregrounded linguistic feature contributes to such and such a literary effect. So if particular linguistic features are supplied with a mimetic interpretation, however tentative or straightforward, then such an interpretation relies heavily on the literary sensitivity of the stylistic critic. As a matter of fact, descriptions of linguistic mimesis are few and far between. As E. L. Epstein (1981: 171) remarks in his essay on 'The Self-Reflexive Artefact', the clearest description of various kinds of syntactic mimesis in poetry is to be found in Donald Davie's *Articulate Energy* (1955). Using Davie's typology of mimetic syntax as a basis, Epstein adds other stylistic traits that may be a reflection of content in form, such as mimetic phonological schemata and phonological and syntactic schemata operating in combination. Epstein's attempt to classify these various types of linguistic mimesis appeals to me, because, as Christopher Norris (1983: 62) concludes, it argues for a very flexible view of mimesis. However, in the conclusion of his essay, Epstein seems to throw all this flexibility to the winds, when he claims that 'Applied with some caution, this approach has the virtue of accounting for certain judgments of value, now made on an intuitive basis, of literary artefacts by a comparatively objective procedure' (Epstein 1981: 195). With the debate of objectivity looming up again, I feel much more at ease in the company of Geoffrey Thurley, when he says that 'There is no such thing as a fully objective or intrinsic criticism' (Thurley 1983: 58). What criticism should do, according to Thurley, is, on the one hand, to describe the literary work in the hope of revealing some of its concealed or suppressed formal material and, on the other, to recommend a particular judgement. True, the descriptive element can be used to support this critical judgement, but in such a mélange there must be no 'therefores' and 'it follows thats' suggesting some objective causal connection between the findings of a formal description and a critical evaluation of their literary significance. (Thurley 1983: 58).

The text in its internal and external context

By now all these relativistic considerations may seem to be as many disclaimers of the relevance of stylistics to literary criticism. Yet, I maintain that, in spite of their limitations, the techniques of stylistics, or rather literary stylistics, can provide a sound basis for the kind of empiricist criticism that I subscribe to. In my view, this kind of criticism does not imply that I have to base myself on 'the text-and-nothing-but-the-text'. To be more precise, the formal description of a text may very well require a study and understanding of its 'background', that is, its social, political, historical, psychological provenance or other extra-textual factors (Thurley 1983: 122). This eclectic approach does not detract from the value of those techniques of literary stylistics which enable the critic to dwell at length on the formal elements of a literary text. This focus of attention is essential, because it is these formal elements which may prove to have the potential to disturb our everyday linguistic orderings of the world (Thomson 1978: xi).

Basing myself on the foregoing observations, I propose to analyse what Oliver Elton called Blake's 'mightiest brief poem' (David V. Erdman 1969: 275):[6]

London

I wander thro' each charter'd street
Near where the charter'd Thames does flow
And mark in every face I meet
Marks of weakness marks of woe.

In every cry of every Man,
In every Infants cry of fear,
In every voice: in every ban,
The mind forg'd manacles I hear

How the Chimney sweepers cry
Every blackning Church appalls,
And the hapless Soldiers sigh,
Runs in blood down Palace walls

But most thro' midnight streets I hear
How the youthful Harlots curse
Blasts the new born Infants tear
And blights with plagues the Marriage hearse.

From William Blake, *Songs of Experience* (1794). Digital JPEG image, plate 46, 'London', Fitzwilliam Museum, Cambridge, accession number: P.125–1950.[7]

To get at least some idea of a significant element of its contemporary eighteenth-century external context, I obtained from the Fitzwilliam Museum, Cambridge, a digital image of Blake's own illuminated version of the poem. The fact is that Blake experimented with relief etchings[8] to illuminate some of his poetry books. It was a laborious and time-consuming process so that in the end he printed only a relatively small number of books. Perhaps most famous are the illuminations of *Songs of Innocence* (1789) and *Songs of Innocence and of Experience* (1794). The plate featuring the text of the poem 'London' shows a child guiding a bent old man on crutches along the cobbled streets, presumably showing him the dreadful sights of the streets of London. Below this there is a smoky bonfire by which a small boy (probably homeless) is warming his hands. The smoke caused by the fire seeks its way into the space of the poem, meaningfully curls round the word 'woe' at the end of the first stanza and ultimately appears to envelop all the aspects of social and personal misery severely criticized in the poem.

Lexical sets generate an internal and external context

Speaking of context, I agree with Winifred Nowottny that criticism of a poem's diction, that is, its choice of lexical items, should be concerned mainly with the interplay among those lexical items which create a certain context inside the poem. Obviously, single lexical items bring to the poem their referential meaning, that is, the semantic potential which derives from their usage outside the text, but this potential is greatly added to, when it is set to work in combination with (or, for that matter, in collision with) other lexical items used in the poem (Nowottny 1962: 46). This inner activity of a poem can be shown by a lexical analysis, which can be based on an intuitive sorting of the lexical items of a poem into lexical sets.

Words are selected for inclusion in a particular lexical set on the principle of loose synonymy, that is, the lexical items selected are related in meaning in the sense that they occur in similar contexts and refer to the same areas of reality or experience.

In Blake's 'London', the most striking lexical sets are those of *misery* and *oppression*. The *misery* set, which is sustained throughout the poem, may be said to comprise the following items: 'weakness', 'woe', 'cry' (three times), 'fear', 'blackning', 'appalls', 'hapless', 'sigh', 'blood', 'blasts', 'tear', 'blights', 'plagues' and 'hearse'. These words are interwoven with the *oppression* set, with items like 'charter'd' (twice; primarily with the sense of 'being granted a (possibly restricting) charter or license', but already with the overtones of 'available to hire: being hired out' – see note 9 below), 'marks' (twice; including the sense of scars resulting from penal branding), 'ban', 'manacles' and 'curse'.

As we observed before, lexical sets in poetry generate two kinds of context: they provide the referential context they have in the external world, and they acquire an internal context built up by their own textual surroundings. It is obvious that, if we add to the foregoing lexical sets three other sets of *movement*, *city* and *physical perception*, which establish the setting and action of the poem, we could very well make an external thematic statement about Blake's 'London'.[9] It would be a statement about what the first-person speaker saw and heard on his walk through eighteenth-century London. The streets and the river Thames are entirely monopolized by commerce.

The degradation of the inhabitants, the misery of those most unfortunate children, the chimney sweeps, the swarms of prostitutes, whose clients infected their wives with venereal disease which blinded their babies. This statement could be expanded on by including Blake's ideas about free love and marriage, his rebellion against Church and State, against their rules and laws, which he saw as suppressing people's individuality. In brief, the poem is a prolonged outcry against the corruption of power. However, such an 'unseemly rush from words to world' (Forrest-Thomson 1978: xi) at this stage of our analysis would entirely ignore the poem's dynamics of expression created by the textual relations set up among the lexical items.

To reveal this text-internal 'meaning', I suggest that we trace the lexical patterns in the poem and try to state the relation among themselves and their relation to other levels of language organization, such as syntax and phonology.

Tracing the lexical patterns through the stanzas, we find that the sets of *misery* and *oppression* are used in association with 'Church', 'Palace' and 'Marriage'. Lexico-semantically, it is apparent that the members of the *misery* set build up in intensity, the range being from 'weakness' and 'woe' in the first stanza to 'plagues' and 'hearse' in the last stanza. Besides this growing intensity in meaning, there is also an increasing frequency, which ends up in a high concentration in the last two lines: 'blasts', 'tear', 'blights', 'plagues' and 'hearse'.

This gradual increase in intensity set in motion by the lexis of the poem is reinforced by the distribution of verbs and nouns over the four stanzas. Thus it appears that the *misery* items in the first two stanzas are all nouns ('weakness', 'woe', 'cry' (twice) and 'fear'), which are syntactically linked up with verbs of perception, in that they are the static objects of 'mark' and 'hear' (twice). In the last two stanzas, however, the *misery* items include many verbs such as 'appalls', 'runs' (in blood), 'blasts' and 'blights', which contribute to the effect that the exponents of misery, which in the first two stanzas are described as the static objects of observation, are turning into an active force after the centre of the poem.

Some foregrounded lexical items

Both in the *misery* set and in the *oppression* set, there are some foregrounded groupings of lexical items as a result of deviant choices from the language code. For example, the item 'charter'd' enters twice in rather unpredictable collocations: 'charter'd street' and 'the charter'd Thames'. Such lexical clashes produce the paradox of equating different concepts, and this equation forces us to consider not only the extra-textual meaning of the juxtaposed lexical items, but also their text-internal meaning as it is set up by the collision. According to the language code, we may expect collocations such as 'chartered liberties' and 'chartered companies/land/town', etc. in which 'chartered' carries the meaning of 'granted, founded, privileged, or protected by (royal) charter'. Another common collocation is as in 'chartered plane or ship', in which it means 'hired' or 'rented'.[10] The item 'street' has its purely physical meaning of 'road', but by extension it also refers to the common people living there.

It is typical of poetry that these surprising combinations do not produce one new unit of meaning. On the contrary, they keep disturbing our cliché-ridden perceptions because we are required to reformulate our intuitions of the language code and, as a result, our intuitions of the world. Thus, bearing in mind the different aspects of meaning yoked together in 'charter'd street', we may arrive at various readings. For example, in its sense of 'privileged or protected by (royal) charter', the modifier 'charter'd' yields heavy irony, if we realize the poem's prevalent atmosphere of oppression. (We are led to reflect that the grant of privileges to one group of people inevitably restricts the freedom of others.)

Similarly, the collocational clash 'charter'd Thames' is quite disturbing. To some extent, the image of freedom called up by the river flowing at its own sweet will corresponds with the concept of liberty associated with 'charter'd'. However, it forcefully clashes with the other meanings of 'chartered', that is, '*institutionalized* liberty' and 'hired out' or 'rented', which induce us to reflect on the idea of a river 'regulated for commerce' or 'hired out to the world of business', as a result of which the river is restrained in its natural freedom.

At the exact centre of the poem, there is the third prominent lexical clash in the *oppression* set, viz., in 'the mind-forg'd manacles'. Here we visualize in one half of the collocation the actual physical process of shaping fetters by heating fire and hammering, whereas the other half of the combination, containing the word 'mind', hints at the mental process of fabricating or inventing restraints of freedom. Obviously, the vigour surrounding the physical process emphasizes the force and intensity of the mental activity, and by implication of the poet's suggestion that the fetters of misery are created in the twisted minds both of the oppressor and the oppressed, who accept the chains.

At this point it is also quite rewarding to look at the syntactic patterning of 'the mind-forg'd manacles', the 'clanking' of which is heard 'In every cry of every Man,/In every Infants cry of fear,/In every voice: in every ban'. This heaping up of coordinated adverbials not only accentuates the groans of universal suffering, but in its last constituent 'in every ban' we can also discover the main instruments of the general oppression. According to the language code, the noun 'ban' includes the following denotations: 'the summoning of the King's soldiers', 'a solemn curse made by the Church' and 'a proclamation of

Marriage'. This lexical and syntactic foregrounding leaves no doubt about the identity of the institutions which the speaker in the poem holds responsible for all this human degradation. As a matter of fact, they figure conspicuously in the poem: 'Church', 'Palace' and 'Marriage'.

In the lexical set of *misery*, most foregrounded lexical collocations appear in the third and in the last stanza. In lines 9 and 10, 'How the Chimney sweepers cry/Every blackning Church appalls', the participle 'blackning' obviously not only refers to the result of the London soot, but also carries the meaning of 'smearing one's reputation'. In line 10, there appears to be a nicely concealed pun in the juxtaposition of 'blackning' and 'appalls', if we trace the etymological origin of the latter verb, that is, 'to wax pale', or 'to cause to lose colour'. This allows us to see the verb 'appalls' in a somewhat different light than its general meaning of 'to dismay' or 'to horrify' which it carries in the language code.

The other two most prominent lexical clashes in the *misery* set are in lines 11 and 12, 'And the hapless Soldiers sigh/Runs in blood down Palace walls', while at the very end of the poem, we observe the stunning clash in 'the Marriage hearse', in which the marriage coach is converted into a funeral carriage.

So far the analysis has been made chiefly on the level of the lexis of the poem, though I hasten to say that it is far from complete. The main object of my efforts has been to reveal the overpowering intensity with which Blake vents his indignation.

The poem's significant syntax

I will now turn to the syntax of the poem and try to demonstrate that also at this level of organization, the patterning greatly contributes to this fiery intensity of expression.

There is a remarkable difference between the overall syntactic structure of the first two stanzas and that of the last two. (The enclosed appendix visualizes the syntactic analysis.) It will be observed that the first two are largely taken up by adverbials, which all play one and the same semantic role, that of 'place'. This locative effect is not only intensified by this congestion of adverbials, but also by the fact that they all have exactly the same formal structure, viz., prepositional phrases. On the other hand, the third stanza is in its entirety[11] and the fourth stanza is almost in its entirety a series of coordinated direct objects of the twice-repeated verb 'hear', thereby bombarding the reader with the things that they should hear.

Blake has apparently taken great pains with the syntactic arrangement of the second and third stanzas. Thus, the inversion of verb and object in line 8 in the third stanza, 'The mind-forg'd manacles I hear', not only adds to the emphasis on 'the mind-forg'd manacles', but also enables the reader to accept the verb 'hear' as the predicator of the third stanza, which, as we have already said, is as a whole its direct object. To cap it all, on re-examining the structure of the third stanza, we make the startling discovery that the poet has all the same smuggled in a pseudo-predicator by employing the device of an acrostic in which the initial letters of lines 9–12 reveal the verb 'hear'. This concealed verb seems to take on the nature of an imperative or an adhortative imply-ing an urgent but muffled plea from the afflicted Londoners to 'hear' about their misery.

The sound patterns in the poem

So far we have collected a large amount of evidence to support the poem's cohesion of expression at the levels of lexis and syntax. We shall now inves-tigate the poem's phonology in order to find out whether its sound patterns contain similar unifying features.

Metrically, the first stanza has an iambic pattern in which, however, the first occurrence of the noun 'marks' in line 4 is foregrounded in that it has first syllable stress. This extrametrical stress, in combination with the syntactic and structural parallelism in the line (i.e. two coordinated direct objects real-ized by two similarly structured noun phrases) as well as the alliteration in 'weakness' and 'woe', greatly emphasizes the word 'marks'. Syntactically, the run-on between lines 3 and 4 adds to this emphasis, as does the repetition, on the lexical level, of the noun 'marks' and the verb 'mark'.

In stanza two, the first three lines show a regular iambic pattern, in which all the stresses are realized. This regularity, however, is disturbed in line 8 with an extra stress on the crucial attributive modifier 'mind-forg'd'. This line stands out not only phonologically, but also syntactically because of the rupture in the syntactic parallelism with the first stanza, which shows regular word-order.

After the lexically, syntactically and phonologically foregrounded line 'The mind-forg'd manacles I hear', the stress pattern is no longer iambic, but tro-chaic. Thus it appears that the third stanza is given prominence not only by this unexpected metrical change, but, as we have seen, also syntactically by the absence of a predicator, which is graphologically conjured up by an acrostic.

The last stanza is found to contain a combination of an iambic pattern in lines 13 and 16 and a trochaic one in lines 14 and 15. The run-on between these trochaic lines emphasizes 'curse' and 'blasts', and, consequently, also the phonologically related words 'hearse' by assonance, and 'blights' and 'plagues' by alliteration. Although there are many other instances of alliteration in the poem, we wish to restrict ourselves to pointing out this final climactic occurrence of this device, which greatly adds to the vituperative quality of the poem's grand finale.

Seeking a delicate balance between the inwardly and outwardly turned meaning

It is needless to say that there is no such thing as an exhaustive analysis. Neither can any analysis, however detailed, ever produce the 'meanings' of a poem in absolute terms. Nevertheless, I trust that this literary stylistic exercise has unravelled some of the threads of this extremely complicated web of linguistic patterns, which were all found to contribute to the poem's intensity of expression, or rather, its vehement public outcry. The literary critic Thurley calls a poem's intensity of expression its 'inwardly turned meaning', which is generated by the interaction of its formal elements, so the poem's artifice.

The other meaning of a poem is turned outwards, in that it carries the poet's intention, that is, what he wants to express. I hope I have succeeded in delineating the critical assumption that a literary work of art, like any other work of art, carries these two sorts of meanings, and that an aesthetic appreciation must somehow find a delicate balance between the two.

Appendix

1. I wander thro' each charter'd street,
   S V   A

2. Near where the charter'd Thames does flow
                    A

3. And mark in every face I meet
   cc   V   A

4. Marks of weakness, marks of woe.
                  DO

5. In every cry of every Man,
            A

6. In every Infants cry of fear,
            A

7. In every voice; in every ban,
                A

8. The mind-forg'd manacles I hear
             DO   S V

9. How the Chimney-sweepers cry
                DO

10. Every blackning Church appalls,
                DO

11. And the hapless Soldiers sigh
                DO

12. Runs in blood down Palace walls
                DO

13. But most thro' midnight streets I hear
      cc   A   A   S V

14. How the youthful Harlots curse
                DO

15. Blasts the new-born Infants tear
                DO

16. And blights with plagues the Marriage hearse
                DO

N.B.

For this analysis, I have chiefly made use of the terminology and general view of grammar presented in Randolph Quirk et al., *A Grammar of Contemporary English* (London 1972). The following abbreviations are used: S = subject, V = verb, A = adverbial, DO = direct object, cc = coordinating conjunction.

Extracted from Verdonk, P. (1984) 'Poetic Artifice and Literary Stylistics', *DQR Dutch Quarterly Review of Anglo-American Letters* 14/3: 215–28. Reprinted in D'haen, Th. (ed.), (1986) *Linguistics and the Study of Literature*. Amsterdam: Rodopi, pp. 42–55.

3

'We have art in order that we may not perish from truth': The universe of discourse in Auden's 'Musée des Beaux Arts'[1]

Brueghel's iconographic downplay

One of the showpieces in the Museum of Fine Arts in Brussels is a sixteenth-century painting which is usually called *Landscape with the Fall of Icarus*[2] by Pieter Brueghel the Elder (1525?–1569). The story of the fall of Icarus is well-known so that a bare outline will do. Icarus was the son of Daedalus, the mythical Athenian craftsman. To escape from imprisonment in a labyrinth on the island of Crete, they flew away on artificial wings fastened to their shoulders with wax. However, heedless of his father's warnings, Icarus ventured too near the blazing sun, which melted the wax, and so he fell and perished in the sea which is still called after him.

Standing before Brueghel's pictorial re-creation of the myth, one can hardly find the unfortunate Icarus and it takes a moment to discover his waving legs sticking out from the green water in the right-hand bottom corner of the picture. Thus the whole tragedy has been reduced to a few strokes of the brush. In the same way, a mere stain beneath the trees, on the left, indicates the presence of a dead man, which might be an allusion to Daedalus. This downplay of the disaster entirely agrees with the indifferent behaviour of the other figures in the painting: the fisherman on the water's edge does not deign to look up, the shepherd gazes upwards with his back turned to the sea, and the beautiful galleon, which may well have witnessed the fatal splash, hurriedly puts to sea with bellying sails. But the real protagonist is the peasant, who also appears entirely unconcerned with Icarus' misfortune: imperturbably, he ploughs furrows behind his horse in a foreground field high above the sea. In this connection, it is interesting to know that there is an old Dutch proverb maintaining that a plough does not stop for a dying man.

Brueghel's representation of the myth has always been a matter of surprise because his source, *Ovid's Metamorphoses,* Book VIII: v. 215–40, also features the fisherman, the shepherd and the peasant, but here they act as witnesses, though not of the fall, but of the father and his son in full flight, whom they therefore believe to be gods (Innes 1955: 184–5). So there is hardly any doubt that Brueghel knew this text, but he gave it an entirely different emphasis by representing Icarus' fall as a minor incident in the cycle of nature and the life of everyday (Deel van 1982: 50–7). As many of his paintings show, there was for Brueghel no place for the pain and suffering of the individual hero or saint. He saw misery and disaster as an integral part of the whole span of human existence. The painter depicts the same impassive attitude towards the great religious miracles: they may be taking place while everyone is engrossed in the ordinary things of life.

Accordingly, in his painting *The Census in Bethlehem,* Brueghel sets the event, described in Luke II, 1–5, in a snow-covered medieval Flemish village. Among the houses and on the frozen river, the villagers are hustling and bustling in their wintry activities. A pig is being slaughtered, firewood is being gathered, children are doing what children have always done in winter: they are throwing snowballs and skating on a pond. Someone is opening a window of an inn in which the Imperial tax gatherers have established themselves to collect the tithes. Completely unnoticed, Joseph is guiding the pregnant Mary, who is seated on a donkey's back, through a crowd of people and carts. The holy people have merged into the common people, and life goes on as the drama of the Nativity is about to unfold.

Similarly, in *The Massacre of the Innocents*[3], described in Matthew II, 16–18, Brueghel shows this tendency to see his own environment and everyday life about him as the stage for the great religious dramas. In this painting, too, the scene is laid in a typical snow-bound village of Brueghel's own time and the terrible event is told with an unerring eye for frightening and harrowing detail (Martin 1984: 28). Dogs are rushing about, horses are tied to trees and the butchering soldiers are wearing the red coats of the notorious Spanish mercenaries – the painting dates from 1567, the eve of the Eighty Years' War.

In these and other paintings, Brueghel appears to reduce the great events in mythology, the Bible or history to matters of little import by situating them in a world which shows complete indifference to the fate of the individual and in which the most extraordinary and prodigious events are happening while all around the ordinary things of life just go on.

The influence of Brueghel's iconographic understatement on Auden's poetic style

It is precisely this reductive iconography of the painter Brueghel which must have appealed to the poet Auden, when in December 1938 he made a tour round the Museum of Fine Arts during a brief stay in Brussels, and conceived of what was to become one of his most-celebrated short poems, 'Musée des Beaux Arts'. I base this assumption on the fact that this juxtaposition of the ordinary and the extraordinary in Brueghel's paintings, which through its trivializing effect creates a particular kind of irony, falls in with the style that Auden adopts in most of his poems published at the end of the 1930s in the collection *Another Time* (1938).The impact of this style is mainly due to a highly effective, though some-times uneasy, opposition between casualness of tone and seriousness of sub-ject. Though I think that style is a more comprehensive category and therefore subsumes tone, the two terms are notoriously difficult to define. Perhaps we can define style as a speaker's or writer's, often characteristic, mode of linguis-tic expression in terms of emotion, effectiveness, clarity, beauty and the like. (See Chapter 10 for a more detailed discussion of the term.) Tone, on the other hand, appears to be related to a particular attitude or perspective conveyed by a speaker's or writer's style. In Auden's poem, the speaker's tone seems to sug-gest his fatalistic or perhaps passive acceptance of human suffering in this world. Indeed, 'Musée des Beaux Arts' might well serve as an illustration: in a casual, almost laconic tone, the poem probes into the place of suffering in the life of humankind:

      Musée des Beaux Arts
    About suffering they were never wrong,
    The Old Masters: how well they understood
    Its human position; how it takes place
    While someone else is eating or opening a window or just
       walking dully along;
5 How, when the aged are reverently, passionately waiting
    For the miraculous birth, there always must be
    Children who did not specially want it to happen, skating
    On a pond at the edge of the wood:
    They never forgot
10 That even the dreadful martyrdom must run its course
    Anyhow in a corner, some untidy spot
    Where the dogs go on with their doggy life and the torturer's horse
    Scratches its innocent behind on a tree.

In Brueghel's *Icarus,* for instance: how everything turns away
15 Quite leisurely from the disaster; the ploughman may
Have heard the splash, the forsaken cry,
But for him it was not an important failure; the sun shone
As it had to on the white legs disappearing into the green
Water; and the expensive delicate ship that must have seen
20 Something amazing, a boy falling out of the sky,
Had somewhere to get to and sailed calmly on.

(Auden 1966: 123–4)

One reason why I began this essay with a brief discussion of Brueghel's *Landscape with the Fall of Icarus* is that it is the only picture which the poem specifically mentions and of which it gives a fairly accurate description in the second stanza. Next, I very briefly discussed the Brueghel paintings *The Census in Bethlehem* and *The Massacre of the Innocents*, because it is generally assumed that it is these two pictures which are alluded to in the first stanza, though it has been pointed out that none of the horses in the latter picture is actually scratching its behind on a tree!

The plurality of contexts of the poem's discourse and the role of the reader

Another reason why I started with a description of the Brueghel pictures is that I want to reconstruct, as far as such a reconstruction is possible, the various external contexts which may be supposed to attach meaning to the poem's formal structures. Thus, on the one hand, the Brueghel paintings represent the immediate context of an art gallery in which the persona is walking about, and, on the other hand, they evoke a much wider context which is somehow disturbing to him.

Wishing to relate these contextual factors to the meanings of the poem's linguistic structures or text, I propose to perform a literary stylistic analysis for which I will exploit, though rather informally, the techniques of discourse analysis. The basis of such an analysis is the assumption that the poem is a representation of a discourse, that is to say a context-dependent communicative activity in which the participants are fictionalized as persona and implied reader. Clearly, the poet pretends such a communicative situation, and the reader goes along with this pretence by reconstructing or imagining a speaker (or persona) and building out of the textual material the contexts in which this quasi-speech activity takes place (Ohmann 1971: 1–19). From what I have said before, it will be clear that I mean by the term 'context-dependent' that the non-linguistic factors of the contexts within which a discourse is conducted are inherently involved in the language of the text which the speaker utters. At this point, it is important to note that this contextual scope also includes the reader's own view of the poem's discourse, which inevitably affects its interpretation. Naturally, this individual perspective varies from reader to reader depending on their different social and cultural backgrounds.

A reconstruction of the contextual factors affecting the poet's discourse and theme

Having set out the method and purpose of my analysis, I will now continue my reconstruction of the contextual factors which may be supposed to have influenced the poem's discourse and theme.

Therefore, I go back again to that winter of 1938, when Auden spent some time in Brussels and paid a visit to the Museum of Fine Arts. Basing myself on his biographers, I wish to argue that, in addition to being artistically affected by Brueghel's iconographic style, Auden was also emotionally susceptible to the painter's theme of the world's indifference to suffering and of life going on side by side with events of the greatest pathos and importance. Humphrey Carpenter, for example, reports that at the time Auden was in Brussels, he had only recently returned from a journey with Christopher Isherwood to China to report on the Sino-Japanese war, and this trip, added to Hitler's coming into power and his recent sad experiences in the Spanish Civil War, had done no more than strengthen his growing belief in universal human failure (Carpenter 1981: 240–6). Writing on the same period of Auden's life, Edward Mendelson sums up the poet's general state of mind in the following words:

> Auden had already begun to accept in himself the dull ordinariness of suffering, but responsibility for others' suffering was a different matter. Writing of the wounded in *In Time of War* [referring to the Sino-Japanese war], he could only 'stand elsewhere' and observe. Now, in Brussels, standing before the Brueghels in the Musées Royeaux des Beaux Arts, he began to sense a more immediate relation (Mendelson 1981: 362–4).

It seems to me that this brief encounter with Brueghel's genius was one of these moments of artistic felicity about which Auden himself once made the following remark:

> I always have two things in my head — I always have a theme and the form. The form looks for the theme, the theme looks for the form, and when they come together you're able to write (Osborne 1980: 328).

This union of form and theme inspired by the Brueghel paintings resulted in a poetic reflection on a universal state of affairs and, by implication, on the human condition, that is, suffering, death and a universal tendency towards sin, which is traditionally ascribed to the Fall of the first human beings as related in the early chapters of the *Book of Genesis*.

So far I have explored the wider context formed by a number of aspects of the cultural and biographical backgrounds which have possibly affected the poem's semantic structure. When we narrow down this larger context, it is interesting to find how closely interrelated it is with the immediate context of utterance. Thus, the title, 'Musée des Beaux Arts', not only anchors the discourse in an immediate situation, but through its implicit reference to the paintings, it also widens the spatio-temporal frame of reference of the poem's theme. For, as I have pointed out in the initial section of this chapter, the Brueghel paintings in the Museum of Fine Arts have both biblical and classical subjects, set in what were for Brueghel contemporary scenes, so that the poem encompasses at least these three time dimensions, plus that of our own time. Indeed, the title is richly suggestive because, in addition to providing this wide-ranging context of space and time, it is also ironic because in the very place which has been designed to exhibit people's potential for beauty, we shall be reminded of the sordid aspects of their existence.

The immediate speech context of the poem's discourse

As a matter of fact, the immediate speech context specified by the title sets the dramatic scene in which the implied reader assumes the role of someone listening to a speaker philosophizing about the ironic fate that human suffering takes place without anybody taking any notice and that the most extraordinary events happen in the middle of ordinary life with everybody going about their business. While presenting this vision of people's fate, the speaker walks up to a few paintings whose names he does not mention and points out some random details to illustrate his *Weltanschauung*. Then the speaker focuses on one particular painting and stops before Brueghel's *Landscape with the Fall of Icarus*, which he appears to see as the epitome of worldly indifference. For that matter, the poet's choice of not to mention the other paintings and only to describe them allusively has an important literary effect, viz., the possibility of universal applicability of the poem's theme because the implied reader is enabled to extend their experience beyond the immediately given.

The poem's deictic structure

Having imagined that there is a speaker, we must now find textual evidence for his utterance. Usually, such evidence can be found in the deictics of a text. They are those features of language which directly relate an utterance to person(s), place and time. (The term comes from a Greek word meaning 'pointing'.) Among the most obvious deictic elements are the personal pronouns and their reflexive and possessive counterparts; demonstratives; locative expressions such as *here*, *there;* the tense forms of the verb; a variety of temporal expressions such as *now*, *then*, *today*, *last week*, *soon*, etc.; and a number of other syntactically relevant features of the context of utterance (Lyons 1977: 657–77). Among these, I reckon the definite article *the* because it shows important similarities with the demonstratives. Thus the fact that it is originally a reduced form of *that* (in its function of demonstratives pronoun) is still reflected in its basic meaning as a specifying agent. For the overall significance of Auden's poem, it is important to recognize that many of these forms can be used either deictically with situational reference, or non-deictically with reference backwards (anaphoric) or forwards (cataphoric) to elements in the text.

Probably the first – perhaps surprising – observation which will be made about the deictic structure of the poem is that there are no first-person pronouns identifying the speaker and no forms of address involving a second person ('you'). This self-effacement, for that matter, is wholly characteristic of Auden, who rejected the conception of the poet intent on expressing their own emotions; it was therefore one of his artistic tenets that a poet should preserve, as he put it himself, a 'necessary impersonality' (Hoggart 1961: 29).

As a matter of fact, there appear to be other textual features, both deictic and non-deictic, which clearly suggest a verbal interaction. I shall explore these features in arbitrary order and relate their implications to my reading of the poem.

Most conspicuously, there is the thematization, that is, the syntactic fronting, of the prepositional group 'About suffering' in the first line. I agree with Traugott that thematization, the choice of what to put first, is a discoursal (so a supra-sentential) rather than a sentential process and, therefore, a kind of deictic, in which the speaker points from one element in the total discourse (the point of departure or 'theme') towards the rest of his statement (Traugott and Pratt 1980: 282–7). Given its prominent place, this starting point may be taken as a reflection of the persona's stream of consciousness in that it gives away what is uppermost in his mind.

Furthermore, it seems to me that the persona's abrupt opening statement 'About suffering they were never wrong,/The Old Masters:' has the rhetorical effect of plunging the reader right into the speaker's conclusion. It is as if the poem opens in the middle of a conversation and I get the impression that in the dramatic sequence of events, the speaker had already been looking at some of the pictures before springing his bold generalization on the reader/listener. In addition, the syntactic delay of 'The Old Masters', which with more deliberateness could have been incorporated into the syntax of the preceding clause, contributes to a casual tone which is sustained throughout the poem.

The poem's rhyme scheme

This casual tone of the poem's discourse is one of the most important influences on its overall meaning. Just as Brueghel, the painter, by his pictorial medium provided his viewers with a fresh insight into the human condition by ironically mingling images of events which are usually regarded as incongruous, the poet Auden exploits his verbal medium to assign a tone to his persona in which the implied reader perceives the same mingling of discordant elements. Indeed, there is general agreement among Auden's critics that the poem's power largely derives from the sustained low-keyed tone of the persona's argument. In particular, Le Page has made a detailed analysis of the factors that bring out this shading in the poem's spectrum of tone: they include the diction and rhythm, the easy-going, under-stressed lines, the predominance of run-on lines, the seemingly purposeless pattern of syllables (only the first three lines have ten syllables resembling blank verse), accent and metre, and finally the unpredictable rhyme scheme (Le Page 1973: 253–8). Though to a large extent I agree with this view, I think that Le Page's observation that the rhyme scheme is unpredictable is not quite accurate. The reader tracing the rhymes will find that they are indeed capricious and sometimes a bit far apart, but they are not entirely unpredictable in that they do interlink the three parts of the first stanza: abcadedbfgfge. Only the last word of line 3 ('place') lacks a rhyming counterpart. The rhyme scheme of the second stanza is even quite regular: aabcddbc. So on the whole the poem's rhymes appear to serve as an appropriate counterpoint to its seemingly rambling syntactic structure.[4]

Other linguistic stylistic markers conveying the persona's casual tone and rhetorical power

In addition to the above widely discussed features, I shall point out below a few more linguistic stylistic markers conveying the persona's casual-sounding tone of voice. Rhetorically, after the powerful generalization with which the poem opens, the rest of the speaker's argument is mainly an exposition in which he indicates specific details in the paintings to illustrate and reinforce the point he is trying to make. This exposition clearly falls into two parts – the first generalizing and the second particularizing, in the sense that in the first stanza a few nameless paintings are considered generally, while the second stanza is entirely devoted to one single painting, Brueghel's *Icarus*. Here, too, the rhetoric is marked by the grammar, the division between generalization and particularization being marked by the syntactic break between the two stanzas, each of which is composed of one sentence.

In fact, the grammetrics[5] of the poem are quite complex: there are two sentences, one covering 13 lines in the first stanza and the other 8 lines in the second; together they consist of a congestion of independent and dependent clauses. Rhetorically, this structural intricacy forces the reader to reconstruct the syntactic process with the result that they are drawn into formulating the persona's argument for themselves.

Another interesting feature on the graphological level[6] (Halliday et al.1964: 50) is the relatively large number of punctuation marks separating, in varying degrees of strength (Quirk et al. 1972: 1054–81), different units of the poem's two sentences. Punctuation marks are auxiliary graphic signs used to denote features of speech such as pauses, emphasis, astonishment, etc. However, they signal not only certain patterns of intonation but also break down the discourse into particular units of information. It appears to me that in either function, this abundance of punctuation marks not only underpins the above-mentioned rhetorical effect of the poem's syntax but also imparts to it a dynamic effect, which, almost physically, guides the reader through the museum room and makes them look at the various details in the pictures one by one, while digesting the persona's exposition of his point of view. Furthermore, the two rambling, meticulously punctuated sentences are clearly imitative of a colloquy between persona and implied reader.

The wider significance of the definite article in its deictic function

In his essay 'Auden and the Audenesque', Bernard Bergonzi reckons a 'copious use of the definite article' among the characteristics of Auden's syntax (Bergonzi 1975: 70). However, Auden appears to have had an uneasy relationship with this part of speech because in the Preface to his *Collected Shorter Poems 1927–1957*, Auden himself writes:

> Re-reading my poems, I find that in the nineteen-thirties I fell into some very slovenly verbal habits. The definite article is always a headache to any poet writing in English, but my addiction to German usages became a disease.

These two statements, added to the fact that, contrary to his habit, Auden left the text of his 'Musée des Beaux Arts' virtually unaltered (Beach 1957), offer sufficient inducement to have a closer look at the implications of its definite articles. As I have said before, the definite article 'the' may be counted among the specific deictics because in many ways it resembles the deictics proper, the demonstratives. Another similarity is, as we have seen, their potential of being used non-deictically as well.

On the other hand, there is a clear-cut semantic distinction between them because the demonstratives carry some referential meaning within themselves, whereas the definite article has no such semantic content of its own. Thus, by their inherent meaning, demonstratives imply proximity, nearness in space or time, be it more or less remote. However, the definite article depends on additional information for its specific reference. This information is supplied inside the text (through anaphoric or cataphoric reference) in case the article is used non-deictically. However, the article is taken to be used deictically when the referential information must be found in the discourse, that is, when the text is related to an appropriate context of use or situation.

Now the fact that the poem does not contain any demonstrative pronoun and that, with one exception[7], all occurrences of the definite article are deictic appears to be a rich source of meaning. This is because the situational context from which the deictic article derives its specific reference may be particular or general. At the same time, however, it must be recognized that there is not always a clear dividing line between particular and general situations; instead, as Quirk et al. have put it, 'there is a scale of generality running from the most restricted to the least restricted sphere that can be envisaged: that of the whole universe of human knowledge' (Quirk et al. 1985: 267).

Obviously, this scale from particular reference to general reference leaves room for ambiguity and I have found this a significant feature in a poem in which the deictic article is so predominant. Especially in the first stanza, where no painting is mentioned by name, the situational reference tends to be rather ambivalent in that it may be interpreted as particular but at the same time as general. For instance, the appellation 'The Old Masters' not only refers to the particular situation of the art gallery and its paintings, but through their iconography the paintings allow us to extend the situation to a much wider frame of reference. In this connection, it is interesting to note that graphologically the words 'Old' and 'Masters' are written with initial capitals. Probably, this is because the expression 'The Old Masters' is felt to have unique denotation in our cultural frame of reference.

Similarly, the definite articles before some other nominal groups, which are crucial in the semantic organization of the first stanza, do not tie down their reference unequivocally to the particular context of the paintings alluded to. Thus, the reference to 'the aged' in line 5, 'the miraculous birth' in line 6 and 'the dreadful martyrdom' in line 10 may be extended to the whole of human history. This potential extension of reference is very significant indeed, considering that 'the miraculous birth' and 'the dreadful martyrdom' are metonymically related to 'suffering', which, as its thematic position in the first line suggests, is probably the main subject of the poem (Servotte 1980: 59).[8] Furthermore, this tendency towards 'generality', is borne out by the fact that according to the rules of English grammar, the reference of the definite article preceding the nominalized adjective 'aged' is essentially generic.

In lines 7 and 8, 'Children who did not specially want it to happen, skating/ On a pond at the edge of the wood', this ambivalent alternation between the particular and the general develops even into a sense of disorientation, brought about by the progression from zero deixis (in 'Children') through the indefinite ('a pond') to the definite ('the edge of the wood'). In effect, the movement is from the ideological[9] context of general experience into the assumed iconic context of a painting – and in these neighbour contexts 'it' – that is, 'suffering', also with zero deixis – takes place.

Surely, one of the poem's themes must be this continuous attempt at blurring the boundaries between general and particular contexts, at merging time past with time present. Becoming more and more aware of this mystification of place and time in the poem's universe of discourse, of this feeling that

> . . .we have no time, because
> We have no time until
> We know what time we fill,
> Why time is other than time was. (from *No Time*, Auden 1966: 192).

I will now look at a few textual features that are exploited to bedevil the reader's temporal experience.

Some textual features bedevilling the reader's temporal experience

In its normal deictic function, in reference to past time, the simple past tense locates the situation about which a statement is made in the past with respect to the time of utterance: 'About suffering they were never wrong,/The Old Masters: how well they understood/Its human position'. However, the simple present tense does not generally refer to a situation which is contemporaneous with the time of utterance and this tense is, therefore, a potential source of ambiguity. Thus, the present tense in line 3, 'how it takes place', undoubtedly generates a significant ambiguity from an interpretive point of view because it is capable of being explained as a grammaticalization of two entirely different speech acts:

1 The persona describes what he sees in the pictures and employs the present tense in its instantaneous use, which signifies an event occurring simultaneously with the present moment and in a definable context.
2 The persona generalizes, in which case the present tense denotes habit, iteration and, by extension, 'eternal truth' (Leech 1971: 2–6).

The first kind of meaning of the present tense might be called 'non-generic', in the sense that it communicates a single, transitory event, whereas the second kind of meaning might be regarded as generic because it expresses an omnitemporal proposition implying that something has been, is and always will be so (Chafe 1970: 188–91). This potential cause of ambiguity is carried on right into the next line 'While someone else is eating or opening a window or just walking dully along' because also the present progressive may be either non-generic or generic. In the non-generic case, the series of events ('eating', 'opening a window' and 'walking') are understood to be in progress at the time of the utterance for a limited period of time. In other words, the events are represented as a process of limited duration within which the other event, 'how it takes place', is temporally located. However, in the generic case, the progressive has an iterative function and is not time-bound. Here it expresses that as suffering takes place, there will always be people going on with their trivial doings.

The present tense progressive in line 5, 'How, when the aged are reverently, passionately waiting/For the miraculous birth. . .', probably has the same double meaning, namely, the non-generic meaning which communicates a single, transitory event bound to a specific place and time or the generic meaning expressing an omnitemporal ever-recurring circumstance.

Another interesting point about this distinction between the non-generic and the generic character of these verbal actions is that it appears to be related to the inferential meaning of the modal auxiliary 'must' in line 6 '. . . there always must be/Children who did not specially want it to happen, skating/On a pond at the edge of the wood'. In fact, this present tense of 'must' can only be generic in meaning expressing an omnitemporal proposition because it is difficult to imagine that the speaker says he 'infers' something to be happening when in fact he sees it happening before his very eyes.

The temporal situation is getting even more bewildering when we take into account that 'must' in line 6 introduces the simple past tense in the next line 'Children who did not specially want it to happen. . .'. It will be recognized that this is unusual in English because the simple past tense normally requires a definite point of orientation, and one of the ways in which this may be specified is the preceding use of a present perfect. Accordingly, it would have been more natural to say 'there always *must have* been/Children who *did* not specially want it to happen', or, conversely, 'there always *must* be/Children who *do* not specially want it to happen'. It will be observed that this temporal ambiguity reinforces the sense of disorientation which we perceived earlier in these lines.

The temporal shift occurring in the opening lines is paralleled in lines 9–13:

> They never *forgot*
> That even the dreadful martyrdom *must* run its course
> Anyhow in a corner, some untidy spot
> Where the dogs *go* on with their doggy life and the torturer's horse
> *Scratches* its innocent behind on a tree. (Italics added)

Again, the movement seems to be from the ideological context of general experience into the iconic context of the paintings. If also here *must* expresses inference based on knowledge acquired by general experience, its generic meaning ties in with the potential extension of reference of the definite article in the phrase 'the dreadful martyrdom'. Thereupon the speaker seems to lead the reader again into the world of the paintings by using the simple present tense of direct report in 'Where the dogs go on with their doggy life and the torturer's horse/Scratches its innocent behind on a tree' involving his immediate perception of what he sees. This latter (non-generic) use paves the way for the simple present tense in the first line of the second stanza 'In Brueghel's *Icarus*, for instance: how everything turns away/Quite leisurely from the disaster. . .', which unambiguously expresses simultaneous commentary on an event in a specific context because the persona has pointed to Brueghel's *Icarus*.

It has already been noted that in the greater part of the first stanza the temporal ambiguities are linked with the ambivalent reference of some of the definite articles. A different kind of correlation is to be observed in the last lines of the first stanza and in the entire second stanza, in which the explicit meaning of the present tense corresponds to the unequivocal reference of the definite articles. As I have pointed out, this shift from ambivalence to monovalence takes place because the persona has made intervening reference to a specific painting.

Furthermore, the ambivalent experience of time, especially where it may be interpreted as an 'omnitemporal' present, must be related to the significant fact that the poem makes use of paintings, artistic representations of reality – and not of reality itself – to illustrate its theme. Immobility, silence, timelessness – these are sensations inherent in the paintings themselves. The 'suffering', 'the miraculous birth', 'the dreadful martyrdom' and the disastrous fall have become the 'foster-child[ren] of silence and slow time'; forever, 'the forsaken cry' will be unheard, and, now that Keats's 'Ode on a Grecian Urn' has forced itself upon the reader's mind, it makes one wonder whether, as a variation upon the immortal lines 'Heard melodies are sweet, but those unheard/Are sweeter', the cries we hear are bitter, but those we do not hear are bitterer.

This haunting question brings me back to the pregnant function of the definite articles in the poem. In his book *Stylistics and the Teaching of Literature*, Widdowson observes that in the last stanza the nominal groups function in such a deictic way that they suggest the immediacy of direct reference to an exact picture. But almost in the same breath, Widdowson emphasizes that a proper description of the linguistic features of a text does not, on its own, lead to a proper interpretation of a poem (Widdowson 1975: 13–14). Of this, to my mind, true observation, the nominal group 'the forsaken cry' in line 16 is a case in point. Clearly, in his description of the picture, the persona has momentarily shifted from the visible to the audible, imagining the cry in his mind's ear.

Similarly, in the frozen world of the picture, the unspectacular and humdrum events of daily life will forever keep in step with the spectacular and the miraculous; forever, the busy ploughman and the dutiful but impassive sun will be the epitome of the world's indifference to human suffering, and the unseeing 'expensive delicate ship' will forever remain 'a painted ship upon a painted ocean'.

Having come to the final stage of my article, I fully realize that any kind of analysis of a poem may lead to an entirely, or at least partly, misleading interpretation because it examines one element in isolation from the others. Therefore, appreciating that a poem is not the sum total of all its elements – its tone, imagery, diction, stanzaic organization, etc. – but that it is all of them at once, I have tried to bring out in my analysis that the poem is a closely knit synthesis in which seemingly discordant elements have been made to harmonize in a forcible poetic statement. The persona's ambivalent tone of high seriousness and self-protective casualness, which has the ironic effect of both mitigating and subtly intensifying the horror of the human condition, is a true image of Brueghel's theme and method; in other words, Auden's poetic genius has turned the paintings into a powerful verbal icon.

My assumption that, in addition to artistic purposes, the persona's irony also serves as a protective shield between the horror of the human condition and the poet's own self may find support in the fact that his collection of essays *The Dyer's Hand* (London 1948) has as its motto Nietzsche's dictum 'We have Art in order that we may not perish from Truth'.

Extracted from Verdonk, P. (1987) 'We have art in order that we may not perish from truth': The Universe of Discourse in Auden's 'Musée des Beaux Arts', *DQR Dutch Quarterly Review of Anglo-American Letters* 17(2): 78–96.

4

Who are the performers of Owen's 'Anthem for Doomed Youth'?[1]

The title's plurality of meanings

On 25 September 1917, Wilfred Owen wrote to his mother: 'I send you my two best war Poems. Sassoon supplied the title 'Anthem': just what I meant it to be.'[2] From Sassoon's memoirs and Owen's biographer Jon Stallworthy we know that, while they were both invalided as nerve patients at Craiglockhart War Hospital at Slateford near Edinburgh, Owen had shown Sassoon a largely unrhymed first draft of a poem for which the latter had suggested as a title 'Anthem for Dead Youth' (Sassoon in Walsh 1964: 35 and Stallworthy 1974: 216–25). Then the poem went through a few more versions and when the final draft, too, was shown to Sassoon, he suggested changing 'Dead Youth' into 'Doomed Youth', which became the final title of this frequently anthologized sonnet (Hibberd 1973: 76):

> Anthem for Doomed Youth
> What passing–bells for these who die as cattle?
>   —Only the monstrous anger of the guns.
>   Only the stuttering rifles' rapid rattle
> Can patter out their hasty orisons.
> No mockeries now for them; no prayers nor bells;
>   Nor any voice of mourning save the choirs,—
> The shrill, demented choirs of wailing shells;
>   And bugles calling for them from sad shires.
> What candles may be held to speed them all?
>   Not in the hands of boys, but in their eyes
> Shall shine the holy glimmers of good-byes.

> The pallor of girls' brows shall be their pall;
> Their flowers the tenderness of patient minds,
> And each slow dusk a drawing-down of blinds.

Owen's delight at the wording of the final title suggested by Sassoon shows his acute sense of its wide-ranging semantic ramifications. Particularly, the word 'anthem' proves to generate many levels of meaning, such as its denotative and connotative meanings, the meanings resulting from its context in the poem, the meaning evoked by its sound associations and the meaning that is suggested by its literary echoes. What Owen did probably not sense was that, on virtually all these levels of meaning, the word 'anthem' lies at the root of the paradox that despite its rejection of formal ceremonies, 'No mockeries now. . .', the poem constitutes in itself a ceremony. Some critics, including Silkin (1979 and 1985) and Lucas (1986), say that this paradox takes the sting out of the poem. Others, including Hibberd (1973), do not see it this way and find the sonnet wholly effective.

However it may be, there is no denying one of history's little ironies that Benjamin Britten used 'Anthem for Doomed Youth' in his *War Requiem*, composed for the consecration in May 1962 of the new cathedral at Coventry built to replace the church destroyed by bombs in 1940. In the text of this work, the Latin Mass of the Dead, the *Missa pro Defunctis*, is ironically punctuated by settings for solo voice of nine poems by Owen (the first in the sequence being 'Anthem for Doomed Youth' and the last 'Strange Meeting'). Further down in this essay, I shall argue that some of the implications and ironies of the title 'Anthem for Doomed Youth' emanate from the dominant sense of the word 'anthem' that was presumably in Owen's mind, namely the strict etymological sense of 'antiphon'. In view of this argument, it is worth noting already at this point that the structure of Britten's composition is also 'antiphonal' in its juxtaposition of the timeless religious language of the mass – ethereally sung by choirboys – with the earthly human language of the poems, sung by the three adult soloists.

According to the definitions in the *Oxford English Dictionary*, 'anthem' denotes (1) a text, usually from the Bible or liturgy, set to sacred music, (2) a song of praise or gladness as used, for example, in the English 'National Anthem' and (3) a composition sung antiphonally by two voices or choirs. As I have said above, it is most likely that it is this etymological sense of 'antiphon' which was uppermost in Owen's mind, and in this connection it is interesting that in the *Book of Common Prayer*, in The Order for Morning Prayer, we find after the Third Collect – the Collect praying for Grace – the rubric 'In Quires and Places where they sing here followeth the Anthem.'[3]

Connotatively, 'anthem' can be associated with a religious ceremony in an ordered community where, sincerely by some and hypocritically by others, life and death are held in respect and surrounded by decorum. Further, it can be associated with other solemnities such as a coronation, a celebration of victory or a commemorative service, which in their turn may conjure up the concomitant sentiments of blustering patriotism.

If we next realize that, both denotatively and connotatively, the attribute 'doomed' carries notions such as 'fated', 'damned', 'cursed', 'condemned to some fate' and 'consigned to misfortune or destruction', it becomes obvious that the syntactic union between 'anthem' and its modifying phrase 'for doomed youth' gives rise to a hybrid range of meanings creating pungent irony. This effect is even further reinforced when we realize that in its ominous prophecy, the word 'doomed' may be interpreted as addressing not only the hundreds of thousands already dead but also the untold numbers yet to die. Presumably, it was Owen's gibe at the armchair heroes at home, the ardent patriots singing hymns and anthems in praise of the young men they had sent to their certain death. Thus, in his edition of Owen's poems, Dominic Hibberd writes: 'To intelligent subalterns like Sassoon and Owen, England seemed full of profiteering and jingoistic clap-trap. The gulf between civilians and combatants was so great that people were using the old phrase "The Two Nations"[4] to describe it.' (Hibberd 1973: 29).

The bitter irony implied in the poem's title is effectively carried on to the octave of the sonnet. Since the conventional paraphernalia of a memorial service would have made a mockery of it all ('No mockeries now for them. . .'), this 'anthem for doomed youth' is orchestrated by the very instruments which have directly or indirectly caused their death. The guns, the shells and the bugles of the two opposing armies are booming, whining and sounding antiphonally in an 'Anthem Macabre', while the staccato rattling of the rifles is a worthy substitute for the hastily and thoughtlessly uttered prayers of a religious ceremony. In connection with the line 'Can patter out their hasty orisons', it is worth noting that the noun 'patter' is used for the kind of gabbling speech with which a cheap-jack extols his wares or a conjurer distracts and deceives his audience. To speak of a priest 'pattering out' prayers would indeed imply a mockery.

Then, at the end of the octave, this grotesque requiem dies down in the final blasts of the bugles, which eases the transition to the subdued tones of the sestet. In answer to the rhetorical question 'What candles may be held to speed them all?' the poem's speaker makes us understand that because the 'doomed youth' are denied a proper burial in the presence of their families and sweethearts, the latter will not find an outlet for their grief in the conventional signs of mourning. The only ritual support left to them is to close the blinds of their homes,[5] which at nightfall is mimed by Nature commiserating with the bereaved by shrouding the earth in darkness.

Evocative sound associations

Of course, this is a banal and unimaginative paraphrase of Owen's sonnet, which does no justice to his masterly control of language on all levels of structure and meaning. Thus, the poem's sound structure is possibly its most powerful rhetorical device. Particularly in the octave, the sound effects are closely related to the sense, culminating in lines 3 and 4, which have almost become the textbook example of alliteration and assonance verging on onomatopoeia:

> Only the stuttering rifles' rapid rattle
> Can patter out their hasty orisons.

And then, to the strains of the title word 'anthem', there are the numerous sound associations evoked by lexical items such as 'passing-bells', 'guns', 'stuttering', 'rifles', 'rattle', 'patter', 'orisons', 'prayers', 'bells', 'voice', 'choirs', 'shrill', 'wailing', 'shells' and 'bugles', which all add force to the cacophony of this gruesome war requiem on the battlefield.[6]

In the sestet, which seems much more concerned with the images of mourning, the sound effects reinforce the meaning structure much less obtrusively, although the underpinning of the metaphor in line 12:

> The pallor of girls' brows shall be their pall;

by the syllable echoes p—l/p—l (possibly with the further echo of 'shall') is too conspicuous to be missed. Besides, the metaphor is also highlighted by a kind of oxymoron, the 'pall', a cloth covering the coffin or bier, being customarily black.

Discourse structure and mind style

Examination of the phonetic texture of the poem, which could be kept brief because Owen's extremely sensitive ear has been highly praised by many other critics,[7] prompts a further stage of investigation into the sonnet's discourse structure. As we proceed to that stage, we begin to discover that the poem is an interpersonal communication in a particular context. With the help of certain features in the printed text of the poem, we shall be able to identify the participants in this communicative act and relate them to a temporal and locational setting. Actually, in my inadequate paraphrase of the poem, I partly anticipated this point by assuming that the text presents a speaker (also known as the persona). Now I will address myself to questions such as these: How does this speaker manifest himself in the poem's discourse? What is the extent of his personal involvement? Are there other speakers involved? Are there any other addressees besides the reader/listener? What is the speaker's location and what is his time reference? These questions are concerned mainly with the so-called 'deixis' of the poem's discourse, which term refers to those grammatical and lexical features which relate the discourse to a time, place or person(s). Another, perhaps the most interesting, question is whether the poem's discourse contains recurrent structural features which somehow reveal the speaker's conceptualization of his experience. For this phenomenon, I shall use Fowler's term 'mind style': 'Cumulatively, consistent structural options, agreeing in cutting the presented world to one pattern or another, give rise to an impression of a world-view, what I shall call a "mind style" ' (Fowler 1977: 76; see also Fowler 1986: 150–67 and Leech and Short 1981: 187–208). To begin with, the speaker clearly manifests himself in the opening lines of the octave and the sestet

> What passing-bells for these who die as cattle?
> What candles may be held to speed them all?

and I will try to show that these speech acts lay the foundations for the whole organization of the speaker's discourse.

First of all, it is obvious that there is a dichotomy between the form and function of these lines, for, though formally questions, in terms of their discourse function, they apparently do not seek information because the answer is supplied by the speaker himself.

Therefore, the speaker's two questions can be regarded in the first instance as rhetorical questions or, to be more precise, as rhetorical wh-questions. In form, such questions have an interrogative wh-element in initial position (e.g., 'What do I care?'), but in their semantic function, they do not expect an answer and have the force of an emphatic statement in which the wh-element is replaced by a negative element ('I don't care.'). So if we regard the speaker's two questions as being used with non-question force, they are semantically equivalent to strong assertions like 'No passing-bells shall be rung for these who die as cattle' and 'There shall be no candles held to speed them all'. However, as we can see, in the poem's discourse, both questions are answered in detail by the speaker himself. So the questions are self-addressed and self-answered and as such they may be termed ratiocinative rhetorical questions giving the speaker ample opportunity to build up a kind of argumentation (Quirk et al. 1985: 826).

Indeed, by using the rigid form of the sonnet consisting of a Shakespearean octave, rhyming ababcdcd, and an Italian sestet consisting of two tercets, rhyming eff egg[8], the poet forces his persona to concentrate on the possibility of formulating some kind of ordered response to the frightful questions.

It is here that I realize that not only the poem's content, as we have seen above, but also its formal realization, namely this question and response structure, exemplifies the denotative sense of 'antiphon' in the title word 'anthem'.

For that matter, this effort on the part of the poet to fit his persona's thoughts into a disciplined mould is also apparent from the poem's grammetrics. By this, I mean the interrelationship between grammatical structure and metrical organization. Thus, there is a tendency in the poem to synchronize grammatical units with metrical units such as the single line (lines 1, 2, 9 and 12), the couplet (lines 3–4, 10–11 and 13–14) and the quartet (lines 5–8). Actually, this tightly structured encasement of the speaker's line of thought is even further reinforced by the fact that none of the run-on lines are 'heavy', in the sense that none of the enjambements interrupts the grammatical structure in the middle of a constituent.

As a deviation from this taut organization, which is of course greatly reinforced by the web of sound patterns throughout the sonnet, there is an 'irregularity' in the speaker's discourse which has not been noticed in the critical literature I have seen. What I am referring to is the stylistic feature that in almost every main clause the verbal predicate is suppressed. In fact, there are only four lines containing such a predicate at main clause level, namely line 4 'can patter out', line 9 'may be held', line 11 'shall shine' and line 12 'shall be'. The few other verbs that the poem contains function as predicates of two subordinate modifying clauses, namely 'who die as cattle' in line 1 and 'calling for them' in line 8, and of a subordinate adverbial clause, namely 'to speed them all' in line 9. This incomplete clause structure requires the reader to establish a bridge of meaning with the nouns which can be associated with the suppressed verbal predicates. In discourse theory, it is generally accepted that human beings are naturally inclined to try to make sense of any spoken or written text which is intended to communicate. Even if there are 'no formal linguistic links connecting contiguous linguistic strings, the fact of their contiguity leads readers/hearers to interpret them as connected. They readily fill in any connections which are required' (Brown and Yule 1983: 224). Thus, when trying to fill in the required connections, they will find that only in two lines, viz., in 13 and 14, the verbal predicates can be recovered from the grammatical structure of the discourse. Following Quirk et al. (1985: 1622–3), I regard the semi-colon as a coordinating mark of punctuation, corresponding most nearly to the coordinating conjunction 'and'. Therefore, the three clauses in lines 12–14 can be seen as coordinated, which enables the reader to retrieve the verbal predicates deleted in lines 13 and 14 from the complete clause in line 12:

> The pallor of girls' brows shall be their pall;
> Their flowers [shall be] the tenderness of patient minds,
> And each slow dusk [shall be] a drawing-down of blinds.

On the other hand, nearly all the other fragmentary main clauses are held together by underlying semantic links. That is, when we try to supply the missing verbal predicates, we mainly rely on lexical linkage. For example, 'passing-bells' and 'toll' or 'ring' belong to the same semantic set. So do 'the anger of the guns' and 'roar out' or 'thunder out'. In the same way, 'prayers' will prompt 'utter' or 'say' and, probably, we will associate 'The shrill, demented choirs of wailing shells' with the verbs 'whine' and 'shriek (out)'. At the same time, of course, this process of inference involves our appraisal of what the poem's speaker tries to communicate (his intended meaning), our awareness of the context and situation of the poem's discourse as well as our socio-cultural knowledge (more generally, the facts about the world): in brief, what is called 'pragmatic' knowledge (see Leech 1983 and Levinson 1983).

Now, what does this semantic and pragmatic exercise yield in terms of a literary stylistic evaluation? I will try to show that it reveals a threefold rhetorical effect.

First, owing to the deletion of the verbal predicates, the nouns to which they are related in the underlying structure are brought into prominence. After all, they are the listener's/reader's mainstay in the interpretive process. Since, as we have noted, most of the nouns involved call up strong sound associations, this prominence results in a highly *audible* performance of this sinister anthem.

Second, if we do fill in the missing links, the din will only increase in intensity because most of the nouns linked with the suppressed predicates prompt verbs which appeal to our auditory sense! Thus, in our mind's ear we hear 'the passing-bells toll', 'the guns roar', 'the shells whine', as well as other sounds evoked by the verbs occurring in the deep structure.

Third, the deletion of finite verbs with their defined tense, mood and person is a clear demonstration of' the speaker's impersonal tone, which, for that matter, seems to be in harmony with his ratiocination initiated by the two rhetorical questions that I discussed earlier.

The persona's ambition to be impersonal

On the subject of stylistic features showing the speaker's ambition to extend the poem's situation beyond personal boundaries, it is significant that there is no first-person pronoun in the poem; nor is there any second person 'you'. On the other hand, there are plenty of third person references: their hasty orisons; no mockeries now for them; bugles calling for them; to speed them all; but in their eyes; shall be their pall; their flowers. For a proper understanding of the grammaticalization of the speaker's detachment, it is important to note that in the English pronominal system, the first person includes the speaker, the second person includes the addressee, whereas the third person excludes both speaker and addressee, that is, third-person pronouns refer to 'third parties' not directly involved in the speech event (see Lyons 1977: 638, and Levinson 1983: 69).

In connection with line 4, 'Can patter out their hasty orisons', there is a grammatical point which is interesting in view of what has been said about third-person references. The point is that 'their' in this line is ambiguous, that is, what is its antecedent? Does it refer to the rifles that stutter out their mockery of prayer for the doomed and dying (as the priest utters his orisons in church, so the rifles patter their orisons on the battlefield)? Or does it refer deictically to the doomed themselves? (So that 'their orisons' equals 'the orisons that are said on their behalf'). The two readings are:

a   The rifles say their [the rifles'] prayers
b   The rifles say their [the young men's] prayers

Though reading (a) is at least possible, reading (b) must be the one intended by Owen, in which case, 'their' must, in performance, bear a marked accent – 'Can patter out *their* hasty orisons' – in coupling with a similar accent on *these* in the first line, and *them* in the line beginning 'No mockeries now for them'.

When I described the genesis of 'Anthem for Doomed Youth' at the beginning of this essay, I wrote that Owen made a fairly large number of drafts of the poem. Indeed, no fewer than seven complete drafts have survived. Interestingly, two of these produce evidence that Owen intentionally forged this armour of impersonality for his persona because from the first and second drafts, he removed all first- and second-person pronouns (Hibberd 1973: 148–50).

For that matter, a comparison of the first line in these four drafts also shows that the poet was consciously working on the grammaticalization of his persona's detachment:

> First draft: What passing-bells for these who die so fast?
> Second draft: What passing-bells for you who die in herds?
> Third draft: What passing-bells for these dumb-dying cattle?
> Fourth draft: What passing bells for these who die as cattle?

The reason why 'you who' had to go is clear now. But the choice for 'these who' in the final version is remarkable because the usual equivalent of the 'the ones who' is 'those who' (Quirk et al. 1985: 872). Few grammarians are explicit about the possible usage of 'these who': Close (1975: 138) clearly states that only 'those', not 'these', will occur in the phrase 'those who', while that great storehouse of knowledge *A Grammar of Late Modern English* by Poutsma (1916: 917) mentions that no instances have been found of the demonstrative 'these' used as determinative in the group 'these who'.

The interesting question is, of course, why did Owen deviate from standard usage? First of all, it is noteworthy that none of the drafts has 'for them who', which would have been in accord with the ultimate predominance of third-person references in his poem. So his choice for 'these who' must have been deliberate. Perhaps Owen's motives can be reconstructed as follows: Both 'for them who' and 'for those who' serve the purpose of sounding impersonal, but 'these who' gives more scope for ambiguity. Thus, for instance, if 'these' is interpreted anaphorically, the phrase 'doomed youth' in the title and 'these who die as cattle' in the first line become identical. At the same time, however, 'these' can have situational reference because the speaker in the poem may assume that he shares with his listeners/readers the extra-linguistic situation of the poem, namely the slaughter-house of the Great War. The irony in this presupposition is, of course, that the speaker knows very well that lots of his countrymen pretend not to know or refuse to face the facts. And, finally, if the proximity expressed by 'these' is interpreted psychologically rather than spatially (Quirk et al. 1985: 374), it might even betray the speaker's personal involvement and thus reveal a chink in his armour of impersonality.[9]

The persona's references to place and time are elusive

Having established that, except for this possible lapse, the speaker hides behind a mask of impersonality, and that there is no addressee apart from the reader/listener, I must next conclude that the speaker's references to place and time are equally elusive. This unfixedness results from various deictic features, which include the following:

1   The above-mentioned suppression of verbal predicates which, potentially, might have provided temporal references to the situation of the speaker's discourse.
2   The present tense 'die', in the clause 'who die as cattle', does not primarily refer to an event occurring at the moment of speech, but rather implies an inherently unrestricted time span (Quirk et al. 1985: 179–81).
3   The finite verbal predicates 'can patter out', 'may be held', 'shall shine', 'shall be', as well as the hypothetical verbal structure in (which may speed

them all) underlying 'to speed them all' do not have a purely temporal reference, because, though present tensed, the auxiliaries 'can', 'may' and 'shall' primarily encode modal notions (Lyons 1977: 677). In brief, it seems as if the speaker's awareness of time is psychological rather than actual or historical.

4 All definite articles, with one significant exception, are used non-deictically because their definite reference can be derived from the linguistic context. The exception is the article defining 'guns' in line 2, which is used deictically, in that it depends for the identification of its referent on the extra-linguistic situation. Just as with the demonstrative 'these' in line 1, that is, if interpreted as having situational reference, the speaker assumes that his listeners/readers know what situation he is referring to. Clearly, with the same ironic effect. Here, too, there is evidence of the poet's awareness of this effect, because the first draft had 'our guns', which, apart from missing this particular ironic point, would have narrowed down the situational context by excluding the guns of the enemy, and that would have worked against the poem's general tendency to widen out the locative and temporal context as much as possible.

5 Finally, there is the speaker's predilection for the use of plural nouns (out of 33 nouns, no fewer than 23 show a plural sibilant suffix). Apart from leaving a trail of hissing sounds throughout the sonnet, these plurals give an emotional colouring of intensity and extent to the speaker's discourse, having at the same time a generalizing effect (Zandvoort 1975: 122).[10]

By now, at least two aspects of the speaker's mind style are taking shape. On the one hand, his successful attempt at an impersonal style is very effective in driving home to his audience, in a pseudo-objective manner, something they know to be inescapably true. On the other hand, there is the speaker's consistent refusal to be tied down to a specific time and place: he does not indicate any clearly defined period, the events are not localized, they could have occurred on either side, in any war. Now, of course, if we look at the poet's life, we could relate his persona's discourse to World War I, to the horrors of trench warfare on the Western Front, but the above characteristics of the speaker's mind style also allow his listeners/readers to universalize a horrifying experience. As Philip Larkin has put it: 'But in the end Owen's war is not Sassoon's war but all war; not particular suffering but all suffering; not particular waste but all waste. If this verse did not cease to be valid in 1918, it is because these things continued, and the necessity for compassion with them' (Larkin 1983: 162–3).

Owen's allegiance to the Romantics and the Victorians

It is a well-known fact that throughout his short life, Owen's poetic reading was devoted mainly to the Romantic and Victorian writers. He almost worshipped Keats and also Shelley, Wordsworth, Tennyson and Swinburne influenced his poetic views profoundly. One of Owen's poetic precepts could have been the following statement by Shelley in his *A Defence of Poetry* 'Poetry turns all things to loveliness; it exalts the beauty of that which is most beautiful, and it adds beauty to that which is most deformed; it marries exultation and horror, grief and pleasure, eternity and change; it subdues to union under its light yoke all irreconcilable things' (Jones 1965: 134).

This allegiance of Owen to the Romantics and the Victorians also shines through the vocabulary of his persona in 'Anthem for Doomed Youth' in that it is pervaded with what in literary criticism is called Romantic idiom. Since also lexis plays an important part in the encoding of ideas and experience, the extensive and repetitive use of words and phrases which are reminiscent of Romantic poetry constitutes a significant element of the speaker's mind style. Thus, through its literary echoes, the Romantic idiom contributes to his achievement of broadening the temporal perspective of his theme, while, at the same time, it is conducive to an ironic distance from his subject because by using it, he suggests, 'by contrast or default, what it [can] no longer express' (Johnston 1964: 205–9).

As a matter of fact, it is again the word 'anthem' in the title which sparks off a sequence of Romantic reverberations. For instance, it is not unlikely that Owen also embraced Sassoon's suggestion for calling the sonnet 'Anthem' because it immediately reminded him of Keats's 'Ode to a Nightingale', 'Adieu! Adieu! thy plaintive anthem fades/Past the near meadows, over the still stream,. . .', and further, it may have appealed to him because it amplifies other Keatsian echoes in the poem. Thus, David Perkins (1976: 279–85) is probably right in his presumption that many readers will be haunted by literary reminiscence in the lines: Nor any voice of mourning save the choirs,—/The shrill, demented choirs of wailing shells, and will not feel contented until they have located their artistic provenance in Keats's ode 'To Autumn':[11] 'Then in a wailful choir the small gnats mourn.' And, tracing the word 'anthem' in other Romantic poets, I came upon these lines in Tennyson's 'Ode on the Death of the Duke of Wellington':

> Let the bell be toll'd:
> And a deeper knell in the heart be knoll'd;
> And the sound of the sorrowing anthem roll'd

> Thro' the dome of the golden cross;
> And the volleying cannon thunder his loss;
> He knew their voices of old.
> For many a time in many a clime
> His captain's-ear has heard them boom
> Bellowing victory, bellowing doom: (11. 58–66)

It may very well be that these lines, too, can be heard in the disturbing Romantic echoes in Owen's 'Anthem'. Anyway, the flag-waving jingoism exuded by these lines and the customary accessories such as 'the sorrowing anthem' and the booming guns 'Bellowing victory, bellowing doom' brilliantly illustrate 'What stuff [Owen's irony] is made of'. Here we are reminded of another letter Owen sent to his mother from Craiglockhart War Hospital in which he wrote: 'Tennyson, it seems, was always a great child. So should I have been, but for Beaumont Hamel.' (Near this place Owen's regiment had been involved in particularly severe fighting. [Bell 1985: Letter 538]).

The semantic roles of the subject constituents in the persona's mind style

Finally, there is still another important aspect of the persona's mind style which I wish to draw attention to. It proves to be encapsulated in the poem's syntax and in order to bring it out, I have analysed the semantic roles embedded in the subject constituents of the poem's clause structure. With some slight modifications, I have used the descriptive terminology from Quirk et al. (1985: 740–54) and for the tentative results of my analysis, I refer to the enclosed appendix. For a detailed discussion about the theory of 'transitivity', I refer to Halliday's article 'Types of Process' (1976: 159–73), while for its application in stylistic criticism, reference is made to Halliday in Freeman (1981: 325–60), to Fowler (1977, 1981 and 1986) and to Leech and Short (1981).

In making this analysis, I was again confronted with the above-mentioned suppression of most verbal predicates in the octave. Since the subject's semantic role is mainly determined in the light of its relationship with the verb and, if necessary, with other clausal elements, I think it is plausible that this cumulative pattern suggests a deliberate obfuscation of this role on the part of the persona.

Besides, my analysis has shown that in order to convey his persona's bemused understanding of who is responsible for what, the poet has used other linguistic resources. To appreciate these resources, I shall give an account of a number of participant roles which potentially underlie the subject function in a clause. Here, the term 'participant role' is a semantic notion refer-ring to the nouns (or more precisely, the noun phrases) encoding the human and non-human beings, as well as the inanimate and abstract entities which participate or play a particular role in the situation described by the clause.

My analysis has yielded the following potential roles of the subject which Quirk et al. specify, viz. 'affected', 'eventive', 'identified' and 'temporal', to which I have added the epithets 'cause' and 'result'. Besides, Quirk et al. mention eight more possible roles of the subject, viz. 'agentive', 'instrument', 'external causer (force)', 'characterized', 'experiencer', 'recipient', 'positioner' and 'loca-tive'. We must note here that of all these roles that of *agentive* participant is the most typical of the subject.

I have enumerated this list of roles for two reasons: first, because it shows the widely varied semantic potential of one and the same syntactic function; second, and perhaps more interestingly, because both the instances in the poem and the examples in Quirk et al. demonstrate that, with the exception of the characteristic correspondence between subject and agent, there is no correlation between the classic subject position in the clause and its potential semantic role.

It is obvious that this indistinct role-marking in the surface structure, on the one hand, and, on the other hand, our tendency to identify the subject position with the agentive role, provide a writer with a welcome linguistic device to create confusion and ambiguity. For instance, a particular repetitive lexico-syntactic structure may suggest a pattern of 'agentiveness', which, upon closer inspection, turns out to be a matter of mere manipulation of our perception. In fact, this somewhat lengthy account was needed to show that this is exactly what the poet Owen has done.

Indeed, after retrieving from the deep structure the suppressed verbs in the octet by lexical linking (as we have seen, the two missing verbs in the sestet can be recovered from the grammatical structure), and having thus reconstructed the semantic roles of the related subjects, I have found that, although just about all the subjects take up their characteristic agent position on the left-hand side of the clause, none of them actually has this role of agentive participant: that is, 'the animate being instigating or causing the happening denoted by the verb' (Quirk et al. 1985: 741).

As a matter of fact, there is only one subject referring to people. Most portentously, it is the pronoun 'who' in the clause 'who die as cattle', which, in accordance with the semantic classification I have adopted, must be assigned the somewhat euphemistic role of 'affected' participant. For the rest, the human element in the subjects is only represented by a few synec-dochical phrases such as, for instance, 'the holy glimmers of good-byes' and 'the pallor of girls' brows', which play various participant roles but not the one of agent.

On the other hand, there is a strong preference for non-human subjects, many of which have the affected role, with great emphasis on the process in which they are involved, but without implying human agency: 'What passing-bells (shall toll)', 'the monstrous anger of the guns (shall thunder out)', '(nor) bells (shall ring)', 'The shrill, demented choirs of wailing shells (shall shriek)' and 'bugles (shall sound)'. These subjects are not agentive. Nevertheless, one tends to ascribe to them the metaphorical character of agents – a process which, for that matter, is commonly occurrent in everyday language. (Quirk et al. 1985: 745 give the appropriate example 'Guns kill'. See also Chapter 8 'Guns don't kill people, people kill people' in Bolinger's *Language: The Loaded Weapon* 1980: 68–88).

The persona has two different voices

Obviously, the moment we become aware of the persona's tendency to humanize inanimate agents, we sense the literary effects which I pointed out earlier: in the octave, the irony emanating from the replacement of the public rituals of death by the baneful weaponry of war and, in the sestet, the pathetic inadequacy of the private rituals of mourning. However, there must be more to it. For, if the theory of mind style is correct, the relation between 'reality' and the way in which its experiencer describes it, is just as important as any other fact, because 'reality' is to a large extent 'constructed' by the experiencer on the basis of their knowledge, expectations, prejudices, etc., and it also constantly changes under the influence of their personal emotions (Dennis Potter expresses similar views in a fascinating interview in *De Tijd* of 2 October 1987, pp. 44–7). And, indeed, if my analysis of the persona's mind style has shown one thing it is that we can hear two entirely different voices of a man who is torn between conflicting emotions and whose conceptualization of experience shifts with them. (See also Adrian Caesar's very interesting essay 'The 'human problem' in Wilfred Owen's poetry' in *Critical Quarterly*, summer 1987, pp. 67–84).

Thus, earlier, we have heard the voice of a man whose speech is imbued with bitter irony, who couches his words in a mould of formal discipline, who displays an almost Olympian impersonality and distance and who fully succeeds in creating an impression of undefinableness of the poem's historical occasion. In brief, a man speaking with authority and feeling in full control of the situation.

This must have been the public voice of Owen, the poet's poet, who had undertaken the mission to raise a public outcry against the war, as well as of Owen, the gallant officer, who felt sure that through good leadership he would actually be able to help his soldiers. About his mission as a poet of protest, he wrote to his mother on New Year's Eve 1917: 'I go out of this year a Poet, my dear Mother, as which I did not enter it. I am held peer by the Georgians; I am a poet's poet.' And in the same letter, he continues to explain why he has to go back to the front: 'But chiefly I thought of the very strange look on all faces in that camp; an incomprehensive look. . . . It was not despair, or terror, it was more terrible than terror, for it was a blindfold look, and without expression, like a dead rabbit's. It will never be painted, and no actor will ever seize it. And to describe it, I think I must go back and be with them' (Bell 1985: Letter 578). And how he took his duty as an officer is apparent from another letter to his mother, which he wrote one month before his death. After having told her that he has been recommended for the Military Cross, he writes: 'My nerves are in perfect order. I came out in order to help these boys – directly by leading them as well as an officer can; indirectly, by watching their sufferings that I may speak of them as well as a pleader can. I have done the first' (Bell 1985: Letter 662).

However, in the poem we can hear a completely different voice of a man whose speech shows a predominant tendency to obscure the subject role by divesting it of its customary human agency. It shows us a man who feels that things have got entirely out of human control. Or is it that he refuses to face the dreadful fact that, after all, it is human beings who must be held responsible for these horrors of war and that, therefore, he reasons himself into the false belief that stronger non-human forces have seized power? At this point, it is worth considering that also the persona's Romantic idiom brings out these two voices: the confident voice of the missionary poet's poet and the doubtful voice of his alter ego. For, as we have seen, the former uses it to an ironic and distancing effect, while for the latter, it is a convenient device to keep reality at bay.

The doubtful voice must be that of Owen, the private man, who appreciates that, most ironically, his poetry is engendered by the very same war which it protests against. In a famous letter of May 1917 to his mother, Owen summed up this inner conflict in one pregnant sentence: 'And am I not myself a conscientious objector with a very seared conscience?' (Bell 1985: Letter 512).

It must also be the voice of the other self of Owen, the officer, who is painfully aware that through his commands he is actually driving the soldiers to their deaths. This awareness emerges from letters he wrote to Sassoon and his mother on two successive days in 1918. On 31 August, he wrote to his mother: 'And now I go among cattle to be a cattle-driver. . .' and one day later to Sassoon: 'And now I am among the herds again, a Herdsman; and a Shepherd of sheep that do not know my voice' (Bell 1985: Letters 647 and 649). But most of all this ambivalence reveals itself in the following passage from a letter he wrote in July 1918 to Osbert Sitwell: 'For fourteen hours yesterday

I was at work – teaching Christ to lift his cross by numbers, and how to adjust his crown; and not to imagine the thirst till after the last halt; I attended his Supper to see that there were no complaints; and inspected his feet to see that they should be worthy of the nails. I see to it that he is dumb and stands to attention before his accusers. With a piece of silver I buy him every day, and with maps I make him familiar with the topography of Golgotha' (Bell 1985: Letter 634).

Without claiming that this analysis is in any way exhaustive, I still think that at least to some extent it reveals the paradoxes and inner conflicts from which presumably all of Owen's war poetry was born, and that it needs an extremely sensitive ear to discern between all the performers of this direful anthem.

Appendix

The semantic roles embedded in the subject constituents of the clause structure of Owen's 'Anthem for Doomed Youth':

What passing-bells [shall toll] (intrans)	AFFECTED[1]
who die (intrans)	AFFECTED
the monstrous anger of the guns [shall thunder out] (intrans)	CAUSE or RESULT[2]
the stuttering rifles' rapid rattle	CAUSE
can patter out their hasty orisons (trans)	
[there shall be] no mockeries (intrans)	EVENTIVE[3]
no prayers [shall be uttered] (intrans)	RESULT
(nor) bells [shall ring] (intrans)	AFFECTED
(nor) any voice of mourning [shall be raised] (intrans)	AFFECTED
(save) the choirs, – the shrill demented choirs of wailing shells [shall shriek out] (intrans)	AFFECTED[4]
bugles [shall sound] (intrans)	AFFECTED
What candles may be held (intrans)	AFFECTED
(. . . in their eyes) shall shine (intrans)	
the holy glimmers of good-byes	EVENTIVE
the pallor of girls' brows shall be (copula)	IDENTIFIED[5]
(their pall)	
their flowers [shall be] (copula)	IDENTIFIED
(the tenderness of patient minds)	
each slow dusk [shall be] (copula)	TEMPORAL[6]
(a drawing – down of blinds)	

[1] With intransitive verbs, the subject frequently has the AFFECTED role elsewhere typical of the direct object (Quirk et al. 1985: 743)

[2] Though the retrieved verb phrase [shall thunder out] is intransitive, the AFFECTED role for 'the monstrous anger of the guns' does not seem particularly appropriate. Therefore, I suggest CAUSE or RESULT, though the latter is not one of the epithets used by Quirk et al.

[3] An important role of the subject is EVENTIVE. The noun at the head of the noun phrase is commonly deverbal or a nominalization (Quirk et al. 1985: 747).

[4] As I have suggested in the body of this essay, if we metaphorize the non-agentive (inanimate) subject, its role is agentive.

[5] The term 'affected' has been extended generally to subjects of copulas. But we can make some further distinctions within the affected role for subjects according to whether the subject complement as attribute identifies or characterizes (Quirk et al.1985: 743).

[6] The subject may have the TEMPORAL role of designating its time (Quirk et al.1985: 747).

Some further reading

Blunden, E. (ed.) (1931), *The Poems of Wilfred Owen.* London: Chatto & Windus.

Day Lewis, C. (ed.) (1963), *The Collected Poems of Wilfred Owen.* London: Chatto & Windus.

Hibberd, D. (ed.) (1981), *Poetry of the First World War.* London: Macmillan.

Press, J. (1969), *A Map of Modern English Verse.* Oxford: Oxford University Press.

Thwaite, A. (1978), *Twentieth-Century English Poetry.* London: Heinemann.

Extracted from Verdonk, P. (1988) 'Who are the Performers of Owen's 'Anthem for Doomed Youth'?', *Parlance. The Journal of the Poetics and Linguistics Association* 1(2): 203–22.

5

The language of poetry: The application of literary stylistic theory in university teaching[1]

This chapter gives an account of a project in literary stylistics which I carried out with fairly advanced students in the English Department of the University of Amsterdam. The objective of the project was to scrutinize a number of theories and techniques that are to be found within the 'New Stylistics' and to exemplify these approaches by analysing a number of twentieth-century poems.

Narrowing down the field

As far as I know, it was Roger Fowler (1975: 4) who coined the term the 'New Stylistics', which, as he pointed out, should not be taken as a common denominator of a particular school of stylistics, but as a pragmatic designation of the output of writings produced approximately between the 1960s and 1990s by scholars mainly in Great Britain and the United States, who were trying to come to grips with the language of literature.

Fowler also provides a brief survey of the characteristics of the New Stylistics, and he concludes that 'theoretical catholicity' is one of them. Indeed, a mere glance at a bibliography on the subject will suffice to appreciate that since the publication of Sebeok's *Style in Language* in 1960, which is usually taken as a convenient starting point for this flood of activity, stylistics has received much impetus from the multifarious developments in linguistics during the same period.

It is therefore obvious that to make a short-range project with students workable, one has to select a limited number of approaches, which should preferably show some kind of interrelation and unity of thought. In narrowing down the field, I developed a predilection for the stylistics originating from the body of research carried out in Britain (also starting in the 1960s) in the neo-Firthian or Hallidayan school of linguistics. Taking my students' linguistic expertise into account, I set out on essentially text-oriented approaches and compiled for them a select bibliography of writings produced mainly in the earlier stage of this British tradition, which has been designated as 'classic' stylistics (D'haen 1986: 3). The items featuring in this reading list are included in the bibliography at the end of this book. As in some respects, British stylistics has been influenced by the Russian formalists, the Prague aestheticians and international structuralism, the working bibliography also included relevant passages from Jakobson (1960), Mukařovsky (1964) and Culler (1975).

After preliminary talks about this theoretical framework, we focused our attention on some of the writings of Leech (1965), Fowler (1971a: 219–37), Widdowson (1974) and Cluysenaar (1976 and 1982) (in fact, we dealt with them in this order) for the actual application of some stylistic models.

Motivation of the project

Having set these bibliographical bounds to the project, I shall now discuss its chief motivation. Though I have no wish to get involved in the old controversy about the relevance of linguistic stylistics to literary criticism, this project has been set up with students of both disciplines on the assumption that a sensitive and effective linguistic perception that leads to subtle stylistic distinctions does provide a secure basis for an aesthetic appreciation of literature. Another motive is the desire to counteract the falling off of a formal knowledge of language due to the present-day educational spirit, at least in The Netherlands. It must be admitted that the average student has learnt to talk quickly and very easily, which is in itself a joyful phenomenon, but I am afraid that this success has often been attained with the sacrifice of the ability to reflect on language with patience and sensitivity.

This is not the place to rehearse the fundamentals of linguistics and stylistics that are needed to evolve such an aptitude for the workings of language. Suffice it to say that with the help of illustrative material I have tried to show my students that literary stylistics is primarily concerned with the relation between linguistic form and literary function. Furthermore, I have emphasized time and again that stylistics should never be reduced to some mechanical ticking off of the linguistic features of a text, but that, on the contrary, intuition and personal judgement (based on observable textual features) are of paramount importance.

Place in the curriculum, duration and teaching format

Before discussing the internal design of the project, I wish to give some factual details about its place in the curriculum, its duration and its teaching format. After completing an 18-month uniform introductory programme, our students split up into three main streams: modern linguistics, historical linguistics (both applied to English) and English and American literature. Each main-stream programme consists of a certain proportion of compulsory and optional courses varying in content, intensity, teaching format and length. Literary stylistics comes under the optional courses, and as it is considered to be an interdisciplinary subject, it can be chosen by literature as well as linguistics students.[2]

The course lasts one semester (which is 13 weeks of our academic year) and usually there are two seminar groups involved with about 15 students each for 2 hours per week, which means that I have 26 hours of actual teaching time for each group.

The classroom model for a project like this is very important and I fully agree with Roger Fowler (1986: 178) that the seminar format ensures maximal involvement of the students while the teacher's role is less dominant. As a result, the students feel more inclined to share their views and ideas and to cooperate on oral and written assignments.

Internal design of the project

As to the internal design of the project, I wish to emphasize that I have found it to be of crucial importance to bring about a firm link between what Leech (1977) called the three levels of exegesis: the *linguistic level* of non-aesthetic discussion, the *literary critical level* of aesthetic discussion and an intermediate level which he called the *stylistic level.* It is on the stylistic level that linguistic statements are selected for their relevance to the aesthetic discussion on the literary critical level. For this selection of relevant linguistic features, I encouraged the students to apply some stylistic theories such as the theory of *foregrounding,* which will be discussed further down, and at the same time to keep an open mind on other aesthetic considerations. As a matter of fact, both my students and I have found this interplay between the non-aesthetic and the aesthetic to be quite revealing and fruitful.

With this objective in mind and after several try-outs in the preceding academic year, when the students came up with a lot of valuable suggestions, I finally decided on the following physical organization of the project.

The first three weeks were spent on introductory talks about the theoretical basis of the project, though I took care that these talks were interspersed with practical applications of the various stylistic models. As a result of this approach, the students became highly motivated to have a go themselves.

After these preliminaries, I handed out a working-schedule (covering the remaining ten weeks) on which the students were asked to enter themselves for the following assignments (at the end of the project, all students were supposed to have done assignment B, while they had a choice between assignment A or C):

Every *even* week – *Assignment A*:

Two or three students were to present an article to the seminar to be chosen from: Leech (1965), Fowler (1971a: 219–37), Widdowson (1974), Cluysenaar (1976: 50–75) and Cluysenaar (1982). These writings were to be discussed in this order. (In order to facilitate discussion, all members of the seminar were supposed to have studied the articles beforehand.)

Every *odd* week – *Assignment B*:

Two or three students had to hand out on paper a stylistic analysis of a twentieth-century poem based on the model suggested in the article discussed in the preceding week.

Assignment C:

Two or three students had to make sure that they had a preview of the stylistic analysis referred to in assignment B so that they could make evaluative comments and lead the discussion when the analysis was presented to the seminar.

It was my role to chair these proceedings, to come up with suggestions whenever the discussion got stuck, to intervene when the discussion was sidetracked, to make notes for subsequent evaluation and so forth.

Analysis of Philip Larkin's 'Going' based on the model proposed by Leech (1965)

At this point, I would like to turn to the presentation of the stylistic analyses resulting from the seminar discussions described above. As I have said, there were some 30 participants in the project so that they must of necessity remain nameless, but all the same I wish to make a point of giving them the share of the credit that is due to them.

The first poem for which we suggest an interpretation based on a literary stylistic analysis is Philip Larkin's 'Going' (1955). We have proceeded on the model of analysis proposed by Geoffrey Leech (1965).[3] In his analysis of Dylan Thomas's 'This Bread I Break', Leech proceeds from linguistic description to literary interpretation. Pointing out that 'a work of literature contains dimensions of meaning additional to those operating in other types of discourse', he expresses the view that linguistic description cannot be applied to literary texts without proper adjustments and he therefore incorporates three stylistic concepts: *cohesion*, *foregrounding* and *cohesion of foregrounding*.

Endorsing the view that it is the linguist's aim to make 'statements of meaning', Leech refers to the work of J. R. Firth (1957: 32–3 and 190–215), the founder of the neo-Firthian or British school of linguistics. Leech points out that 'meaning' in the above quotation must be given a wider sense than usual, sometimes including every aspect of linguistic choice: semantics, vocabulary, grammar or phonology, and though Leech mentions it later in his paper, it is convenient to anticipate and to add here another aspect conducive to meaning, viz., context of situation. In Firthian linguistic theory, meaning is looked upon as a complex phenomenon, its various aspects being relatable to features of the external world as well as to the several levels of linguistic analysis. Context of situation refers to the whole set of external world features considered to be relevant to the analysis of an utterance at these levels (Firth 1957: 192). Leech adds to this that, prototypically, in literature we have to construct such a context from the text itself.

We shall now suggest an interpretation of Larkin's poem in the light of a linguistic analysis extended with the above-mentioned stylistic categories of description: cohesion, foregrounding and cohesion of foregrounding.

> Going
> There is an evening coming in
> Across the fields, one never seen before,
> That lights no lamps.

Silken it seems at a distance, yet
[5]   When it is drawn up over the knees and breast
It brings no comfort.

Where has the tree gone, that locked
Earth to the sky? What is under my hands,
That I cannot feel?

[10]   What loads my hands down?

February (?) 1946 Philip Larkin, *Collected Poems* (1988: 3)

Cohesion

Leech defines *cohesion* as 'the way in which independent choices in different points of a text correspond with or presuppose one another, forming a network of sequential relations'. So what is of interest is the way in which these linguistic choices form patterns of intra-textual relations on any of the levels of linguistic description: phonology, grammar, semantics and pragmatics.

The cross-references to the postponed subject *an evening* in line 1 are only made by grammatical means, viz., by the pronominal *one* in line 2, by the pronoun *that* in line 3 and by a high concentration of the pronoun *it* in three consecutive lines: 4, 5 and 6. It is noticeable that there is no attempt at repetition of the noun *evening* by means of lexical items so as to reinforce its contextual meaning. In part, this meaning is conveyed grammatically. The article *an* modifying *evening* (1) as well as the earlier-mentioned pronominal cross-references (*one, that* and *it*) carry a suggestion of indefiniteness. This notion is reinforced by the cohesive grammatical structure of the poem: two long declarative sentences, which, evidently, do not contain enough information about *an evening* to prevent the following three relatively short WH-questions in lines 7, 8 and 10.

Furthermore, there is the repetition of three negative elements: *never* in the clause *never seen before* (2) expresses *unfamiliarity* with *an evening*, while *no* in the descriptive clauses *That lights no lamps* (3) and *It brings no comfort* (6) conveys its negative aspects.

The most obvious grammatical pattern in this poem is the selection of the simple present tense in lines 3, 4, 6, 8, 9 and 10. As a matter of fact, the passive *is drawn up* (5) and the aspectual verbal forms *is coming in* (1), *seen* (2) (here we assume the underlying structure 'one that has never been seen before') and *has gone* (7) also have a present tense form in their explicit or implicit auxiliaries. In fact, there is only one past tense: *locked* in line 7. This predominance of the present tense seems to suggest an inescapable immediacy.

Foregrounding

Referring to the theory of aesthetics and language from the Czech School (see Garvin 1964), Leech interprets *foregrounding* as 'a motivated deviation from linguistic, or other socially accepted norms'. Elsewhere (in Fowler 1973: 75), he defines foregrounding as 'the violation of rules and conventions, by which a poet transcends the normal communicative resources of the language, and awakens the reader, by freeing them from the grooves of cliché expression, to a new perceptivity'.

In our poem, there are many foregrounded groupings of lexical items as a result of the following deviant choices from the language code:

i 'an evening is coming in' (1)
ii '(an evening) That lights no lamps' (3)
iii 'Silken it (an evening) seems at a distance' (4)
iv 'it (an evening) is drawn up over knees and breast' (5)
v 'It (an evening) brings no comfort' (6)
vi '(the tree) that locked earth to the sky' (7–8)

In (i), (ii) and (v), the noun *evening* which normally has the feature of ínanimateness is given a human feature. In (iii) and (iv), the same noun is also used in highly unpredictable collocations. If we set up the frames *Silken . . . seems at a distance,* and, *When . . . is drawn up over the knees and breast,* the noun *evening* is not available for selection in these positions. A normal choice, particularly in the second frame, would be, for example, the nouns *sheet* or *blanket.*

If we take the verb *lock* in (vi) to mean 'to fix or to join firmly together', the choice of the noun *tree* is abnormal, not to mention the semantic oddity of the collocation *locked earth to the sky.*

The above instances of lexical foregrounding are clear illustrations of metaphorical language in which linguistic forms should be given something other than their normal (literal) interpretation.

There is grammatical deviation in the pattern *Silken it seems at a distance* (4) in which the subject complement *silken* is preposed.

Furthermore, the syntactic ambiguity of *What is under my hands,/That I cannot feel?* (8–9) could be regarded as a way of foregrounding this WH-question. The clause *That I cannot feel* can be seen as an adverbial (of result): 'so that I cannot feel', though it also seems possible to regard the constituents *what* and *that I cannot feel* as being in an attributive relationship.

There is also an example of internal deviation in this poem, viz., in the stanzaic structure. The poet deviates from his own pattern and thereby from our expectations created by the poem, when he concludes with a one-line stanza after three stanzas consisting of three lines each. As a result, the last stanza is foregrounded and placed in focus.

Cohesion of foregrounding

The third stylistic descriptive statement with which Leech extends the linguistic categories of description is *cohesion of foregrounding.* By this is meant the manner in which 'the foregrounded features identified in isolation are related to one another and to the text in its entirety'. So this feature may occur when certain foregrounded elements, though deviant from normal language use, form a cohesive intra-textual pattern and thus become normal in the context of the poem as a whole.

With regard to this stylistic category, it may be observed that in our poem there is such a predominance of deviant lexical collocations which are foregrounded against normal usage (particularly with the noun *evening*) that they take on a normality in the context of the poem as a whole and can be regarded as a form of cohesion.

Further extended foregrounding is observed in the phonology of the first six lines of the poem in which there is a striking predominance of sibilants: there are fourteen /s/ or /z/ phonemes.

Linguistic stylistic description 'locked to' literary interpretation

Now that we have pointed out several linguistic and stylistic features of the poem, we must ask the question 'To what extent are these features artistically significant?' It will be clear that a satisfactory answer to this question will narrow (or perhaps even close) the gap between linguistic stylistic description and literary interpretation.

For a possible interpretation of the poem, we still need a *context of situation,* which we must infer from the text itself. The situation that suggests itself to us is that of the hour of death of the I-person in the poem. We shall take this situation as a starting point and examine to what extent the cohesive and foregrounded features fit in with this particular level of interpretation.

The association of *an evening* with imminent Death is conveyed by the grammatically cohesive patterns that suggest 'indefiniteness', 'unfamiliarity', 'negative aspects' and 'inescapable immediacy', as well as by the foregrounded lexical patterns in which this noun occurs: *an evening* is given animate features;

it is coming in and it has never been seen before. So it is not just any evening. It seems to have come unexpectedly (cf. 'death's dateless night', Shakespeare, *Sonnet 30*), because people have not lit their lamps. However, the ensuing darkness will persist because this 'evening' *lights no lamps*. It seems useless to try and keep away the darkness of this evening of Death as one would keep away the darkness of an ordinary evening: with lamps. The predominance of sibilants in the first six lines describing the coming of the evening can be seen as reinforcing the stealthy way in which Death is approaching.

In the second stanza *evening* seems *silken. . .at a distance* but *when it is drawn up over knees and breast, it brings no comfort*. The idea of a (silken) sheet or blanket suggests itself. The image of being covered may be associated with dying. However, the I-person is not dead yet, because then the sheet would also have covered his head. The 'sheet of Death' is only seemingly silken and *brings no comfort*.

The third stanza differs very much from the previous ones, which consist of two long sentences. Here we are confronted with two relatively short questions following each other without stopping for an answer. This seems to indicate the persona's growing anxiety at his approaching death. The questions concern his decreasing consciousness of his surroundings. He can no longer see the tree *that locked earth to the sky*. Is it the 'tree of life' (*Genesis* 2: 9)? His diminishing sensibility is also apparent from the fact that he can no longer feel what is under his hands, or, alternatively, that because something (Death?) is under his hands, he cannot feel at all any more (see our earlier discussion of the syntactic ambiguity of *What is under my hands,/That I cannot feel?*). This becoming numb may be seen as a symptom of dying.

We have already observed that the last one-line stanza is foregrounded and therefore gets the maximum of attention. One is inclined to interpret this as the last moment before actual death. Death has now enveloped the I-person entirely and he feels its terrible weight: *What loads my hands down?* This last question also remains unanswered, only silence remains. It is the silence of Death: the I-person is no longer 'going' (we now fully understand the title of the poem!); he is 'gone'.

A brief exposé of a stylistic model proposed by Widdowson (1974)

The most important feature of Widdowson's stylistic model (1974: 202–31) seems to be the idea that a literary text can be construed as a 'secondary language system', a micro-language, formed by the relations which writers set up between the language items within their text. For the interpretation of any text, Widdowson continues, we must recognize not only these intra-textual relations but also the extra-textual relations that exist between the language items occurring in a text and the code from which they derive. The intra-textual relations set up between linguistic items within a literary text create contextual meaning, while the extra-textual relations yield the significance which the items have according to the code, that is, their referential meaning.

In Widdowson's view, it is typical of literature that these two sets of relations do not join to produce one new unit of meaning. On the contrary, 'they overlap to create a unit of meaning which belongs to neither one nor the other: a hybrid unit which derives from both code and context and yet is a unit of neither of them' (1974: 206).

Elsewhere, Widdowson has written that if stylistics is to make any valuable contribution to criticism, literature must be studied as a mode of communication, and in such a study, means and ends must be given equal attention and shown to be interdependent (1980: 235–41). For an appreciation of what writers try to convey, we must study the means they are using in relation to the linguistic resources they can draw on. Since such an examination does not yield enough information about the communicative effect of the writer's linguistic means, we must also know what ends are achieved on that score. According to our understanding, this concept of style emphasizes the contributions of 'form' to 'content', in brief, style is looked upon as 'meaning'.

Analysis of Jon Silkin's 'Death of a Son' based on the model proposed by Widdowson (1974)

After this very brief exposé of Widdowson's stylistic approach, I wish to examine its applicability to the interpretation of poetry and we present here an analysis of Jon Silkin's poem 'Death of a Son' (from Allott 1950: 383–5)[4]:

Death of a Son
(*who died in a mental hospital, aged one*)

Something has ceased to come along with me.
Something like a person: something very like one.
And there was no nobility in it
Or anything like that.

[5]   Something was there like a one year
Old house, dumb as stone. While the near buildings

    Sang like birds and laughed
        Understanding the pact

    They were to have with silence. But he
[10] Neither sang nor laughed. He did not bless silence
        Like bread, with words.
            He did not forsake silence.

    But rather, like a house in mourning
    Kept the eye turned in to watch the silence while
[15]   The other houses like birds
            Sang around him.

    And the breathing silence neither
    Moved nor was still.

    I have seen stones: I have seen brick
[20] But this house was made up of neither bricks nor stone
        But a house of flesh and blood
            With flesh of stone

    And bricks for blood. A house
    Of stones and blood in breathing silence with the other
[25]   Birds singing crazy on its chimneys.
            But this was silence,

    This was something else, this was
    Hearing and speaking though he was a house drawn
        Into silence, this was
[30]   Something religious in his silence,

    Something shining in his quiet,
    This was different this was altogether something else:
        Though he never spoke, this
            Was something to do with death.

[35] And then slowly the eye stopped looking
    Inward. The silence rose and became still.
    The look turned to the outer place and stopped,
        With the birds still shrilling around him.
            And as if he could speak

[40]   He turned over on his side with his one year
       Red as a wound
       He turned over as if he could be sorry for this
       And out of his eyes two great tears rolled, like stones,
                                              and he died.

In our analysis, we shall proceed in agreement with Widdowson's proposal 'to pick on features in the text which appeal to first impression as unusual or striking in some way and then explore their ramifications'.

One of the striking features in this poem is the use of the pronominal *something* in the first two stanzas. *Something* usually refers to an inanimate object, but here it is used with reference to the son, a human being. In the subsequent stanzas, however, the child is referred to by means of the personal pronouns *he, him* and the possessive *his,* which is in agreement with the rules of the code. As a result of this overlap of intra-textual and extra-textual reference of *something,* it acquires a hybrid meaning, giving the son both inanimate and human attributes.

A similar process is found in lines 19–24: 'I have seen stones: I have seen brick/But this house was made up of neither bricks nor stone/But a house of flesh and blood/With flesh of stone/And bricks for blood. A house/Of stones and blood in breathing silence. . .' After the son has been compared to a house in the preceding stanzas: *a one year/Old house, dumb as stone* (5–6) and *a house in mourning* (13), the persona tells us explicitly that *this house was made up of neither bricks nor stone* (20). In this way he breaks the rules of the code, taking away some of the features of the referent *house* and then makes up for the deficiency by placing the deviant items *flesh* and *blood* in a pattern with *house: a house of flesh and blood/With flesh of stone/And bricks for blood* (21–3). In the very next line, however, the feature *stone* returns in the phrase *A house/Of stones and blood* (23–4). As a result, the noun *house* also gains a hybrid meaning conveying both animate and inanimate qualities.

The above observations show that the poet does not only sever the extra-textual relations by referring to a person as *something* and by presenting a house *of neither bricks nor stone* (20), but also breaks the intra-textual relations he has set up within his poem. First he constructs the phrase a *house of flesh and blood* (21), which requires us to give the noun *house* a significance beyond that which it carries in the language code, and then he diminishes this contextual meaning again by referring to the extra-textual features of the referent *house,* reintroducing the feature *stones,* though preserving the deviant item *blood,* which yields a *house of stones and blood* (23–4).

The poet also breaks up intra-textual relations within the context of the poem without recurrence to extra-textual relations with the code. In the second stanza, the boy is compared to a house and consistent with this deviant intra-textual pattern, the other children (if we assume that they are also mental patients in the same hospital) are referred to as *the near buildings (6)*. Apparently, these children are lively and cheerful, as we can gather from the highly deviant clause *the near buildings/Sang like birds and laughed* (6–7). This deviation holds for the lexical collocations only, because the syntax is entirely regular: subject – predicator – adverbial (of manner). However, in the fourth stanza we find: *The other houses like birds/Sang around him* (15–16). It will be observed that the prepositional phrase *like birds* has been given a different place, viz., following the subject and preceding the predicator. In this position, the phrase still functions as an adverbial, but it is now related not only to the process denoted by the verb (as in lines 6–7), but also to the subject. *The other houses* (15) can thus be construed as bird-like in other ways besides their singing. Many of the adverbials in this position show their relationship with the subject by allowing a paraphrase like 'They were like birds when they sang around him', showing a complement relationship between the subject *they* and the adverbial *like birds.* This syntactic shift prepares us for the poet's severance of the intra-textual relations set up by him between *the near buildings* (6), *the other houses* (15) and the other children, because in the seventh stanza, he no longer compares these children to buildings or houses but only to birds, which are *singing crazy* on the chimneys of the one remaining 'house': the dying boy. The boy and the other children are no longer of a kind: 'A house/ Of stones and blood in breathing silence with the other/Birds singing crazy on its chimneys' (23–5).

Another stylistic feature that arrests our attention is the frequent repetition of one and the same lexical item, viz., the noun *silence.* Widdowson remarks that literature, and indeed all art, creates 'patterns out of deviations from normality and these patterns then represent a different reality from that represented by the conventional code'. What are the patterns involving the word *silence* in this poem and what different realities are created by them?

The first occurrence of *silence* in line 9 is not entirely unexpected, because we have already been told that there was *something. . .like a one-year-/Old house, dumb as stone* (5–6). However, the collocational pattern in which the word *silence* is used deviates from the conventions of the code: 'While the near buildings/Sang like birds and laughed/Understanding the pact/They were to have with silence' (6–9). So we have here another instance of overlapping of extra-textual relations which link the word *silence* with the code ('condition of not speaking') and intra-textual relations which link it with the contextual situation in which it seems that the cheerful children felt free to sing like birds and to laugh, because they understood *the pact they were to have with silence.* At one level of meaning, *silence* may be taken to refer to the dying boy, as in lines 17–18: *And the breathing silence neither/Moved nor was still,* and, being mental patients themselves, the other children would of necessity have some mysterious bond with the dumb little boy ('the pact they *were to* have with silence').

The other contextual patterns in which the word *silence* is placed also accrete to it a wealth of meanings over and above that which can be recovered from the code.

Thus the lexical patterning in the third stanza creates obvious biblical echoes: *He did not bless silence/Like bread, with words./He did not forsake silence* (10–12).

In line 14, *Kept the eye turned in to watch the silence,* there is a collocational clash with the verb *watch* expressing visual perception and its abstract object. Here *silence* is within the boy; in lines 23–4 and 29 the boy is within *silence: A house/Of stones and blood in breathing silence* (23–4), and *he was a house drawn/Into silence* (28–9), while the boy is *silence* in lines 17–18, and probably also in line 26: *And the breathing silence neither/Moved nor was still* (17–18), and *But this was silence* (26).

In lines 29–30, *silence* is again related to religion: *this was/Something religious in his silence,* and we notice that after *He did not bless silence/Like bread, with words* (10–11), *something* (the dying boy) acquires a religious attribute. The structurally identical lines 30–1: *Something religious in his silence,/Something shining in his quiet* emphasize the link between *something religious* and its parallel *something shining:* the religious feature seems to be shining through now, the persona can see it. The son has become quite different from the *something* of the first line.

In line 36, *The silence rose and became still,* the word *silence* is again used in a highly deviant lexical environment. We feel inclined to relate this line to lines 13–14: *like a house in mourning/Kept the eye turned in to watch the silence.* Of a house in mourning, the curtains are lowered, its inhabitants cannot look out ('they keep their eyes turned in') and inside reigns the silence of grief. In line 36, we find *the silence rose and became still.* Does this mark the end of mourning? Did the curtains rise *(the silence* [of mourning] *rose)* because the house is no longer in mourning and is there an end to the acute pains of grief *(and became still)*?

We are perfectly aware of the fact that we have touched upon only very few of the manifold contextual problems and their resultant meanings in this moving poem and that this brief discussion has raised more questions than it has answered. Nevertheless, we think we have shown that, at any rate in this poem, 'form' and 'content' are interdependent, in other words, that style is 'meaning' (for more on this very complex issue, see Leech and Short 1981: 12–73). The poem's style reflects the disorderly thoughts, the confrontation with different realities and unrealities, caused by the untold grief of the persona for the death of his small son.

Analysis of Sylvia Plath's 'Ariel' based on the stylistic model proposed by Cluysenaar (1982)

We now turn to Anne Cluysenaar (1982), who has expressed the view that a consideration of fairly obvious lexical and syntactic features of a literary text can be made to yield semantic information that may be found relevant to its literary description and evaluation. Since Cluysenaar's paper was primarily intended for those engaged in teaching English literature to non-native speakers, she recommended a simple approach to observe these formal properties. Hence there is no need to discuss this approach separately.

We propose to analyse Sylvia Plath's 'Ariel' (1965) along the lines suggested by Cluysenaar, though we will also make use of some extra-textual information, such as the fact that Ariel[5] was the name of Sylvia Plath's horse. We will also take into account the poet's symbolic use of colours, which can be found in her other poems as well.

     Ariel
     Stasis in darkness.
     Then the substanceless blue
     Pour of tor and distances.

     God's lioness,
[5]   How one we grow,
     Pivot of heels and knees! – The furrow

     Splits and passes, sister to
     The brown arc
     Of the neck I cannot catch,

[10] Nigger-eye
     Berries cast dark
     Hooks —

     Black sweet blood mouthfuls,
     Shadows.
[15] Something else

     Hauls me through air —
     Thighs, hair;
     Flakes from my heels.

> White
> [20] Godiva, I unpeel —
> Dead hands, dead stringencies.
>
> And now I
> Foam to wheat, a glitter of seas.
> The child's cry
>
> [25] Melts in the wall.
> And I
> Am the arrow,
>
> The dew that flies,
> Suicidal, at one with the drive
> [30] Into the red
>
> Eye, the cauldron of morning.

At the lexical level of the poem, we find that the largest set of lexical items refers to parts of the body: *heels* (6), *knees* (6), *neck* (9), *thighs* (17), *hair* (17), *heels* (18), *hands* (21), *eye* (31). That *neck* (9) refers to the horse is clear. With the exception of *eye* in the last line, the other items seem to refer either to the rider or to the horse, and in line 6 perhaps to both. This lexical string denotes the physical aspect of the ride. However, the ambiguity as to the possessor of the *eye* in line 31 illustrates that the action described is more than just physical. For *eye* contains a whole range of possible references, of which that to a part of the body is only the most obvious one. One might conclude that the predominantly physical process ends in line 21, where the persona is liberated from all that captivates her, here symbolized by the shedding of her physical being.

The next conspicuous set of lexical items is formed by words referring to colours: *blue* (2), *brown* (8), *black* (13), *white* (19), *red* (30), of which *black* is reinforced in *darkness* (1), *nigger-eye* (10), *dark* (11) and *shadows* (14) and *red* in *blood* (13). *Blue* and *brown* are fairly neutral and undramatic colours and do not have the strong symbolic implications which black, white and red have in Sylvia Plath's poetry. (Cf. *black* in 'Daddy', and *red* and *white* in 'Tulips'.) All colours mentioned – with the possible exception of *white* (19) – have reference to the real landscape or the physical setting of the poem. *Blue* (2) and *brown* (8) are merely part of this setting, whereas *black* (13), *white* (19) and *red* (30) point to the symbolic dimension of the ride. So here, as in the previous lexical string, we find a transition from the physical, the natural to the symbolic level.

The third lexical string is formed by items referring to nature: *tor* (3), *furrow* (6), *berries* (11), *air* (16), *wheat* (23), *seas* (23), *dew* (28). It is significant that with the first four items, the persona seems to experience nature as something external. The last three items, however, apart from possibly functioning at a literal level, are used as images to express the rider's sensation of personal disintegration and unification with nature:

> White
> Godiva, I unpeel
> Dead hands, dead stringencies.
>
> And now I
> Foam to wheat, a glitter of seas. (19–23)
>
> And I
> Am the arrow,
>
> The dew that flies
> Suicidal, . . .(26–9)

Pondering over this sense of disintegration and the rider's complete identification with nature, we are tempted to regroup the above lexical set into the subsets [*tor, furrow, wheat*], [*air*], [*seas, dew*] and to add [*red/Eye* (30–1), *cauldron* (31)] assuming that they refer to the rising sun. The result is that such a lexical framework comprises the four elements: earth, air, water and fire, of which, according to pre-scientific ideas of physiology, all matter is composed.

Continuing this line of thought, we notice that the string of lexical items referring to water can be extended further: *foam* (23), *melts* (25) and perhaps also *the . . .blue/Pour* (2–3).

Though we are anticipating one of the possible readings of the poem, we wish to point out here the irony in *The dew that flies/Suicidal* (28–9), if we bear in mind that water is universally thought of as a life-giving force.

Even a brief look at the syntax suffices to say that the poem's grammar is extremely complex and in some lines highly ambiguous. The appendix shows an attempt at a syntactic analysis, which reveals a number of striking characteristics that are conducive to the overall meaning of the poem.

The marking of the syntactic constituents shows the boundaries of the sentences, clauses and phrases and also where they do not coincide with a line-end. It will be noted that there is a very large number of run-on lines, in many of which the syntactic pull is particularly strong because the run-on occurs within a phrase. This feature has a marked effect on the verse-movement, because after the opening line *Stasis in darkness,* which true to its wording is actually the only still point in the whole poem, the reader is hurried forward and thus seems to join in the rider's rush throughout the poem to *red/Eye, the cauldron of morning* (30–1).

There are probably a number of causes that can be assigned to the poem's overall impression of syntactic complexity and ambiguity. We notice some verbless clauses, for example, in lines 1–3. Furthermore, there are a number of obscure syntactic relationships, for example, the phrases *sister to/The brown arc/Of the neck I cannot catch* (7–9) and *Black sweet blood mouthfuls* (13). Assuming that our analysis makes sense, we observe that at several places a given syntactic constituent is delayed, for example, *Shadows* (14), *Thighs, hair* (17) and *Flakes from my heels* (18). It is also difficult to know whether *Flakes* is a verb or a noun and whether it is related to *Something else* (15). Another such disturbing question concerns *unpeel* (20). Is it really a transitive verb or is it intransitive? Whatever it may be, the syntax of the poem seems to be well-adapted to its subject, since these complexities and ambiguities are a clear reflection of the fleeting impressions of the surrounding landscape that rushes past as well as of the whirling thoughts caused by the rider's ecstasy and impetuous urgency.

The first and most literal reading of the poem offers a description of a horse ride, with horse and rider setting out in the dark of an early morning galloping in ecstasy towards the rising sun. Interwoven with this first reading and never entirely separate from it is a more symbolic one in which the ride takes on a spiritual dimension. In the literal reading, the *Stasis in darkness* is that of horse and rider poised for action. *Stasis,* however, which also carries the meaning of 'stoppage' or 'stagnation', can be seen as applying to the inner state of the persona: totally passive, withdrawn from life. The ride becomes a way of escaping from this stagnation and of finding release in the fiery sunrise, the beginning of a new day.

It is important to realize that this process of liberation is not initiated by the persona, but that it is brought on by a force outside. In the beginning it is the horse, in line 15, it is *Something else* and although towards the end the rider has completely merged with the movement *(I am the arrow)*, the source of the motion is still outside the persona.

When *Something else* (15) propels the rider through the air, all inessentialities and restrictions are shed. There is purification *(white* in line 19), the rider having become as naked as the mythical heroine Godiva, there is disintegration *(Thighs, hair; /Flakes from my heels)* and a complete merging with nature. At last the rider reaches unity, which until then had not been total (cf. *The brown arc/Of the neck I cannot catch,* lines 8–9).

The lines *The child's cry/Melts in the wall* (24–5) stand out rather oddly. They are obscure, but they seem to convey impotence and inability to communicate. In spite of this, the persona regains self-confidence: *And I/Am the arrow* (26–7), speeds on and finds ultimate release in the *red/Eye, the cauldron of morning.*

That this is the key phrase in the poem is made perceptible by the fact that, whereas the rest of the poem is neatly divided into three-line stanzas, this last line stands apart. It is the culmination of the ride, and it is rich in ambiguity. Though the word *eye* fits into the first lexical string of parts of the body, its immediate context suggests a number of different readings. For example, the word *arrow* (27) leads us to associate *the red/Eye* (30–1) with the 'bull's eye': the persona has reached the ultimate goal of the ride. When we interpret *eye* as something that is central or is felt to be central, that is, the 'core' of something, another reading suggests itself: *Eye* as *I*. This reading is supported by the process of 'unpeeling', the shedding of inessentialities as described in the central stanzas of the poem. The *Eye/I* then is the persona's pure, raw, red essence, the core of being.

It gradually becomes clear that the ecstatic ride, the gallop for liberation may also be a ride towards destruction:

> And I
> Am the arrow,
>
> The dew that flies
> Suicidal, at one with the drive
> Into the red
>
> Eye, the cauldron of morning. (26–31)

The rider has escaped from the *hooks* (12) and *dead stringencies* (21) have been shaken off. *Stasis* has been turned into motion, darkness has become light. Yet this light is fiery, aggressive, and the rider could be consumed by it. The rider has become *wheat, dew,* both symbols of fertility, but the dew will evaporate in the heat of the sun. *Stasis,* though negative in its meaning of 'stagnation', etc. is positive when it implies 'a state of balance or equilibrium', whereas *morning,* which has positive connotations when it is seen as an image of the birth of a new day, of new hope and energy perhaps, acquires a negative shade of meaning as a result of its being equated with *cauldron* (i.e. in its sense of 'a state of unrest or upheaval'). Thus the poem ends on a superbly ambiguous note.

In her book *Introduction to Literary Stylistics* (1976: 32) Anne Cluysenaar postulates that 'each [literary] work sets up, by the way in which its particular elements interact, a balance of forces which must be understood as a unique structure'. Such 'dominant structures' are linguistic patterns which may reveal meaningful events at any level of linguistic form. These events must be related at all levels with each other and with formal poetic (and other) structures and to wider aspects of meaning.

Following these precepts, we have based our reading of this poem mainly on its 'dominant' lexical and syntactic structures and have also related the latter to the verse movement. In other words, what we have attempted is to bring out the poem's unique balance of formal – semantic interactions.

Epilogue

Obviously, the above three stylistic analyses form only a small part of the total output of the project (actually 15 poems were submitted to an analysis), in which about 30 students took part (and, I may say, they all carried out their assignments with a great deal of enthusiasm and a strong motivation to make the thing a success). Yet these three analyses are fairly representative of the students' level of achievement.

During the evaluation of the project, the general feeling of the students was that they had learnt to look at poetry with different eyes: they had learnt to ask questions about the language of a poem that they might otherwise have ignored.

Earlier on, I said that having to make allowances for my students' knowledge of linguistics at the time of the project, I had to work with essentially text-oriented approaches. I am well aware of the limitations of these models and that the recently developed functionally, that is, socially and communicatively, oriented dimensions of analysis will add to the literary critical potential of stylistics. On the other hand, an account of textual structure and its semantic implications will keep its *raison d'être* in literary stylistics. Besides, I think that the stylistic analyses presented in this chapter are by no means too formalist and that they consistently show what Short (1986: 161) refers to as 'the inferential approach to language'. In other words, the meanings attached to the foregrounded, cohesive and parallel structures in these three poems are based mainly on the reader's intuition and his or her social and cultural experience.

Anyway, what I have been striving to bring about in my students has never been, and probably will never be, better expressed than in the memorable words that Peter Porter wrote in 1978:

It is the duty of art [poetry in this case] to make palatable somehow the real tragedy of the world. It must tell the truth about the facts of that tragedy at the same time. This is a tall order but one which poets have to face up to. One way of doing so, I believe, is to question the machinery of language, to try to test the worth of the words we use to describe our feelings, I don't mean games with words, but a constant awareness of the shapes language makes of itself. Such questioning means that poetry can never hope to be very popular. Yet its feelings should be universal.

Appendix

'Ariel', Sylvia Plath   Notes

1. <u>Stasis</u> <u>in darkness</u>.
       S   A   1. We assume: 'There is (a) stasis in
                                           darkness.'

----

2. <u>Then</u> <u>the substanceless blue</u>→→
       A   S
                                       2–3 We assume: 'Then follows the
                                            substanceless blue pour of tor
                                            and distances'

3. <u>Pour of tor and distances</u>.
                  S
4. <u>God's lioness</u>,
       Vocative   4 Ariel is also a Hebrew name
                                          signifying 'lion of God'

----

5. <u>How</u> <u>one</u> <u>we</u> <u>grow</u>,
       A   SC   S   V   5–6 We assume: 'How we grow one,
                                            (how we become) a pivot of heels
                                            and knees!'

6. <u>Pivot of heels and knees!</u> – <u>The furrow</u>→
              SC   S

----

7. <u>Splits and passes</u>, <u>sister to</u>→→
       V (coord.)   SC   7–9 We assume: 'I feel/am (like) a
                                               sister to the brown arc of the neck
                                               I cannot catch.'

8. <u>The brown arc</u>→→
       SC (contd.)
9. <u>Of the neck I cannot catch</u>,
          SC (contd.)

----

10. <u>Nigger-eye</u>→→
          S   10–12 and 14 We assume: 'Nigger-eye berries
                                                     cast dark hooks – (dark) shadows.'

11. <u>Berries</u>   <u>cast</u> <u>dark</u>
    S (contd.)   V DO
12. <u>Hooks</u> —
    DO (contd.)

---

13. <u>Black sweet blood mouthfuls,</u>
               DO   13 We assume: 'I remember/I still taste these mouthfuls of black sweet blood when eating the nigger-eye berries.'

14. <u>Shadows.</u>
    DO (contd from 12)

---

15. <u>Something else</u>→
           S   15–17 We assume: 'Something else hauls me, thighs, hair, through air.'

16. <u>Hauls</u> <u>me</u> <u>through air</u> —
    V   DO   A
17. <u>Thighs, hair;</u>
    DO (contd)

---

18. <u>Flakes</u> <u>from my heels.</u>
    V   A   18 We assume: 'Something else (15) flakes from my heels.'

---

19. <u>White</u>→→
    Vocative
20. <u>Godiva,</u>   <u>I</u> <u>unpeel</u> →
    Vocative S V
    (contd)   19–20 Alternatively: 'Like White Godiva I unpeel –' in which case 'White Godiva' functions as an adverbial.

---

21. <u>Dead hands, dead stringencies.</u>
               DO   We assume: 'I unpeel

　　　　　　　　　　　　　　　　　(shed) (my) dead hands, dead
　　　　　　　　　　　　　　　　　stringencies.'

22.　And now I →
　　　cc　 A　S

23.　Foam to wheat, a glitter of seas.
　　　　V　　　　　　SC　　　　　　　23　We look upon 'to foam' as an
　　　　　　　　　　　　　　　　　　　　　intensive verb here; hence 'to
　　　　　　　　　　　　　　　　　　　　　wheat, a glitter of seas' is marked
　　　　　　　　　　　　　　　　　　　　　as a subject complement.

24.　The child's cry→
　　　　　　S
25.　Melts in the wall.
　　　　V　　　A
26.　And I→
　　　cc　S

27.　Am the arrow,
　　　V　　SC　　　　　　　　　　　27–29　We assume: 'I am the arrow
　　　　　　　　　　　　　　　　　　　　　　(and) the dew that flies suicidal.'
　　　　　　　　　　　　　　　　　　　　　　(One would expect 'suicidally'. Cf.
　　　　　　　　　　　　　　　　　　　　　　*Webster's Third New International
　　　　　　　　　　　　　　　　　　　　　　Dictionary* (1976): 'The ouzel. . .
　　　　　　　　　　　　　　　　　　　　　　flies suicidally through a
　　　　　　　　　　　　　　　　　　　　　　waterfall.')

28.　The dew that flies,→
　　　　SC (contd)
29.　Suicidal,　　at one with the drive
　　　SC (contd)　　　　　A

30.　Into the red→→
　　　　　　A　　　　　　　　　　　　30–1　We assume an appositive
　　　　　　　　　　　　　　　　　　　　　　relationship between 'the red eye'
　　　　　　　　　　　　　　　　　　　　　　and 'the cauldron of morning'.

31.　Eye, the cauldron of morning.
　　　　　　　　A

Note

'→' marks run-on lines

'→→' marks a 'stronger' run-on line because the run-on occurs within a phrase.

For this analysis, we have chiefly made use of the terminology and general view of grammar presented in Quirk et al., *A Grammar of Contemporary English* (1972). The following abbreviations are used: S = subject; A = adverbial; SC = subject complement; V = verb; DO = direct object; cc = coordinating conjunction.

Extracted from Verdonk, P. (1989) 'The language of poetry: the application of literary stylistic theory in university teaching', in Short, M. (ed.), *Reading, Analysing and Teaching Literature*. London: Longman, pp. 241–66.

6

Poetry as text and discourse: The poetics of Philip Larkin[1]

'Strange to be ignorant of the way things work.'

Larkin's poetics in brief

While working on the relationship between text and discourse in poetry, I came across Philip Larkin's well-known mini-essay 'The Pleasure Principle', which he first published in the 1950s and re-published in 1983 in his collected prose pieces, ironically entitled *Required Writing* (Larkin 1957 and 1983: 80–2). The essay gives an account of Larkin's own poetics, and its style is so straightforward and thereby persuasive that I cannot resist the temptation to quote the opening paragraph in full:

It is sometimes useful to remind ourselves of the simpler aspects of things normally regarded as complicated. Take, for instance, the writing of a poem. It consists of three stages: the first is when a man becomes obsessed with an emotional concept to such a degree that he is compelled to do something about it. What he does is the second stage, namely, construct a verbal device that will reproduce this emotional concept in anyone who cares to read it, anywhere, any time. The third stage is the recurrent situation of people in different times and places setting off the device and re-creating in themselves what the poet felt when he wrote it. The stages are interdependent and all necessary. If there has been no preliminary feeling, the device has nothing to reproduce and the reader will experience nothing. If the second stage has not been well done, the device will not deliver the goods, or will deliver only a few goods to a few people, or will stop delivering them after an absurdly short while. And if there is no third stage, no successful reading, the poem can hardly be said to exist in a practical sense at all.

Right after setting out these principles, Larkin makes the provocative remark that 'All modes of critical derogation are no more than different ways of saying this, whatever literary, philosophical or moral terminology they employ. . .'. In spite of this curt dismissal of literary criticism, I can't get away from the impression that Larkin's poetic theory is in a way reminiscent of what T. S. Eliot wrote in his essay 'Hamlet' (1919; reprinted in Eliot 1951: 141–6) when introducing the term 'objective correlative': 'The only way of expressing emotion in the form of art is by finding an 'objective correlative'; in other words, a set of objects, a situation, a chain of events which shall be the formula of that *particular* emotion; such that when the external facts, which must terminate in sensory experience, are given, the emotion is immediately evoked.' Although this is not the place to discuss the manifold theoretical problems underlying Eliot's concept, I wish to endorse at least one of the objections which has been raised to it, namely that it is hardly likely that a poet can be so absolutely in control, and so transparently present in the text, that any given situation or chain of events will express for the poet and evoke in the reader precisely the same *'particular* emotion' (Vivas 1944).

The reader and the context are vital in a poem's discourse: The third stage in Larkin's poetics

Having expressed this reservation, I still think that Larkin's meta-linguistic account of his own manner and aims in writing poetry provides interesting material for comparison with the main principles and methods of a literary stylistics which is founded on a pragmatic approach to language. Such an approach does not stop at a consideration of the formal structures of language, but seeks to explain how these structures are actually used and experienced by the participants in an act of communication performed in a particular context (Brown and Yule 1983; Levinson 1983).

To begin with the most fundamental principle of such a literary pragmatic approach, I subscribe to the view that a poem, and for that matter all other literary genres, can be regarded as a verbal composition which represents an utterance or discourse between the author and the reader.[2] Discourse may be defined here as a context-dependent interpersonal linguistic activity whose form depends on its social purpose, which in our case is a message in a certain literary form transmitted from author to reader.[3]

Working in reverse order, I think it can be argued that the tenet that literature is a mode of discourse falls in with the third stage of Larkin's tripartite structure, the stage of the reader's response and of pragmatics, in which readers, as verbal creatures, display their habitual communicative behaviour by responding to the poet's verbal structure. Readers do so because the verbal structure encodes a discourse in which a speaker invites them, and sometimes even provokes them, to create conceivable contexts for it. On this point, the literary pragmaticist fully agrees with Larkin that the reader is a vital link in the poem's discourse and that, as he puts it, the poem does not exist in a practical sense at all, if there has been no successful reading. Again, in literary pragmatic terms, the poet's text becomes a meaningful discourse only at the time when it is being read, that is, when the reader starts to build up interpersonal and socio-cultural contexts by imagining plausible circumstances and motives which could have given rise to the discourse gradually taking shape.

Indeed, it is an established fact that language in use, that is discourse, is governed by a wide range of contextual factors, which may extend from the phonological, grammatical and semantic context (sometimes designated as the co-text) to broader contexts such as the situation within which the discourse occurs, the identities, beliefs, attitudes of the participants and the relations holding between them. Even more broadly, readers might also take into account any social, psychological, historical or cultural contexts if these prove to have a bearing on the act of communication.

With regard to the interpersonal aspects of the poem's discourse, it is only natural that, in order to deepen their insight into the poet's situation, attitudes and feelings, and, indeed, into their identity, readers might also avail themselves of all the knowledge and experience they have gained from previous similar contexts.

In addition, for a profound understanding of the socio-cultural contexts of the poem's discourse, the reader should also have experience of institutionalized stylistic registers developed from literary genre conventions such as the epic, the lyric, the pastoral, the sonnet and many others. These literary traditions are facts of society and history, and awareness of them makes the reader and the poet equal (and congenial) participants in a socio-linguistic community (Fowler 1981: 134).

A final and obvious remark we can make about the conception of poetry as discourse is that, because it allows, perhaps we should say, persuades readers to create their own contexts of meaning, it enables them to account for the artistic axiom that different readers in different times and places will attach different sets of contexts to one and the same verbal structure. It will be noticed that this view, too, corresponds with Larkin's description of the reader's response in the third stage of a poem's generative process. At this point, both the title of Larkin's essay, 'The Pleasure Principle', and the view expressed in it that '. . . at bottom poetry, like all art, is inextricably bound up with giving pleasure . . .' (Larkin 1983: 81), remind me of Roland Barthes's *The Pleasure of the Text*. In one of his intriguing aphoristic statements, Barthes writes:

> Classics. Culture (the more culture, the greater, more diverse, the pleasure will be). Intelligence. Irony. Delicacy. Euphoria. Mastery. Security: art of living. The pleasure of the text can be defined by *praxis* (without any danger of repression): the time and place of reading: house, countryside, near mealtime, the lamp, family where it should be, i.e., close but not too close (Proust in the lavatory that smelled of orris root), etc. Extraordinary ego-reinforcement (by fantasy), the unconscious muffled. This pleasure can be *spoken:* whence criticism (Barthes 1976: 51).[4]

The formal structure of a poem's discourse: The second stage of Larkin's poetics

This *jeu d'esprit* seems to form the appropriate transition to the formal structure underlying a discourse, which contains all kinds of cues for the reader as to how the poet intends the discourse to be interpreted. We could regard this formal structure as the *medium* of discourse (Fowler 1986: 85), while in linguistics it has become customary to designate it as 'text' to distinguish it from 'discourse'. Whereas we have seen that the treatment of poetry as *discourse* coincides with the third stage of Larkin's conception of the genesis of poetry, the treatment of poetry as *text* may be said to correspond with the second stage, in which Larkin visualizes the poet constructing a verbal device as an outlet for the emotions he was obsessed with in the first stage of the poem's creation.

In his poetic precepts, Larkin rightly emphasizes the interdependence of the various stages in the creative process. Similarly, in pragmatic stylistics, text and discourse are interdependent. So they are not categories for separate parts of language, but aspects of language used as critical tools enabling us to focus on particular readers' perspectives. For example, I do not want to forfeit the possibility of investigating the formal features of the written text as a possible source of meaning. Indeed, I share the view that literature, by its very nature, breeds its own formalism (de Man 1980: 122), which in poetry is most evident, of course, in its phonological tissue (metre, rhythm, assonance, rhyme, onomatopoeia, etc.) and in its spatial arrangement in lines and stanzas. Each in its own way, these physical aspects of textual organization convey some secondary meaning and guide the reader's experience and perspective. Further, I am in full agreement with Leech, who has argued that the contribution to meaning made by the literary text as a formal object lies primarily in the principle of iconicity, that is, 'its very physical substance imitates or enacts the meaning that it represents' (Leech 1987: 86).

In the previous paragraphs, I have looked briefly at the productive and the receptive end of the linguistic interaction between the poet and the reader and found them to fall in with the third and the second stage, respectively, of Larkin's definition of the poetic process. I have not yet examined to what extent the first stage of this process fits in with my methodology of literary stylistics. As I think that this point had better be discussed by means of a concrete example, I intend to come back to it in the course of a practical analysis of one of Larkin's own poems further on in this essay.

But first I wish to add a few more points of a theoretical nature, in particular about certain linguistic features in poetic texts whose effects have often been treated only within the text, that is, in terms of their formal properties, and not outside the text, that is, in terms of their pragmatic properties, or, more explicitly, as signals in a poem's language alerting us to a communicative interaction between the poet and the reader.

Here I am alluding to textual devices, such as deviation and parallelism, which in linguistic poetics are usually subsumed under the concept of foregrounding. Very briefly, deviation refers to a writer's conscious or unconscious violation of some linguistic rule of phonology, morphology, syntax or semantics or an infringement of a particular linguistic usage (e.g. in a particular social community) or of some literary genre or convention. Parallelism is, in a sense, the opposite of deviation, in that it is based on extra regularities, not irregularities, in the poem's language. This effect is usually achieved by repetitive patterns on any of the already indicated levels of language organization.

Now, the original theory of foregrounding claims that by using these unorthodox or highly patterned structures, the poet exploits the language aesthetically and, as a result, provokes the reader into seeing a particular structure in a new light.

Referring for a more detailed treatment of the theory of foregrounding to Garvin (1964), Leech (1966, 1969) and Culler (1975), I here wish to call attention to the empirical research in this field by van Peer (1984, 1986). In a number of psycholinguistic experiments, he has investigated whether readers' responses tally with the aforementioned basic claims of the theory, and in general, his findings confirm the predictions derived from these tenets.

However, rather than claiming to have proved the correctness of the theory, van Peer emphasizes that his experiments were primarily focused on the pragmatic nature of foregrounding devices in literary texts, that is, on the question of what mechanisms are triggered off by such devices in the literary reading process. Here, too, Larkin's three-stage poetic process appears to offer an intriguing parallel, in so far as this empirical research was based on the assumption that foregrounding is a dynamic concept, which seeks to provide a link between specific textual features on the one hand and aspects of text production as well as of text reception on the other.

Now of course, van Peer (1986: 12) makes mention of the fact that Culler (1975) and Werth (1976) clearly demonstrated that foregrounding devices also occur in non-literary texts, thereby exploding Jakobson's theory that linguistic parallelism as such provides a kind of automatic discovery procedure for poetic patterns. This theory has its origin in Jakobson's famous definition of the poetic function: 'The set *(Einstellung)* toward the MESSAGE as such [i.e., the formal properties of language], focus on the message for its own sake, is the POETIC function of language.' (Jakobson 1960: 356; italics and capitals as used in the original). In other and simpler words, poetic function consists merely in linguistic form for the sake of form; the literary text becomes a static artefact whose aesthetic qualities are constituted mainly by distinctive linguistic patterns. Strictly speaking, Jakobson's use of the term 'function' in his concept of 'poetic function' is a contradiction in terms (remarkably enough, it is not so in the rest of his well-known functional typology of language in the same essay of 1960); it is certainly not in line with the common view that in a functional or pragmatic approach, language is regarded as an instrument of social interaction rather than as an instrument set in isolation. However, when Culler, Werth and others (e.g., Fowler 1981: 80–5) rejected this formalist tendency, which appeared to conceive of foregrounding as a kind of litmus test of poetic quality, they did not contest the potential significance of the theory of foregrounding for literary stylistics. As a matter of fact, it seems that this significance can now be sustained, by placing literary stylistics within a pragmatic theory viewing language as part of a complex social process, in which literature is one of the varied modes of discourse.

The actual creative process of a poem: The first stage in Larkin's poetics

I now propose to demonstrate in greater detail the interesting parallels between Larkin's witty account of the poetic process and the principles of pragmatic stylistics by analysing one of Larkin's less known poems, 'Talking in Bed' from *The Whitsun Weddings* (1964: 29).

Talking in Bed

Talking in bed ought to be easiest,
Lying together there goes back so far,
An emblem of two people being honest.

> Yet more and more time passes silently.
> Outside, the wind's incomplete unrest
> Builds and disperses clouds about the sky,
>
> And dark towns heap up on the horizon.
> None of this cares for us. Nothing shows why
> At this unique distance from isolation
>
> It becomes still more difficult to find
> Words at once true and kind,
> Or not untrue and not unkind.

Though well aware of what Brooks (1975 [1947]) called 'The heresy of para-phrase', I agree with Fowler that a preformulated literary thesis, or hunch, or a perceptive preliminary reading is part of the critic's normal procedure (Fowler 1971: 219–21). In fact, such a first cursory reading of a poem may produce an initial response, which, in broad outline, is presumably comparable to what happens in the first stage of the poem's genesis, when, according to Larkin's poetic theory, the poet becomes obsessed with some emotional concept. At any rate, after such a preliminary reading of the poem to be analysed, we arrive at the following:

In 'Talking in Bed' the poet confronts us with the dead-end situation of two well-meaning people whose relationship, which ought to have been an emblem of intimate companionship and harmony, has degenerated into long painful silences and feelings of total isolation. It seems an exemplum of the paradoxical human predicament that our need for company makes us reach out to the other person, but that once a relationship has been established, we become all the more aware of our constitutional loneliness.

As I have said in the introductory paragraphs, if we conceive of a poem as a mode of discourse, we are not primarily concerned with its verbal structures as elements of a static object, but as elements of a dynamic communicative process between the author and the reader. The poem's verbal constituents are dynamic in the sense that, although presented simultaneously, they are encountered by the reader as a kinetic process of fulfilled and frustrated expectations and of ever changing emotions stirred up by directive impulses in the text whenever it is read. It is through the analysis of such impulses that our initial response will be reinforced, enlarged, changed and refined.

Thus, the very title of the poem arouses false expectations, because instead of witnessing a discourse situation within the poem of two people talking intimately, giving us the feeling that we are overhearing a conversation which is not meant to be shared, we can only hear the voice of one speaker, who, for that matter, never speaks directly as an 'I'.

Though, in my discussion of the poem, I often use the terms 'speaker' or 'persona', I wish at this point to make the following observations about these concepts. It is a commonly accepted fact that the moment authors start writing, they create personae both for themselves and for their readers. It is also generally acknowledged that these personae will not flesh out either the poet himself or herself or any of his readers as they 'really' are. Even so, the literary pragmaticist holds that there is what one might describe as a sliding scale of correspondence between the authors and their personae. For instance, a text may give out irony signals warning the reader not to assume any correspondence between the author and his or her persona at all. Such ironically marked personae form part of the content in relation to which authors set up their discourse with the reader (Sell 1986: 302–3). Now in the poem under discussion, there do not seem to be such irony signals, so that we may probably conclude that its persona is pretty close to the poet's own experience and sensibility. Of course, this assumption does not rule out the possibility that the business of being in bed with somebody else is something Larkin imagined as the strongest way of making his point; not least by ironic contrast with the togetherness in poems of the *aubade* tradition up to and beyond Donne's 'Sun Rising'.

Thus, one rhetorical effect of the already noted absence of the deictic 'I' may be that we are not provided with an excuse to focus our attention mainly on the poet's persona. We cannot see him as an individual severed from ourselves, whose predicament, however much we are asked to identify ourselves with it, still remains essentially his. Just because there is no objectifying intermediary, we are not allowed to duck out of this distressing situation; we are, as it were, directly drawn into this bed of estrangement and loneliness.

If we do try to anchor the speaker in a particular situation, he turns out to be quite elusive. This is evidenced by the poem's topography, marked by a sequence of literal and figurative adverbial adjuncts of place, 'in bed', 'there', 'outside', 'about the sky', 'on the horizon' and 'at this unique distance from isolation', which, as anchors for the speaker's physical or mental presence, are hardly specific.[5] Indeed, the diffuseness of location justifies the impression that the persona is both a participant in the poem's discourse situation and an external onlooker commenting on it.

The speaker's attempt to disorientate the reader

At this point, we seem to have every reason to believe that this attempt to disorientate the reader is deliberate because, in conjunction with the speaker's detached and impersonal manner, it not only reinforces the feelings of distance and estrangement between these two people, but also raises the disturbing question: Whom does the speaker address in his bitter conclusion 'None of this cares for us'? On the face of it, the pronoun 'us' seems to refer to the two people most directly involved, the speaker and his lover, but on closer consideration, we cannot get around the pertinent suggestion that it may also refer to all of us, the readers, in which case, this specific situation of human loneliness becomes emblematic of the human condition. Besides, all relationships are in a sense opaque to the outsider, so that any alleged understanding of them is in essence a projection of our own experience.

Furthermore, this disorientating effect caused by the speaker's elusive whereabouts is heightened by his equivocal tone, which becomes particularly manifest in the way he verbalizes his emotional experience of the situation.

To begin with, there is the parallelism between form, syntax and function of the verbal nouns 'talking' and 'lying' in the first stanza:

> Talking in bed ought to be easiest,
> Lying together there goes back so far,
> An emblem of two people being honest.

This instance of foregrounding gives prominence to the tension between these two words created by the pun on 'lying'. A tension, for that matter, which seems to mirror the strained relations between the speaker and his lover, the more so as the potentially double meaning is further reinforced by the implication of the third line 'An emblem of two people being honest'. In fact, this line conceals another significant ambiguity in the phrase 'two people being honest', because its underlying structure is either 'two people who are honest' or 'two people who are being honest'. In the former structure, the so-called habitual present expresses the meaning 'two people who are constitutionally honest', but in the latter, the present progressive could conceivably mean 'two people who are pretending to be honest' (Leech 1971: 25). Actually, this ambiguity is reinforced by the noun 'emblem', in that it not only denotes a formal sign or attribute, but may also suggest pretence. However that may be, it seems that the poem is not allowed to resolve into anything as reassuring as 'An emblem of two people being honest'.

Since modal verbs are often associated with particular pragmatic uses, they too are unmistakable signals to the reader, showing the speaker's attitude to his situation. Let us consider, therefore, the case of 'ought to' in the first line. It is instructive here to contrast its implied meaning with that of a possible alternative auxiliary, viz. 'must' in its sense of 'logical conclusion'. The latter modal implies that the speaker judges the conclusion he has drawn from things already known or observed to be necessarily correct or at least to be most likely correct. However, 'ought to' implies that the speaker has his doubts about the soundness of his conclusion. So, unlike 'must', 'ought to' expresses the speaker's lack of confidence (Quirk et al. 1985: 224–7).

Indeed, the persona uses the most subtle linguistic means in the verbal structuring of his experience so as to convey his agonized ambivalence. How could it happen that two people have drifted so far apart that, even at moments of ideal intimacy, they are unable to derive any emotional or spiritual comfort from each other's company? By omitting conjunctive words to express semantic relationships between the two clauses 'Talking in bed ought to be easiest/Lying together there goes back so far' and the noun phrase 'An emblem of two people being honest' in the first stanza, he shows again his equivocation about any causal connection. As a result, readers may find themselves speculating on possible connections and thus vicariously experience the speaker's dilemma.

By now, any sense of confidence and security, which we might have derived from what on the surface seemed a sententious description of an ideal, has been sufficiently sapped by the speaker to prepare us for the bitter disillusionment expressed in the first line of the second stanza: Yet more and more time passes silently. And even here the speaker cannot help being ambiguous in his wording, because the phrase 'more and more' can be either adverbial or adjectival in function, and as such it only seems to lend additional force to the unremitting process of growing apart.[6]

The systematic suppression of human animacy

Although it is common enough to attach metaphoric animacy to an inanimate subject noun like 'time' in the clause 'time passes silently' as an alternative to the personal pronoun structure 'we pass the time in silence', *all* the subjects refer to inanimate beings, so that they form a foregrounded pattern in the poem. If we assume that foregrounding is dynamic by nature, such a prominent textual scheme adds an extra significant element to the discourse structure inviting the reader's interpretation. Here this additional significance may be derived from the common socio-psychological fact that human animacy involves behavourial notions such as intentions, action or interaction, control, responsibilities, etc. so that its systematic suppression in the poem's textual structure may induce us to see the whole poem as an extended metaphor of the inherent impotence of human beings to deal with their relationships.

Lexico-semantically, this reading of the poem is underpinned by the imagery in the lines:

> Outside, the wind's incomplete unrest
> Builds and disperses clouds about the sky,
>
> And dark towns heap up on the horizon.

The poem's speaker is obviously the victim of conflicting emotions, which cause him to abstract from his situation only particular features and to assign these features suggestively to the game that the wind is playing with the clouds outside. The image of the wind's incomplete unrest, building and dispersing clouds about the sky mirrors the innate instability underlying the relationships established between human beings. Like the clouds, they seem solid enough on the face of it, but in reality, they prove to be unsubstantial and easily dissolvable. Nor, for that matter, can we derive any sense of harmony or order from the ominous cloudscape suggestive of dark towns 'heaping up' on the horizon. Note that also phonologically, the strong stresses are heaping up: 'And dárk tówns héap úp. . .'.

This dominant structure of deletion of human animacy, and thereby of potential agency in the subject, shows that the poet has on purpose rejected the possibility, inherent in the English language, of regular alternation between animate and inanimate subjects. In fact, by restricting his choice to mainly one semantic realization of the subject, which statistically is unlikely to occur to the same degree of consistency, the poet has, for the purposes of foregrounding, deviated from the norms of the language as a whole. It is useful to designate this type of deviation as external deviation or as global frequency deviation (Werth 1976), to distinguish it from internal deviation, an example of which will be considered in the next paragraph.

Significantly, there is only one subject referring to animate beings, namely 'two people' in line 3, which operates on the level of the prepositional complement clause 'two people being honest'. Now the fact that the head of this subject is semantically realized by an animate noun may be regarded as an instance of internal deviation (see Leech 1985: 39–57) because it is a deviation from a norm established within the text of the poem by the aforementioned pattern of inanimate subjects. Here, too, the process of foregrounding is dynamic in that it defeats the readers' expectations and thus alerts them to some significance additional to the propositional meaning. Thus, this isolated instance of an animate subject amid inanimate ones could be seen as mimetic of these two people's feeling of utter loneliness and of their having to struggle against the indifferent, mechanical forces that rule the world of humans and visit on them the sufferings and ironies of life and love. This Hardyesque theme is also intimated by the aforementioned imagery of the cloudscape, while the indifference of nature clearly comes out in the lines:

> None of this cares for us. Nothing shows why
> At this unique distance from isolation
>
> It becomes still more difficult to find
> Words at once true and kind,
> Or not untrue and not unkind.

This condition of complete estrangement is made even more poignant by the ambiguous meanings which on closer consideration turn out to be concealed in the notable line 'At this unique distance from isolation', which alludes, of course, to what the talking in bed ought to have been. Apart from its usual meanings such as (1) 'single', 'one and only', (2) 'unequalled', (3) 'uncommon', 'exceptional', etc. the adjective 'unique' forcefully reminds us of its Latin root *unus*, 'one'. For that matter, the Latin etymologies of the nouns in the colligation also merit our attention, because 'distance' is composed of the morphemes *di*, 'two' and *stare* 'stand apart', while 'isolation' is etymologically related to *insula*, 'island'. As a result, the whole line becomes rather unsettling due to the suggested meaning of 'oneness' or 'singleness', which shows through its lexical items and seriously subverts its propositional meaning.

Larkin's negative prefixes

In his review of *The Whitsun Weddings*, Christopher Ricks pointed out one of the hallmarks of Larkin's style: those negative prefixes 'un-', 'in-', 'im-', 'dis-', etc. 'which define the limits and shades of the world, and which coldly confront our flimsy illusions' (Thwaite 1973/4). They also figure conspicuously in 'Talking in Bed', where we even find them in double negatives: 'incomplete unrest', 'not untrue and not unkind'. Apart from the disturbing realization that even 'unrest' is 'incomplete', it is significant that the negative prefixes are attached to words which in their affirmative forms indicate what the relationship between these two people ought to have been: complete, (full of) rest, true and kind.

Further, this use of the negative prefix reinforces the already detected faltering tone of the poem's speaker. This becomes particularly apparent in the final stanza, where he seems to be groping for the right words, evidently realizing that his relationship has come to a dead end. Simultaneously, the metre and rhyme scheme break down so that the poem itself enacts the persona's faltering and his climactic realization that

> It becomes still more difficult to find
> Words at once true and kind,
> Or not untrue and not unkind.

The last two lines state a terrible truth: human relationships may reach a point where truth and kindness are mutually exclusive, the former causing pain and the latter being untruthful so that in the end all communication is invalidated (Kuby 1974: 66). Having come to this bitter realization, the reader will almost unavoidably hark back to the pun on 'lying' in the second line and grasp that the emblem has belied what it promised to stand for.

As I said earlier, in the conception of literature as an interpersonal linguistic activity between the author and the reader, the reader is taken to build up all kinds of contexts, which may very well involve inter-textuality, that is, relating the text to be interpreted to another text. Thus, it is not unlikely that the pun on 'lying' calls to mind very similar puns in the opening lines and the concluding couplet of Shakespeare's Sonnet 138 (Booth 1977: 119 and 476–81):

> When my love swears that she is made of truth,
> I do believe her though I know she lies,
>
> . . .
>
> Therefore I lie with her, and she with me,
> And in our faults by lies we flattered be.

My account of Larkin's poetic principles in the introductory part of this essay would not be complete unless I mentioned that 7 years later, he came back to them in another of these aphoristic mini-essays, simply called 'Writing Poems' and first published in the 1964 *Bulletin* of the Poetry Book Society, whose selectors he thanked for the compliment they had paid to *The Whitsun Weddings*:

> Some years ago I came to the conclusion that to write a poem was to construct a verbal device that would preserve an experience indefinitely by reproducing it in whoever read the poem. As a working definition, this satisfied me sufficiently to enable individual poems to be written . . . The fact is that my working definition defines very little: . . .it leaves the precise nature of the verbal pickling unexplained.

(Larkin 1983: 83–4)

Since I cannot explain this either, I have chosen a line from 'Ignorance', also occurring in *The Whitsun Weddings,* as a motto for this essay and cannot resist the temptation to quote the first six lines of this poem:

> Strange to know nothing, never to be sure
> Of what is true or right or real,
> But forced to qualify *or so I feel,*
> Or *Well, it does seem so:*
> *Someone must know.*
>
> Strange to be ignorant of the way things work.

Bearing these memorable lines in mind, I have nevertheless tried to uncover some of the meanings of 'Talking in Bed' as a mode of discourse, and to link these with the poem's 'inwardly turned meaning' (Verdonk 1984), that is the meaning generated by its structuring elements, in the firm belief that here a verbal device has been constructed which will reveal a deeply human experience every time this reader goes to it.

Extracted from Verdonk, P. (1991) 'Poems as Text and Discourse: The Poetics of Philip Larkin', in Sell, R. D. (ed.), *Literary Pragmatics.* London: Routledge, pp. 94–109.

7

Poetry and public life:
A contextualized reading
of Heaney's 'Punishment'

Introduction

Seamus Heaney is an Irish poet, who writes in English. He was born and educated in Northern Ireland, the eldest son in a Catholic farming family. His life as a poet has coincided with the most recent period of the Northern Irish Troubles, as they are euphemistically called. This mini biography signifies a life lived in a world of cultural, political and religious division. His poem 'Terminus' from *The Haw Lantern* (1987) contains these lines:

> Two buckets were easier carried than one.
> I grew up in between.
>
> My left hand placed the standard iron weight.
> My right tilted a last grain in the balance.

In the first instance, 'Terminus' is about what Heaney called his 'in-between boyhood', but in a wider perspective, these lines present an appropriate image of his later position between two worlds of experience. Though their double weight means a heavier burden, the poet prefers to carry two buckets so that he can keep his balance. Indeed, in a country like Ireland, it is safer to carry two buckets, otherwise one might end up in one of the camps which keep the country divided against itself. Therefore, Heaney has always been anxious not to become the mouthpiece of either of the contending parties, though much of his poetry is deeply affected by this mood of discord. This classic conflict between the artist's autonomy and his dependence is the starting point of my contextualized stylistic reading of Heaney's much-discussed 'Punishment' from his collection *North* (1975b), which contains some of his most 'committed' poems.

For such an approach, it is necessary to treat the poem as a contextualized discourse, which means in this case a context-bound and interpersonal act of communication. Though aware of the intricacy of the notion of context, I see it as comprising both the wider social, cultural and historical backgrounds and the narrower context of the immediate situation of utterance. After relating the poem to some of its cultural, political and artistic contexts, I distinguish the following basic components of its immediate situational context.

First, it is assumed that the actual readers of the poem are an element of its context, in that their interpretations are inevitably affected by their own beliefs and attitudes.

Second, being bent on communicating with the author, readers will search his poem for clues to its context of place and time. Obviously, authors may be expected to provide such clues because they wish to draw the reader into the text's situation.

Third, there is the interpersonal context to consider, that is, what is the nature of the references to the poem's speaker and to the reader?

The fourth and last contextual component that exerts influence on the language of a text is the genre of discourse. In fact, this element is closely connected with the interpersonal context, because speakers/writers are normally inclined to adapt their style to the discourse genre they are engaged in, for instance, conversation, advertising, journalism or literature.

Having thus placed the poem in its contextual framework and having assessed Heaney's rhetorical and stylistic strategies, I come to the conclusion that the poet has proved himself a successful performer in his balancing act between his artistic and political commitments.

The debate between artistic and political commitments

One of Seamus Heaney's prose books is entitled *The Government of the Tongue* (1988). It is an ambiguous title because it appears to hold a hint of an old conflict: should the tongue (in the sense of the poet's individual talent as well as the common linguistic resource) be governed or should it be the governor? It is the conflict between art's isolation and participation, between its autonomy and dependence and, more in particular, between poetry and public life. In the title essay of his book, Heaney proposes the following modus:

> The fact is that poetry is its own reality and no matter how much a poet may concede to the corrective pressures of social, moral, political and historical reality, the ultimate fidelity must be to the demands and promise of the artistic event (Heaney 1988: 101).

This is very much a self-conscious statement and that on two accounts. Though an Irish poet, born and bred in Northern Ireland, he appears to be regarded as a representative English-language poet: witness the inclusion of a generous selection from his poetry in *The Penguin Book of Contemporary British Poetry*, edited by Blake Morrison and Andrew Motion (1982). On more than one occasion, he has expressed his anxiety about this dilemma, for instance, in his inaugural lecture as Oxford Professor of Poetry. Then he said that he always feels the pull of the claims and counter-claims exerted by the terms 'English literature' and 'Irish' or 'Anglo-Irish literature'. Using a forceful image to make his point, he claimed that all writers in his position 'are caught on the forked stick of their love of the English language itself. Helplessly, they kiss the rod of the consciousness which subjugated them' (Heaney 1990: 9).

Finding a myth

The other, probably even more compelling, reason for this balancing between the poetic and the political is the fact that Heaney's life as a poet has been virtually coterminous with the most recent period of the Northern Irish Troubles. In the early 1970s, when he had become a public figure, he came under increasing pressure to display in his work his concern and involvement, and his artistic anxieties about having to respond in direct terms must have felt relieved when he had been reading a book entitled *The Bog People: Iron Age Man Preserved*, written by the Danish archaeologist P. V. Glob and published in 1969 (Heaney 1980: 57–8; Haffenden 1981: 57). It reports on the excavations of bodies of Iron Age people buried in bogs in north-western Europe, particularly in Denmark and Ireland. What he found in the book revived his own childhood images of bogland, and it provided him with symbols and a mythical background enabling him to put the contemporary political scene in a wider historical and cultural perspective. At about the same time, he had moved from Northern Ireland to the south, to Dublin, which must have created a perspective of geographical distance as well.

From these new imaginative and physical viewpoints, he was able to look back towards Northern Ireland as a country of the mind and he wrote a sequence of poems published in a limited edition as *Bog Poems* (1975a), which were subsequently included in a larger collection significantly called *North* (1975b).

One of these bog corpses described and photographed by Glob is that of a girl. Her peat-covered body was entirely naked, her hair was shaved off, a blindfold was tied over her eyes and she wore an oxhide collar around her neck. Probably, she had been punished for adultery. The following poem tells us how strongly Heaney identifies himself with this girl, both personally and socially:

> Punishment
>
> I can feel the tug
> of the halter at the nape
> of her neck, the wind
> on her naked front.
>
> It blows her nipples
> to amber beads,
> it shakes the frail rigging
> of her ribs.
>
> I can see her drowned
> body in the bog,
> the weighing stone,
> the floating rods and boughs.
>
> Under which at first
> she was a barked sapling
> that is dug up
> oak-bone, brain-firkin:
>
> her shaved head
> like a stubble of black corn,
> her blindfold a soiled bandage,
> her noose a ring
>
> to store
> the memories of love.
> Little adulteress,
> before they punished you
>
> you were flaxen-haired,
> undernourished, and your
> tar-black face was beautiful.
> My poor scapegoat,

I almost love you
but would have cast, I know,
the stones of silence.
I am the artful voyeur

of your brain's exposed
and darkened combs,
your muscles' webbing
and all your numbered bones:

I who have stood dumb
when your betraying sisters,
cauled in tar,
wept by the railings,

who would connive
in civilized outrage
yet understand the exact
and tribal, intimate revenge.

(Heaney 1975b)

The shifting identity of the poet's persona

When saying that *Heaney* strongly identifies himself with the Iron Age girl, we touch on the question as to how far the 'persona' or 'speaker' in a poem can be identified with the poet. It is a literary convention that the moment authors start writing, they create personae both for themselves and for their intended readers. Obviously, these personae do not flesh out either the writers themselves as they 'really' are or any of their actual readers. Even so, with regard to the author/persona relationship, it can be held that there is what we might describe as a sliding scale of correspondence between these two. So at one end of this scale, a text may signal to the reader not to assume any correspondence whatsoever between the author and his or her persona, while at the other end, the distance between the two may be practically negligible (Verdonk 1991: 101–2). As a matter of fact, within the poem under discussion there appears to be such a line. Thus, in the first nine stanzas, the speaker and the poet need not necessarily be identical. However, in the last two stanzas, the identity gap seems to be as good as bridged because the speaker is felt to be very close to the poet's own experience and sensibility. It is even arguable that it is Heaney who is imagining the bog girl of Glob's account as the 'sister' of those Northern Irish girls who were tarred, feathered and tied to railings as a punishment for going out with English soldiers. And, for the same reason, it is plausible that it is Heaney who passes the ambivalent self-judgement. In support of this assumption, I could point to Heaney's own idea of his poetry as a revelation of identities:

> . . .poetry as divination, poetry as revelation of the self to the self, as restoration of the culture to itself; poems as elements of continuity, with the aura and authenticity of archaeological finds, where the buried shard has an importance that is not diminished by the importance of the buried city (Heaney 1980: 41).

The actual reader as an element of the poem's context

Whether they are correct or not, it has only been possible for me to draw these particular inferences about the poet's identity and self-definition, because I have played an active role as an actual reader by contextualizing the poem, at least to a certain extent. Thus, I have gathered some information about Heaney's dilemmas arising from his double cultural identity as well as from the tensions between his artistic and political commitments. Furthermore, I have gained an impression of the mythical background which enabled the poet to relate the past to the present and so to universalize sectarian violence in Northern Ireland.

How far my first reaction to the poem differs from what Heaney would have liked to hear from his intended reader, I do not know, but what it does show in general terms is that the actual reader of a text is an element of its context, that is, the whole complex of factors affecting its meaning and interpretation. To put it differently, in the interactive process between the author, text, and actual readers, the latter are not only affected by the text, they can also exert influence on its interpretation (Mills 1992: 182–205). Clearly, this influence differs from reader to reader because they do not bring to texts the same presuppositions and assumptions. They are female or male, belong to a different time or generation, come from different cultural and societal back-grounds and, therefore, not surprisingly, have different beliefs and attitudes. For instance, some critics have perceived 'Catholic' and 'Republican' attitudes in 'Punishment'. In particular, the last two stanzas have raised several eyebrows at Heaney's position on IRA violence. Is the speaker's understanding also a condoning (O'Brien 1975: 404–5, cited in Corcoran 1986: 116)? And Blake Morrison (1980: 109–10), though not wishing to suggest that 'Punishment' in particular and the Bog poems in general uphold the Republican cause, is critical of the mythical framework, which he feels to be a form of 'explanation' (the scare quotes are Morrison's). In fact, he finds that the whole procedure of *North* lends an historical respectability to sectarian killing in Ulster. It will be obvious that these and other criticisms have also become part of the poem's context because readers taking cognizance of them may very well become prejudiced in their interpretation.

These responses as well as my own appear to bear out the assumption offered in this chapter that once readers are drawn into a text's contextual orbit, so to speak, they not only decode or interpret meanings but also encode or create them. On the other hand, this premise does not imply that the interpretation of a text can result in a free-for-all. For though a lot of research has been done on the role of readers, on how they negotiate with a text, that is, accept or reject it, or respond to it in any other way, the fact remains that the primary impetus for all these responses virtually always comes from the text. So the text is our common starting point because it is generally acknowledged that there is, as a rule, a considerable interpretive consensus about a great deal of its linguistic features. Therefore, I would like to propose a stylistic analysis of Heaney's 'Punishment' that is conditioned by a dynamic interaction between the poem's text and its context.

The poem as a contextualized discourse[1]

Such an approach requires that I should regard the poem as the representation of a discourse. Because this word has become one of the most overworked terms in linguistics, I have to specify that it is used here as a description of the whole complicated process of interaction between people producing and interpreting texts. Furthermore, it is evident that these communicative activities are always pursued in a particular context. What is said, how it is said and how it is comprehended is always partly determined by a wide variety of contextual factors. In actual fact, we can even say that the context or situation precedes the discourse to which it is related.

Though the notion of context is open to many interpretations, I will be using it here in its sense of the whole environment in which a discourse occurs, ranging from the narrower context of utterance, that is, the more immediate situation of the discourse, to the much wider context of social, cultural or historical factors. Of course, such a contextual framework is infinitely extendable so that I can only hope to touch on a fraction of it in my discussion of Heaney's poem. Thus, I have so far looked briefly at some of its cultural, political and artistic backgrounds and will now bring into focus some aspects of its context of utterance. But in doing so, I have to make some brief excursions into a few technical matters. In particular, I will be examining those features of a text that reflect the major components of its context of utterance, which comprises (1) the physical and temporal situation of the participants in the discourse, (2) the channel or medium of expression, (3) the relationships obtaining between the participants and (4) the genre or type of discourse.

The spatial and temporal context

To begin with, we have to distinguish between contexts in which the participants in a discourse are in each other's presence sharing the same place and time, like in face-to-face conversation, and contexts in which the participants are physically separated. For instance, in telephone conversations or live radio or television broadcasts, the participants share the same time (unless, of course, there is a time difference), but not the same place, while in the case of letters and most other types of written texts, the participants (i.e. the addresser and addressee) share neither time nor place: what is 'here and now' for the addresser becomes 'there and then' for the addressee, and the other way around.

Presumably, because they are verbal creatures, readers follow their communicative instincts by searching a text for clues as to how they must visualize or reconstruct a particular context of place and time. In 'Punishment', we can see how the poet provides such clues. For instance, by his use of the definite article the first-person speaker assumes that 'the tug of the halter', 'the nape of her neck', 'the wind on her naked front', 'the bog', 'the weighing stone', etc. are as 'definite' for the reader as they are for himself. Similarly, by using the present tense in 'I can feel', 'It blows', 'it shakes', 'I can see', 'I almost love you', etc., the speaker suggests that his present is the readers' present and that his place is their place. So by creating the impression that the poet and the reader share a number of contextual factors, this stylistic device has the obvious effect of drawing the reader into the situation.

The interpersonal context

In addition to this spatial and temporal perspective, a discourse is also related to an interpersonal context, which comprises the identities of the speaker or writer and the addressee, including their social relationship. In everyday face-to-face conversation, as we have seen, the speaker and the listener can normally identify each other, but in all the other discourse types mentioned, the situation is obviously different. So even a simple written message like 'Meet me here tomorrow' cannot be properly interpreted without knowing its interpersonal context, that is, the identity of the sender hidden behind the pronoun 'me' and that of the addressee implicitly referred to by the imperative 'meet'. (Obviously, we must also know the spatial and temporal context, i.e. the exact place and time, intimated by the adverbs 'here' and 'tomorrow'.)

Poetry, for that matter, shows a wide variety of interpersonal contexts. For instance, poems written in the first person may be addressed to an identified or an unidentified 'you' inside the poem. Other poems are addressed to an outside 'you' or to no one in particular. Still other first-person speakers may address the west wind, a Grecian urn or a ship. Neither need the first-person speaker be a human being. Thus, we may be hearing a hawk speaking to no one in particular as in Ted Hughes's 'Hawk Roosting'. Then there are also instances in which the first-person narrator, though human, cannot possibly be the poet. For example, the narrator in T. S. Eliot's 'Journey of the Magi', is one of the three Magi in a reminiscent mood asking an unidentified listener to write down his recollections. Finally, though it would not be difficult to still add other types of discourse situations, there are of course also many poems in which the speakers efface themselves completely by not referring to themselves in the first person at all.

Nevertheless, however bizarre or unorthodox the discourse situation within a poem may be, a 'frame' discourse between the poet and the reader, a silent communion, so to speak, is always taken for granted. In fact, part of the interest of a poem comes from this double perspective. Thus, as a result of the poet's discoursal strategies, the reader may feel estranged from the situation or, conversely, may feel deeply involved with it. It may also be that the identities of the participants in a poem's discourse undergo some change, which makes it necessary for the reader to reassess the situation. In this connection, I have already pointed out the shifting identity of Heaney's persona in 'Punishment'.

Apart from this aspect, the presence of the persona is quite conspicuous and his impact on the poem seems to be very strong. Indeed, the poem's first word is the pronoun 'I' and it returns at repeated intervals in equally prominent positions in the opening or closing lines of several stanzas. Up to line 22, the speaker addresses an assumed audience in the outside world, giving a perceptive account of how he imagines the girl's punishment to have been and describing graphically the effects on her body of its long immersion in the bog. Then, about halfway through the poem in line 23, the speaker begins to direct his words at the girl so that the earlier audience now finds itself listening in to what is essentially a very intimate address. Stylistically, this intimacy is greatly reinforced by a relatively high frequency of the second-person pronoun 'you' acting in conjunction with the dominant pattern of the first-person pronoun 'I'. Even so, this reader does not feel left out. On the contrary, all the time I have a feeling that the speaker is working around to his own predicament which he wants to share with me. This impression is supported by textual evidence because the pronoun 'you' addressing the bog girl, which is such a dominant stylistic feature of the preceding stanzas, has vanished from the last. It is here that the speaker expresses the essence of his moral and artistic dilemma.

Spatial and temporal deixis

Our discussion in the preceding two paragraphs has clearly shown that language contains a category of words and phrases which directly relate an utterance to a speaker's or writer's place and time and which therefore take their meanings in part from the situational context in which they are used. For instance, you cannot interpret the meaning of 'here' in the utterance 'The book is here', without knowing where the speaker is situated. These words or phrases are called deictics, while the linguistic phenomenon in general is called deixis (from a Greek word meaning 'pointing').

Some obvious examples of deictics include the spatial terms 'here', 'there', the demonstratives 'this/these' and 'that/those'; temporal expressions like 'now', 'then', 'today', 'yesterday', etc.; and the present and past tenses of verbs. Hence, the cited instances of the present tense verbs from our poem are deictically used because they indicate the time to which the speaker relates the events he describes. In this case, it is of course an imaginary present, which, as we have seen, also 'positions' the reader.

One of the uses of the definite article 'the' can also be called deictic. It does not point to things close to or further away from the speaker, like 'this' and 'that', but to things within the speaker's world either already shared or to be shared with the addressee (Traugott and Pratt 1980: 280). For example, the article 'the' in 'Do you remember when we met at the university?' refers back to something already shared by speaker and addressee. On the other hand, from the question 'Have you already visited the castle?' the addressee is to conclude that it must be 'the castle in the speaker's town', that is, that it is anchored in the speaker's context, and that the addressee is therefore invited to share the speaker's familiarity with it.

Similarly, when the speaker in 'Punishment' uses the definite article in the instances quoted above, that is, 'the tug of the halter', 'the nape of her neck', 'the wind on her naked front', 'the bog', etc., he wants his experience and emotions to be absorbed into the reader's world. On the other hand, the speaker's use of the indefinite article 'a' in 'she was a barked sapling', 'her blindfold a soiled bandage', 'her shaved head like a stubble of black corn' and 'her noose a ring' seems to signal that he has not yet internalized these observations, in other words, that they have not yet been incorporated in his world of experience.

Though it does not weaken my argument that Heaney's use of the deictic article has the effect of thrusting the reader into the situational context of the poem, there is a more exact if at first sight more prosaic explanation for some of the instances of the article in that, for example, 'the halter', 'the bog', 'the weighing stone' and 'the floating rods and boughs' may refer to certain details in the photographs of the girl illustrating Glob's book on the bog bodies. Of course, Heaney may not have had the actual photographs in front of him when writing the poem and some of the things he describes may very well be the product of his imagination. But, however it may be, this does not detract from the deictic or 'pointing' function of this specific use of the article because the pictures were actually present in the poet's immediate context of utterance.

It was Henry Widdowson (1975: 10–13) who first pointed out this particular use of the article with reference to the poem 'Leda and the Swan' by Yeats, who is presumed to have made use of a reproduction of Michelangelo's picture on the subject. Furthermore, both Halliday (1966: 59) and Widdowson made the interesting observation that this function is a common feature of the English language used in tourist guides and exhibition catalogues. In these, too, the article's function is deictic because it points to external objects (e.g., paintings, sculptures, altars in churches, gates of castles, etc.) which are supposed to be part of the immediate situation or context when the reader reads about them: 'To reach the battlements, visitors will pass the dungeon head on their right and the guard room of the north west tower' (from a visitors' guide to Saltwood Castle in Kent).[2]

Interpersonal deixis

In addition to the deictics which situate a discourse in a context of place and time, there are other deictic words which mark out the participants in a discourse as speaker or writer and addressee and therefore indicate the interpersonal context. These interpersonal deictics include the first- and second-person pronouns 'I', 'we' and 'you' and of course their related forms like 'me', 'myself', etc. I have already pointed out the dominant position of these interpersonal deictics in 'Punishment' and gone into their stylistic effect on my reading of the poem.

Furthermore, the interpersonal context of a discourse is filled in by what are usually called social deictics. These can reveal information about the social identities of the participants including their attitudes, statuses, and roles and the permanent or temporary social relationships obtaining between them. Obvious examples are forms of address, honorifics (i.e. titles given to people as a sign of respect or honour), words denoting kinship, markers of intimacy and, of course, dishonorifics (Levinson 1983: 89). The latter include, for instance, any kind of address term discriminating against women, race, class or political and religious views. As Kate Clark (1992: 208–24) has shown, naming is a powerful ideological tool which also tells a lot about the views and beliefs of the namer. Different names for people point to different ways of seeing them. Clark illustrates her assertion with the example of the varied references to people who use violence to achieve their political aims. Are they terrorists, guerrillas, freedom-fighters, rebels or resistance fighters? Clearly, these labels suggest different degrees of legitimacy and approval.

So from the socially deictic terms used by the speaker in 'Punishment', we can also make certain inferences about his motives for addressing the bog girl as 'little adulteress' and 'my poor scapegoat'. At first sight, there appears to be affection and compassion in the modifiers 'little' and 'my poor', while in the first instance, the name 'adulteress' may have been prompted by the archaeologist's conjectures about the reason for the girl's penalty. At the same time, one might wonder whether it is the girl's presumed adultery that incites the perverted sexual thrill which, by his own admission, the poem's speaker derives from the sight of the shrivelled but fully preserved corpse, imagining her nipples hardened by the wind blowing on her naked front. And whether it brings out 'the artful voyeur' in him, gloating over the exposed inner parts of her head and body:

> I am the artful voyeur
>
> of your brain's exposed
> and darkened combs,
> your muscles' webbing
> and all your numbered bones:

The allusion in the last line to a Catholic psalm about Christ saying 'They have pierced my hands and feet; they have numbered all my bones' throws into relief the biblical associations of the name 'scapegoat'. It is the scapegoat of the Mosaic ritual (*Leviticus* 16: 8) which is symbolically loaded with the sins of the people and driven into the wilderness and therefore used as an allusion to Christ in Catholic worship. Indeed, there appears to be a causal chain involved in this name-giving, because the label 'adulteress' has biblical links too.

She figures in the gospel story about the woman who is taken in adultery and is therefore to be punished by being stoned to death. But Jesus says to the scribes and Pharisees: 'He that is without sin among you, let him first cast a stone at her' (*John* 8: 7). The ensuing silence is of course an admission of their own sins for which they wanted to make the adulterous woman the scapegoat. By now, it is becoming clear why it is these names that emerged from the speaker's consciousness. He realizes that, though his pity is close to love, if he had lived at the time of the bog girl, he too would have remained silent and would not have had the courage to defend her:

> My poor scapegoat,
>
> I almost love you
> but would have cast, I know,
> the stones of silence.

The poet's self-rebuke continues and the 'weighing stone' which kept the girl's body down in the bog now weighs heavily on his conscience, because in his own days, he also stood by doing nothing when Northern Irish girls, the bog girl's 'betraying sisters', were punished for befriending British soldiers. Their heads too were shaved and tarred by extremists, who then chained them to railings as a deterrent to others. Of course, he used to join in the civilized voices of protest, but in fact, he had allowed it to happen, concealing his deep-rooted understanding of the interminable urge for public vengeance:

> I who have stood dumb
> when your betraying sisters,
> cauled in tar,
> wept by the railings,
>
> who would connive
> in civilized outrage
> yet understand the exact
> and tribal, intimate revenge.

The poet must learn to live with his own punishment, which is that his art forbids him to take sides. He must remain 'the voyeur', the prying observer, who must be 'artful', that is, not only devious but also literally 'full of art'. Yet, it is this very same artfulness which enables the poet to draw the bitter analogy between a victim of tribal retribution in the Iron Age and the victims of sectarian violence in these Christian days.

The egocentricity of deixis

My final observation about deictics is that they are 'speaker-centred'. Since human beings are inclined to see themselves as the centre of things, speakers locate their discourses predominantly in relation to their own viewpoint. (I hasten to assure the reader that this is of course not intended as a moralizing observation.) Being after all a potential speaker too, the addressee plays the game and relates the meanings of 'here and now' or 'there and then' to the place and time in which the speaker or writer is anchored. In fact, this egocentricity is the quintessence of deixis and of high relevance to literary analysis. Hence, authors very often begin a narrative using a number of definite articles. As we have seen earlier in Heaney's poem, this creates stylistically the impression that the writer and the reader already share some knowledge about the situational context so that the reader is quickly drawn into the narrative. Consider as another example of this stylistic device the opening sentences from D. H. Lawrence's short story *The Shades of Spring* (1985): 'It was a mile nearer through the wood. Mechanically, Syson turned up by the forge and lifted the field-gate. The blacksmith and his mate stood still, watching the trespasser'.

The genre or type of discourse

Yet another contextual feature which the language of a text chimes in with is the genre or type of discourse. Actually, the matter of genre is closely linked with the interpersonal context, because in a discourse situation, speakers and writers tend to adapt their language, that is, their style, to all kinds of conventions imposed by their social roles and settings. This is a reciprocal process, in that also the addressees of a discourse are tuned in to these socialized stylistic conventions. Thus, if we have made ourselves familiar with a particular discourse genre, we have usually also developed a sense of what is stylistically appropriate in a given situation.

In any speech community, there are naturally innumerable discourse genres and I will therefore only mention the following widely divergent examples: neighbours having a friendly chat over the garden fence, a journalist interviewing the United States President on TV, managers meeting in the boardroom, a child talking with her grandparents. As these instances show, we can often distinguish various subgenres within a particular discourse genre. So the speech events I have just mentioned would presumably come within the genre of conversation. Likewise, within the discourse genre of the mass media, we could distinguish subgenres like television, radio, newspapers and magazines. Then, of course, further subgenres can be distinguished within each of these: for example news reports, documentaries, quiz shows, etc. within TV discourse.

Since the communicative process I have in mind also produces texts which in a particular culture are recognized as literary, the phenomenon of literature will also be identified as a discourse genre. Here, too, there are broad subgenres like prose, poetry and drama, each of which can be further classified: for example, the novel and short story within prose; lyrical, epic and narrative genres within poetry; and comedy, tragedy and farce within drama.

Being imaginative compositions, literary texts are commonly associated with highly individual stylistic expression. However, like most if not all discourse genres, literature is at the same time subject to a great many conventions. Hence, the language of poetry is characteristically self-involved, which is most evident in its phonological tissue (metre, rhythm, alliteration, rhyme, etc.), its spatial arrangement in lines and stanzas, particular semantic phenomena like imagery, figures of speech (metaphor, simile, oxymoron, irony, etc.) and parallelistic patterns in its sounds, vocabulary or syntax. Furthermore, there are of course the specific conventions developed in subgenres such as the epic, the lyric, the sonnet, the pastoral, etc.

As we have seen, learning the genre conventions of non-literary discourses is in fact a matter of socialization. In the same way, we will have to acquaint ourselves with the practices of literary discourses if we wish to establish a satisfactory rapport with their artistic originators.

Some genre characteristics of poetry

The form in which I have written the foregoing sections has made me embarrassingly aware that I have separated certain aspects of poetry which in fact cannot be separated. The discourse of poetry is a tightly knit network of textual and contextual elements which constantly reinforce each other in meaning. Therefore, whenever we examine one or other element individually, we are doing something that is artistically unpardonable. On the other hand, if we wish to communicate with each other about a poem or any other work of art for that matter, we must be practical about it and reconcile ourselves to this inadequacy. In this spirit, you are asked to read the following discussion about some formal features which are stereotypical of the discourse of poetry, but should be viewed as part of the complex artistic, social and cultural process I have tried to describe briefly in the preceding paragraphs.

In an attempt to track down Heaney's rhetorical or stylistic strategies, if this is at all possible, I must indulge in a certain degree of idealization because in reality, language is by no means as neatly organized and partitioned as I am going to make it out here. So it is assumed that, prompted by his artistic talent, and consciously or intuitively, the poet has chosen certain linguistic structures in preference to others which are potentially available in the language he is using. From this, we could conclude that the artistically or rhetorically motivated choices he has made together form the poem's stylistic design. Clearly, it is these choices that dominate the structure of the poem's discourse.

Furthermore, it is assumed that the poet has made his choices on particular levels of the structure of language. Though there are various models distinguishing different numbers of levels, in this chapter, I shall be making use of the following six-level model of structure:

1. GRAPHOLOGY   (TYPOGRAPHICAL FEATURES)
2. PHONOLOGY   (SOUNDS, RHYTHM, ETC.)
3. LEXIS   (VOCABULARY)
4. SYNTAX   (GRAMMATICAL STRUCTURES)
5. SEMANTICS   (CONSIDERATIONS OF MEANING)
6. PRAGMATICS   (CONTEXTUAL FEATURES)

Needless to say, any choice on any of the levels of graphology, phonology, lexis and syntax is co-determined by considerations of meaning, that is, the semantic level, as well as by a wide variety of contextual features, that is, the pragmatic level.

To begin with, one of the contextual elements I mentioned earlier is that 'Punishment' is included in a collection entitled *North* (1975b), which brings up various associations, especially after reading the other poems. For me, it offers evocations of the grimness of the landscape and climate in northern Europe, the northern origin of the Vikings, who invaded and settled at several places in the north of Ireland, the northern homelands of the Anglo-Saxons fighting their endless inter-tribal wars and clinging to their rigid codes of honour and revenge, the supposedly consonantal or guttural accents of the northern peoples, and, of course, there is the allusion to present-day Northern Ireland with its contemporary conflicts and violence, the place where the poet grew up and where his attitudes and beliefs were formed. To bring out this context, the poet has made a specific choice on the phonological level. Instead of using end-rhyme as an organizing device, he has chosen to structure his poem by internal sound patterns in the form of alliteration, which is the repetition of the consonant sound at the beginning of two or more words. The way Heaney handles this verse form is strongly reminiscent of the staple verse line of Anglo-Saxon poetry, which consisted of two half-lines bridged by a pattern of alliterating heavily stressed syllables and was founded on a centuries-old

Germanic oral tradition. Presumably, the poet's choice also intimates his idea that the alliterative tradition forced itself upon Irish literary culture. In 'Traditions', a poem included in *Wintering Out* (1972), the first book he published after he had left Northern Ireland to live in the Irish Republic, he wrote: 'Our guttural muse/was bulled long ago/by the alliterative tradition'.

In addition to many alliterative pairs like '*b*lows', '*b*eads', '*r*igging', '*r*ibs', '*b*ody', '*b*og' and so on, some of the alliterative patterns in 'Punishment' are even repeated: in the first and second stanzas, we find 'the *h*alter at the *n*ape', 'of *h*er *n*eck', 'on *h*er *n*aked front', 'it blows *h*er *n*ipples'; similarly, the third and fourth stanzas are linked by the following patterns: 'a *b*arked *s*apling', 'a *s*tubble of *b*lack corn', 'her *b*lindfold a *s*oiled *b*andage'. Clearly, this patterning has a cohesive function, linking words together at the level of sound. At the same time, these alliterations, in conjunction with the pounding rhythm of the basic system of two or three stresses, reinforce the semantic interrelationships of many sets of words. Undoubtedly, you will have noticed many disturbing combinations like 'the frail rigging of her ribs', 'her drowned body in the bog', 'her blindfold a soiled bandage', 'the stones of silence', etc. On the lexical level, Heaney uses yet another stylistic device of Anglo-Saxon poetry, namely the kenning, which was also a feature of Old Norse poetry, for that matter. It is a kind of compressed metaphor consisting of a compound of two words used instead of a common word. The sun, for instance, could be referred to as 'world candle', and a ship, as 'wave cleaver'. In 'Punishment', you will now recognize a similar device in the descriptive images of the parts of the girl's body, which due to their age-long submergence in the bog have become vegetable objects: her nipples are 'amber beads' (amber is a yellowish fossilized resin), her body when it was thrown naked into the bog was a 'barked sapling' (a young tree with its bark stripped off), but when it was dug up, her bones were hard as oak ('oak-bone'), her exposed brain resembled a fir cone ('brain-firkin') and her shaved head was like a 'stubble of black corn'.

If you linger a little longer on the lexical level, you will furthermore notice that these Nordic associations are also accentuated by the poet's preference for vocabulary of Anglo-Saxon origin. Nearly all the concrete and earthy imagery is deeply rooted in the Germanic core of the English language, while a minority of words stemming from its French or Latin influx such as 'connive', 'civilized', 'exact', 'intimate', 'revenge', etc. are employed to refer to the abstractions related to the ambivalent attitude the poet takes in the last stanza.

There is one descriptive term of French origin, though, which deserves our special attention. It is the word 'cauled' occurring in the disconcerting lines 'when your betraying sisters,/cauled in tar,/wept by the railings'. The poet has coined his word from the noun 'caul', which was formerly used for a netted cap worn by women to enclose their hair. The reason why he has chosen this obsolete word must be that it has another meaning which turns out to be bitterly ironic. As it is, a caul was also used to describe the inner membrane enclosing the foetus before birth, which sometimes envelops the head of the child at birth. 'Being born with a caul on one's head' was held to be a charm bringing good luck. The word becomes even more intriguing if we extend it to the Northern Irish girls' 'sister', the Iron Age girl drowned in the bog, because a caul was supposed to be a preservative against drowning. According to *Brewer's Dictionary of Phrase and Fable* (Cassell's edition of 1980), they were once advertised for sale and frequently sought after by mariners. This digression leads me to the maritime imagery used to describe the wind blowing on the bog girl's skeletal body in the opening stanzas: 'the wind blows her nipples . . . it shakes the frail rigging of her ribs'. This description conjures up an image of sails filling out, with the wind shaking a poor arrangement of ropes, shrouds, and stays supporting the mast of a ship, which is eventually wrecked. What is left are some 'floating rods and boughs'.

On the graphological level, which involves the poem's layout, the basic two- or three-stress pattern lends a long and narrow shape to the poem with the short lines often embracing one semantically comprehensible unit, for example, 'I can feel the tug', 'it blows her nipples', 'it shakes the frail rigging', 'body in the bog', 'the weighing stone' and so forth. This peculiar structure appears to be iconic of the process of excavation. Just like the archaeologists have dug up the girl's body by removing the soil layer after layer, the poet, too, in trying to contain his emotions reveals them bit by bit. Interestingly, this implied sense of the poem's shape would be in keeping with Heaney's view of poetry as 'a dig, a dig for finds that end up being plants' (Heaney 1980: 41).

Most of the phonological, lexical and graphological features I have been able to distinguish tend to show that this particular discourse is a poem, an artefact. Yet there is a counter-force loosening this cohesive structure. This force is the poem's syntax, the grammatical arrangement of its sentences, which in itself is quite regular but all the same disturbs the tight order of the poem by not respecting the line units. In fact, in several places, it even exceeds the stanzaic units. Now, in conjunction with the absence of end-rhyme, which would have marked off the line boundaries, the syntactic pull of these enjambed or run-on lines carries the reader steadily through to the end. For me, the poem has a strong narrative element and when reading it aloud, I associate it with ordinary speech. In this way, the poem becomes a double-edged discourse accommodating both the 'artfulness' of poetry and the 'ordinariness' of everyday human speech and goes a long way towards fulfilling the poet's artistic ambition to strike a balance between poetry and public life.

Suggestions for further work

1   In this chapter, it is argued that there is as a rule a considerable consensus about the interpretation of texts. If this were not the case, communication would become very difficult. On the other hand, it is also arguable that the actual reader of a text is an element of its context, in that s/he actually influences its meaning and interpretation. Read in small groups of students the poem 'Edge' by Sylvia Plath (1965) and try to establish the degree of common understanding and at what points in the text opinions begin to differ considerably. Work out for yourself the reasons for your individual response. Your answers to these questions may well lead to a contextualized stylistic analysis of this poem.

2   Describe the discourse situation in Seamus Heaney's 'Making Strange' from *Station Island* (1984). It appears that the speaker in the poem is caught between two persons. Are there indications in the poem that we need not take this situation literally? If so, could the discourse situation be interpreted as symbolic of the poet's divided self? You will notice that the poem features a relatively large number of imperatives: '*Be* adept and *be* dialect,/*tell* of this wind', etc. Knowing that the pronouns *I*, *we*, and *you* are interpersonal deictics, can you work out why these imperatives have a deictic function, too (cf. Leech 1969: 183–4)? Finally, can you point out some deictics in this poem which draw the reader into the situation of the text?

3   Describe the discourse situation in Tom Paulin's 'A Lyric Afterwards' (in Morrison and Motion 1982) and suggest a contextualized reading. Do you agree with the following critical assessment: In poems by . . . Paulin . . ., we are often presented with stories that are incomplete, or are denied what might normally be considered essential information. The reader is constantly being made to ask, 'Who is speaking?', 'What are their circumstances and motives?' and 'Can they be believed?' There is, moreover, leisure to ponder these questions at length. (Morrison and Motion 1982: 19)

4   In Stevie Smith's poem 'Not Waving but Drowning' (in MacGibbon 1978), the discourse situation is quite complex. We seem to hear several voices. Whose are they? It is said that Stevie Smith was inspired to write this poem by a bizarre and sad newspaper story about a drowning man whose friends thought he was waving to them. Though you have not read the report, you can see in what respect Stevie Smith has changed the situational context of the accident. What is the effect of these changes on your interpretation of the poem?

5 In 'The Tollund Man' from *Wintering Out* (1972), Seamus Heaney relates an Iron Age victim of a sacrificial ritual to the victims of contemporary Irish sectarian atrocity. Make a fully contextualized analysis of the poem, using the model suggested earlier on in this chapter.

6 In his book *The Haw Lantern* (1987), Seamus Heaney included a sequence of eight sonnets entitled 'Clearances' commemorating his mother's life and death. Reading sonnet four, 'Fear of affectation made her affect', instantly calls to mind Heaney's image of the forked stick on which writers not writing in their mother tongue feel caught because of their love of the English language. From his first collection onwards, language has been a recurrent topic in Heaney's poetry. This sonnet is about language as an instrument of alienation and division. Write a contextualized analysis of this sonnet. I suggest the title 'Betrayal through Language'. Perhaps you could make use of the following statement; 'he [Heaney] delights in language, relishing it . . . as something that embodies politics, history and locality, as well as having its own delectability' (Morrison and Motion 1982: 13).

Extracted from Verdonk, P. (ed.) (1993) *Twentieth-Century Poetry: From Text to Context*. Routledge, London, pp. 112–33.

8

The liberation of the icon: A brief survey from classical rhetoric to cognitive stylistics

In the late 1970s, I was asked to teach a refresher course in English grammar to advanced literature students at the University of Amsterdam. Because neither the students nor the teacher, for that matter, particularly liked the idea, I tried to sweeten the pill by having a closer look at the grammar of some of the early modern poets such as Eliot, Cummings, Yeats, Auden and a few others. At the time, I did not know that by teaching the grammar of poetry, I was following in the footsteps of a 2000-year-old tradition.[1] For in the training schools for rhetoricians in classical Rome, the critical reading of poetry was the business of the grammarian. He was responsible for the preliminary training that was compulsory for admission to the higher school for rhetoricians. It was here that the sons (*sic*) of the well-to-do citizens in Rome were moulded into orators for the public debates in the Senate, for the law courts and for all kinds of ceremonial occasions where people had to be either praised or censured.

Indeed, right from its genesis, the ancient art of persuasive speech has had a close affinity with literature. Aristotle (384-322 BC), the father of rhetoric in the Greek-speaking world, and his inheritors Cicero (106-43 BC) and Quintilian (c. 35-100 AD), the best-known exponents of Latin rhetoric, frequently emphasized in their handbooks that the reading of poetry was crucial for the making of the perfect orator.[2] Apparently, they held the view, like many do now, that in some ways literature is a persuasive discourse too. Actually, centuries before rhetoric made its entry into the culture of the ancient Greeks as a theoretical system, forceful eloquence had been the hallmark of their literature from its very beginning. In the great Homeric epics, verbal agility was invariably put on a par with physical prowess and, unsurprisingly, the oratory of the epic heroes was in later centuries a favourite object of study in the training schools for rhetoricians. If these literary instances of oratorical power are a reflection, as some classical scholars have claimed (Lawson-Tancred 1991: 2–5), of a natural inclination of the ancient Greeks to verbal assertiveness and competition, this may well account for their later fascination with the theory of rhetoric and perhaps even more with its practical application in the political and judicial institutions of the dawning democracies in the Greek city-states of the fifth- and fourth-century BC.

The relationship between rhetoric and poetics was definitely a matter of cross-fertilization, for if the rhetoricians spiced their oratory with expressive images from poetry, the classical poets and their commentators in their turn frequently tapped the theoretical resources of rhetoric. For instance, in his famous handbook *De Oratore* (55 BC), Cicero expresses the view that the ideal orator is he whose style succeeds in 'winning over, instructing and stirring men's minds' (1942a: II. 285). In response, we hear the echo of these aspirations in Horace's verse essay *Ars Poetica* (c. 20–23 BC), in which the ideal poet is described as having 'blended profit and pleasure, at once delighting and instructing the reader' ([1929] 1991: 479).

The basic concepts from rhetoric which were incorporated into poetics can be primarily traced back to the three compositional tasks of the orator. The first of these was *inventio,* by which the classical rhetoricians did not necessarily mean the ability to think up something entirely new, but rather the intellectual skill of the orator to search for a persuasive content and argumentation in the arsenal of knowledge and experience he had personally built up. If this source ran dry, there were always the rhetorical handbooks which contained almost endless lists of themes (Cicero's *topica)* and commonplaces (*loci communes)* with which an argumentation could be constructed.[3] This view of *inventio* is entirely in line with the classical literary tradition, in which an effective transmission of received wisdom is of greater importance than inventiveness in the modern sense of the word, that is, originality of content. Pope's neo-classical dictum 'What oft was *Thought,* but ne'er so well *Exprest* in his *Essay on Criticism* ([1711] 1965: 143–68) is the very epitome of this cultural tradition (Baker-Smith 1990:993). The second compositional task was *dispositio,* the strategic arrangement of the chosen content and argumentation. The orator's third task, *elocutio,* was concerned with the effective wording or style of a particular line of thought. From this it follows, by the way, that the modern study of style does not have its roots in poetics but in classical rhetoric. Obviously, the orator also had to deliver his conception. Therefore, two further tasks were imposed on him: *memoria,* the technique of how to learn his oration by heart, and *actio,* which referred to the actual delivery of his speech.[4] Though this description of the compositional and performative tasks of the orator is necessarily brief, it will be noted that, in somewhat anachronistic terms, classical rhetoric is essentially pragmatic because it provides a communicative framework for the interaction between a speaker, an utterance (including the speaker's intended persuasion) and an audience.

After the fall of the western Roman Empire in the latter half of the fifth century, rhetoric apparently went underground, because after some four centuries of political chaos and intellectual darkness, it surfaced again in the medieval and early Renaissance universities in Western Europe. The links with classical antiquity appeared not to have been severed entirely, because the Church had preserved the ancient studies and had adapted them in some degree to their educational programme. Thus, rhetoric became part of the Seven Liberal Arts curriculum, consisting of the *Trivium* (rhetoric, grammar, logic) and the *Qua-drivium* (arithmetic, geometry, music and astronomy).

Since there was no longer scope for public speeches in institutions of government and justice at that stage of political history, rhetoric shifted its interest to literature, thereby once more showing its well-nigh inseparable link with poetics. It seems unique to Western culture that for some 2000 years there was only one monopolistic literary discipline and that its theoretical concepts were the only available tools for the composition and analysis of literature. Be that as it may, rhetoric finally lost its attraction during the Romantic Period because by that time it had cast off all its classical characteristics of logic and systematicity. It had become focused entirely on *elocutio*, or style, which because of its prescriptive artificiality was rejected by the Romantic poets, who aspired to creative freedom, spontaneity and emotional engagement.

Surprisingly, in the latter half of the twentieth century, which after all has witnessed a general decline in classical studies, we have seen a revival of interest in rhetoric. As we have observed earlier, the full scope of classical rhetoric provided a threefold communicative framework comprising the interaction between a speaker (or writer), a discourse and an audience (or reader). It is this communicative triangle that happens to fit in with some recent developments in literary studies and in linguistic sub-disciplines such as pragmatics, text linguistics, discourse studies and argumentation theory. This list should have included stylistics, but I have singled it out because as a typical interdiscipline it has benefited from shifts of emphasis in both linguistic and literary theories. Since these changes are most evident in the role of the audience (or reader), it will be the pivotal point of the following brief overview.

Though, as we have seen, rhetoric in its widest scope is definitely audience-directed, it is remarkable that its huge theoretical apparatus does not mention a single word about the possibility of an active role of the audience in the process of meaning production. The audience was only the passive object of the intended persuasive effects of the text. This situation remained unaltered when the Renaissance humanists and writers rediscovered Aristotle, Cicero and Quintilian, and, in point of fact, throughout the following centuries things remained as they had always been. Interestingly, it has been suggested that perhaps the reason for this ready acceptance of the classical ideas about the relative weakness of the listener or reader lies in the corresponding power of the Word in the Judeo-Christian tradition, which cast the listener or reader in an equally submissive position (Bauschatz 1980: 266).

It may be amazing but even the most influential literary theories formulated in the first three decades of this century perpetuated this passivity of the reader. In Russian Formalism, the Prague Linguistic Circle, Practical Criticism and New Criticism, the formal autonomy of the text was fully maintained and there was no role for the reader in the activation of meaning.

Between the 1930s and 1970s, the ideas of New Criticism probably exerted the greatest influence on English and American literature, including modern English and American stylistics, and even in present-day critical and educational practice, this influence is still manifest. As we have seen, the New Critics regarded a literary text as an autonomous artefact signalling its own intrinsic meaning, which was therefore recoverable from its internal verbal structure only. The literary text was, as it were, to cite the title of a book by a well-known New Critic, locked up in a verbal icon (Wimsatt [1954] 1967). In his poem 'Ars Poetica', the American poet Archibald MacLeish, who had finely tuned antennae for the literary critical trends of his time, very aptly summed up the idea about the text as 'object' in his dictum 'A poem should not mean/But be' (1935: 123). How persistent but also attractive this idea is, is illustrated by the fact that only recently a literary critic of a Dutch weekly wrote in a review of Graham Swift's *Last Orders:* 'The book is, before it is about something' (Paul 1997: 67–8).

But also the most important linguistic theories of the twentieth century did not accommodate listeners or readers of texts as co-producers of meaning. For both structuralism, which set the trend from the 1920s to the1960s, and Chomsky's generative grammar, which took over the linguistic throne in the 1960s, saw language as an autonomous system of formal relations divorced from its natural environment of actual communication.

Reverting our attention to the development of stylistics, we see that, after its emergence as an offshoot of Saussurean linguistics, it gradually gained acceptance on the European continent in the first half of the twentieth century. When, in the 1960s, stylistics reached the academic scene in Britain and the United States, its introduction was no doubt inspired by the ideas of Practical Criticism and New Criticism, which through their preoccupation with the text had created a favourable climate for the analysis of literary texts in terms of their verbal forms only, without regard to their external context. Indeed, stylistics at the time was dominantly formalist and it happily embraced the close reading techniques from Practical Criticism and New Criticism as well as the concepts of defamiliarization and foregrounding from Russian Formalism and the Prague Circle. In brief, the British and American pioneers of stylistics also left the reader out in the cold.

It was not until the 1970s that post-formalist theories were advanced in which the literary text was no longer seen as an autonomous object, but as a discourse, that is, as a contextualized socio-cognitive interaction in which meaning is not unidirectional but rather a matter of negotiation between speakers or writers on the one hand and listeners or readers on the other. The verbal icon was liberated and the text came out to enter a free exchange of signification to which also readers were assumed to contribute. It was the heyday of Roland Barthes, who heralded the transition from structuralism to post-structuralism, of Wolfgang Iser's reader response criticism, Umberto Eco's model reader and Stanley Fish's affective stylistics.[5]

Around about the same time, there was a similar development in linguistics. For linguistic models were constructed which centred on the question of how meanings are negotiated in a contextualized socio-cognitive interaction. Broadly speaking, the study of meaning in such a non-linguistic context belongs to the domain of pragmatics. However, due to the great complexity of these contextual factors, pragmatics has come to intersect with a number of other areas of study including discourse analysis, sociolinguistics, ethnolinguistics, speech act theory and cognitive linguistics. It is precisely this new emphasis on the pragmatic perspective of language in use that has revived classical rhetoric. Clearly, this revival does not involve the formal study of its vast Greek and Latin terminology so that we should not be surprised if the term rhetoric is nowadays used rather flexibly to suit current ideas in modern linguistics and literary theory.

Being a true interdiscipline, stylistics once again climbed on the bandwagon, switching from a strictly formalist approach to pragmatic, socio-pragmatic, rhetorical and cognitive approaches. Accordingly, many stylisticians now view literary texts as part of a complex social and cultural process, that is, as discourses, and although the formal structure of the text remains the object of close attention, a shift in focus has occurred to the perspective of the reader. One of the possible answers to the question of how the role of the reader as an animator of meaning could be described is offered by what is now commonly called schema theory. Here I shall give a very brief account of this theory[6] and later apply it to one of Philip Larkin's poems.

Psycholinguistic research and experiments with artificial intelligence have shown that in an interactive relation with a text, readers interpret the discourse they consequently derive from this, with the help of pre-existing knowledge structures, which are commonly referred to as schemata. Readers have built up these cognitive patterns in the course of their personal and social lives about all kinds of experiences and things in the world around them. As a result, readers can formulate certain expectations about the discourse they are interpreting. They can categorize the information it contains, quickly digest familiar information, fill in less explicit or missing information and add, when needed, new information to their existing reservoir of knowledge.

Two other terms which are also frequently used to refer to pre-existing knowledge structures are frame and script. For example, our average store of experiential knowledge about TREES,[7] in the sense of woody plants which can live for many years, may contain such elements as root, stem or trunk, bark, branches, twigs, leaves, the colour green, and perhaps even castle (in the sense of the leafy head of a tree) and probably many other features or qualities typical of trees. Such a complex of features or qualities of a particular phenomenon is also known as a frame. If subsequently our schema of the GROWING PROCESS OF TREES is activated, it will contain a temporal or logical order, for instance, the trees begin to develop new buds, these buds swell, open up and put out leaves, new shoots grow, annual rings are formed, then the leaves whither again and fall from the trees and so on, until the next cycle of the same events. Such a sequence of events has a kind of narrative structure and is therefore also called a script. In this paper, I shall only use the term schema, because the terms frame and script sometimes overlap and an attempt to distinguish between these terms would lead me too far afield.

It is evident that we have numerous knowledge schemata at our disposal, for example, we have common assumptions about all kinds of aspects of time and place, about people and their behaviour, about our body and its parts, about social and cultural phenomena, about abstract concepts, etc. Of course, many of our schemata such as those about men and women, and about various socio-cultural and historical events, will be slanted ideologically. Furthermore, we have cognitive units for all sorts of linguistic phenomena such as the expected order of phonemes, words and syntactic structures. If, for example, we see a definite article, we expect the next constituent to be a noun (possibly premodified by an adjective) and next a verb and so on. As a result, we can distinguish two strategies of reading and interpretation which support and propel each other: one moves from larger to smaller parts, the so-called top-down strategy, and the other from smaller formal details to larger portions, the so-called bottom-up strategy.

From what I have said about them so far, it will be obvious that our cognitive schemata are far from being static structures. They are actually to a very large extent flexible and adaptable, in that they can be confirmed, dismantled, reorganized, reinforced or renewed. In cognitive stylistics, therefore, it is assumed that, in particular, literary texts have the potential of inducing readers to adjust or revise partly or entirely their existing schemata. In fact, being culturally conditioned, readers expect this discourse genre to shed a new light on their common assumptions. These adjustments or revisions, however, are likely to be temporary or to be stored as sub-schemata, which may or may not influence readers when they return to the humdrum things of their everyday lives and have to fall back again on their socialised and generally accepted schemata.

Added to this, we must realize that these schema revisions motivated by the reading of literary texts undoubtedly vary in detail from reader to reader because their individual experiences will be different. This variety, though, will not result in interpretive chaos, because in spite of the uniqueness of our personal experiences, most of our cognitive schemata are largely filled with conventional perceptions and representations of what we regard as our reality. To make all this a bit more concrete, I propose that we make a brief literary excursion into a poem by Philip Larkin:

The Trees

The trees are coming into leaf
Like something almost being said;
The recent buds relax and spread,
Their greenness is a kind of grief.

Is it that they are born again
And we grow old? No, they die too.
Their yearly trick of looking new
Is written down in rings of grain.

Yet still the unresting castles thresh
In full grown thickness every May.
Last year is dead, they seem to say,
Begin afresh, afresh, afresh.

(Larkin: [1974] 1979: 12)[8]

We treat the poem as a discourse, that is to say, as a particular language utterance produced by a speaker at a certain moment, in a certain context and situation, and intended to be heard and interpreted by a listener, who in this case happens to be a reader. In literary analyses, this reader is often construed as a model reader or ideal reader. But I shall not follow that line here, because such a constructed reader would ultimately be a clone from my own schemata. So whenever I use the term reader or readers, my mind is on myself. This does not mean, however, that my reading will be solely subjective. In part it will also be intersubjective because, as we have seen, many components of my schemata will be shared by other readers. In other words, there will always be a considerable convergence on what is contextually relevant between readers with more or less the same socio-cultural background.

Schema theory also implies that the moment readers recognize the genre of a discourse, such as for instance a letter or a newspaper report, they will immediately activate their pre-structured knowledge about the appropriate structure and style conventions of the genre involved. This reader has recognized Larkin's text as a poem, and will therefore call up the schema associated with this discourse genre. It will include the knowledge that the language of poetry is highly self-involved, which is most evident in its connective phonological tissue, in its spatial arrangement in lines and stanzas, in semantic phenomena like imagery and figures of speech and in parallelistic patterns on all levels of language organization.

In this particular instance, I have also built up a schema of the supposed historical and psychological personality of the poet Larkin, which has been recently enriched by the publication of Andrew Motion's authorized biography in 1993, 8 years after Larkin's death. This biography contains no less than five references to 'The Trees' (Motion 1993: 371, 395, 421, 445, 488), but with one exception, to which I shall refer later, I will make no use of this contextual information, at least not consciously.

We shall now move on to the poem itself. The very first word in the title is the definite article 'the'. Evidently, it does not refer to trees mentioned earlier in the discourse or to something unique which is common knowledge and therefore already shared by speaker and listener, like 'The sun sets in the west'. All the same, informed readers will not be surprised because in literary discourses, the definite article is quite often the very first word. The rhetorical effect is that readers get the feeling that they share their knowledge schema, which has thus been activated, with that of the narrator or, as in this case, with that of the poet's persona. As a result, readers are drawn as it were into the discourse, they feel a degree of involvement, and they are therefore encouraged to further explore not only their prestructured knowledge of 'trees' but also to call up any other related cognitive structures. Besides, it produces in readers the sensation that the poet's persona wants his experience and emotions to be absorbed into the reader's world. Interestingly, this deictic function of the definite article appears to provide evidence that readers do make use of cognitive schemata in their interpretation of discourses.

The first line 'The trees are coming into leaf' is likely to confirm the reader's corresponding schema about the beginning of a yearly repeated event in nature. However, knowing the discourse genre of poetry, the reader may be expected to transform these bare facts into a metaphorical message for humankind, particularly because this message is suggested, though not explicitly expressed, in the second line 'Like something almost being said'. Clearly, this line necessitates an adjustment or even a complete revision of the reader's schema about THE GROWTH OF TREES, for trees coming into leaf are not supposed to be able to speak. It is only natural, though, that readers still want to know the message of the trees, and searching through their mental knowledge stores, and perhaps simultaneously renewing them, they are likely to produce their own version of the content of the message.

In the third and fourth lines, we find the same discursive process as in the first two lines. The third line 'The recent buds relax and spread' confirms the reader's existing schema of a particular natural phenomenon, though the verb 'relax' in this context seems deviant or foregrounded and may well lead to a slight adjustment of the relevant schema. However, the fourth line 'Their greenness is a kind of grief' requires a drastic revision of the reader's experiential knowledge and therewith presents a challenge to metaphorization. At this point, the reader may tentatively infer that the silent message of the trees is an annually repeated reminder of the fact that this ritual of nature implies a paradox. For, on the one hand, there is the promise of new life and continuity as expressed in the phrase 'their greenness', and on the other hand, there is the sense of finiteness and mortality, which is alluded to in the qualified phrase 'a kind of grief'. Since according to cognitive linguists, metaphors are the foundation of the human conceptual system, many readers may well feel inclined to relate this disquieting paradox to the human condition, in particular to the cycle of birth and death.

There is no more space in this paper, to continue this cognitive and metaphoric excursion. Now it only remains for me to draw your attention to an interesting meeting point between schema theory and the ideas on foregrounding and parallelism originating from formalist literary theories. Foregrounding and parallelism were seen as the essence of poetry, but at the time that formalism was fashionable, they were never related to the active role of the reader in the negotiation of meaning. Recent publications (among others, Cook 1994; Semino 1995 and 1997) have pointed out that schema theory might fill this void, by hypothesizing that notably through the foregrounded or unorthodox formal aspects of poetry the cognitive schemata of readers are activated, interconnected and completely or partially revised.

For an illustration of this process we shall return to the poem. Here we see that the schema in which the reader's knowledge is stored concerning cyclic events in nature is likely to be stimulated by the cyclic *abba* rhyming pattern of all three stanzas. This CYCLE schema is naturally associated with a MOVEMENT schema, and for this the reader finds formal and therewith cognitive support in the repetitive patterning of present participle forms such as 'coming', 'being', 'looking' and 'unresting', which characteristically express a sense of movement, particularly in terms of progress and continuity. Another schema which will be activated under the influence of the CYCLE schema is one pertaining to the concept of REPETITION or RENEWAL. This schema will in particular be triggered off by the high frequency of the semantic notion of 'repetition' in words such as 'again', 'yearly', 'new', 'written down in rings of grain', 'every May' and of course, 'Begin afresh, afresh, afresh' in the second and third stanzas. This cognitive concept of REPETITION will be stimulated even further by the repeated echoes of the same sound patterns in 'greenness'/'grief', 'written'/'rings', and by the ambiguous contrast between 'still' and 'unresting' in the line 'Yet still the unresting castles thresh'.

This brings me to further evidence for the working of cognitive schemata, namely the way in which readers notice ambiguities and respond to them. In conformity with the activated schemas of TREES and their GROWING PROCESS, readers are likely to interpret the word 'grain' in the phrase 'rings of grain' in the first instance as 'the natural circular patterns of lines in the wood of trees', thus the annual rings of growth. Likewise, prompted by their expectation roused by the phrase 'the unresting castles', readers will initially interpret the verb 'thresh' as 'move violently'. But because the words 'grain' and 'thresh' both appear at the end of two successive lines, they are likely to catch the reader's eye long enough for calling into action a totally different schema, namely that of GRAIN WHICH HAS RIPENED AND, THEREFORE, IN THE CYCLIC COURSE OF THINGS HAS TO BE HARVESTED AND THRESHED. Readers familiar with poetic discourse are intellectually and emotionally sensitive to such rich ambiguities, and will include in their interpretations the extra layers of meaning generated by them. Actually, if they fail to register this particular ambiguity, they would miss the restatement of the poem's central paradox that growth, continuity and fulfilment inevitably involve transitoriness and mortality.

The last poetic convention I shall touch on very briefly is that readers acquainted with this genre of discourse will usually be susceptible to the rhetoric of the poet's persona. This reader has the impression that a subconscious polemic between the persona's split personalities produces a tension in the poem between, on the one hand, his wonder at the vitality of nature, and on the other, his deep conviction that all life is finite. But these two contradictory emotions are not in balance, because the fervent exhortation at the end of the poem 'Begin afresh, afresh, afresh', which is already somewhat hedged in by the preceding comment clause 'they seem to say', is drowned out by the persona's acute sense of human mortality. So in the end, this reader experiences the poem as a lament about human existence.

I think this is the most suitable moment to come back to the only exception I said I was going to make to the non-activation of my knowledge schema about Larkin's biography. As it happens, this contradictory response of the poem's persona to nature's yearly renewal appears to correspond with a similar ambivalent attitude of the supposed historical personality of the poet to having written this emotive lyric. For in an attempt at self-protecting irony, Larkin scribbled underneath the manuscript of this poem the scathing comment 'Bloody awful tripe' (Motion 1993: 372).

Extracted from Verdonk, P. (1999) 'The Liberation of the Icon: A brief Survey from Classical Rhetoric to Cognitive Stylistics', *Journal of Literary Studies* 15(3/4): 291–304.

9

Painting, poetry, parallelism: Ekphrasis, stylistics and cognitive poetics

The Dance
In Brueghel's great picture, The Kermess,[1]
the dancers go round, they go round and
around, the squeal and the blare and the
tweedle of bagpipes, a bugle and fiddles
tipping their bellies (round as the thick-
sided glasses whose wash they impound)
their hips and their bellies off balance
to turn them. Kicking and rolling about
the Fair Grounds, swinging their butts, those
shanks must be sound to bear up under such
rollicking measures, prance as they dance
in Brueghel's great picture, The Kermess.
William Carlos Williams, *Selected Poems* (1985)

Ekphrasis in classical rhetoric

Poems describing a work of art, like 'The Dance' by William Carlos Williams, are traditionally associated with a literary sub-genre called ekphrasis, which is a transliteration of a Greek word meaning 'description'. (The spelling ecphrasis is also current.) However, contrary to what might be expected, the term has its origin not in poetics but in classical rhetoric, the art of persuasion. Here ekphrasis was usually defined as a self-contained description, often of a common topic, which could be inserted at an appropriate place in a piece of oratory so as to enhance its persuasive powers. For this purpose, the teachers of ancient rhetoric required an ekphrasis to be so vivid that it would bring the event or object described before the mind's eye of the listener. To give a typical example, I quote below a brief passage from *Rhetorica ad Herennium* (Rhetoric for Herennius), an early Latin handbook, written perhaps around 84 BC by an anonymous author, who addressed it to an unidentified Herennius.[2] This is what he has to say on *descriptio*, the Latin equivalent of ekphrasis:

Vivid Description is the name for the figure which contains a clear, lucid and impressive exposition of the consequences of an act, as follows:

> But, men of the jury, if by your votes you free this defendant, immediately, like a lion released from his cage, or some foul beast loosed from his chains, he will slink and prowl about in the forum, sharpening his teeth to attack everyone's property, assaulting every man, friend and enemy, known to him or unknown, now despoiling a good name, now attacking a life, now bringing ruin upon a house and its entire household, shaking the republic from its foundations. Therefore, men of the jury, cast him out from the state, free everyone from fear, and finally, think of yourselves. For if you release this creature without punishment, believe me, gentlemen, it is against yourselves that you will have let loose a wild and savage beast. ([Cicero] 1989: IV.xxxix.51)

Cross-fertilization between rhetoric and poetics

It will not be difficult to see that precisely this type of rhetorical figure of description is a prime candidate for evolving into a literary figure, though without necessarily losing its persuasive features (Cockcroft 2003: 54). Indeed, there was a lot of cross-fertilization going on between rhetoric and poetics, with the rhetoricians spicing up their oratory with expressive images from poetry, and the poets tapping the rich resources of rhetoric (Verdonk 1999: 293). For example, in his rhetorical handbook *De Oratore* (*On the Orator*) (55BC), Cicero holds that the orator has three main functions, namely 'the winning over, the instructing and the stirring of men's minds' (1988: II.xxviii.121). In the literary camp, these rhetorical aspirations are echoed in Horace's verse essay *Ars Poetica* (c. 20–23 BC), where the ideal poet is described as having 'blended profit and pleasure, at once delighting and instructing the reader' (1991: 333).

Ekphrasis as a literary figure

Now, literary ekphrasis, as it ultimately evolved from rhetoric, can be taken in a wider and a narrower sense. In the wider sense, it is a detailed description of any real or imagined object or scene, or of an abstract idea, mental image or state of emotion. In the more restricted sense, ekphrasis is associated with poetry addressing not only works of visual art, such as paintings, tapestries and sculpture, but also architectural art, and functional artefacts such as goblets, vases, and weaponry like swords, shields and suits of armour. In this case too, all these objects may be real or fictional. At this point, it appears useful to follow Hollander's example in his fine book on ekphrasis, entitled *The Gazer's Spirit: Poems Speaking to Silent Works of Art* (1995), by making a distinction between 'actual' and 'notional' ekphrasis. Actual ekphrastic poems are engaged with particular and identifiable works of art or artefacts, whereas in the case of notional ekphrasis, the artistic objects addressed are purely fictional (1995: 4).[3] In antiquity, and long after, notional ekphrasis abounds, and it has become an established convention to regard Homer's description of the making of the legendary shield of Achilles in the *Iliad* as its generic prototype (1974: XVIII.483–608). Homer's masterpiece was emulated several times in later epics, including Virgil's description of Aeneas's shield in *The Aeneid* (Virgil 1974: VIII.626–731), while in our times it has been transferred to a modern anti-heroic setting by W. H. Auden in his bitter poem 'The Shield of Achilles' (1966: 294–5). These and many other classical instances of notional ekphrasis also inspired a great many English poets, from Chaucer, Spenser and Shakespeare to the Romantics, with, I think, Keats's 'Ode on a Grecian Urn' as the acme of perfection.[4]

Perhaps unsurprisingly, a bird's eye view of Western art history shows that different periods have different ekphrastic agendas. For instance, it is remarkable that in the twentieth century so many poets, both inside and outside Britain, produced such a lot of actual ekphrastic poems addressing real and identifiable paintings, and it is even more remarkable that for some unexplained reason the sixteenth-century Flemish painter Pieter Brueghel the Elder became their special favourite (Kranz 1975). His pictures provided an inspiration for poets such as John Berryman, Walter de la Mare, Sylvia Plath, Wislawa Szymborska, William Carlos Williams and, notably, W. H. Auden, who perhaps set this fashion with his justly celebrated ekphrastic poem 'Musée des Beaux Arts', which specifically mentions Pieter Brueghel's *Landscape with the Fall of Icarus* and alludes to a few other pictures by the same artist (Verdonk 1987). William Carlos Williams, for that matter, wrote no fewer than ten poems on paintings by Brueghel, which were all collected in his book *Pictures from Brueghel and Other Poems* (1962), for which he was awarded the Pulitzer Prize for Poetry only 2 months after his death in March 1963. Williams's poem 'The Dance', which will be discussed later, had been published earlier in *The Wedge* (1944) and was subsequently included in *Selected Poems* (1985).

The bond between poetry and the visual arts

Considering notional and actual ekphrasis in a wider perspective, it appears that in the history of Western art, there has traditionally been a strong bond between poetry and the visual arts. Thus, in the opening chapter of his *Poetics,* Aristotle (384-322 BC) yokes the two arts together in the fundamental statement: 'Some artists, whether by theoretical knowledge or by long practice, can represent things by imitating their shapes and colours, and others do so by the use of the voice' (Dorsch 1983: 32). The keywords here are 'represent' and 'imitate', the latter being a translation of the Greek word *mimesis.* Indeed, though using different media, poetry and painting were long regarded as imitative arts, because they both used mimetic representation to depict humans and objects in their relationship to the outside world.

This close affinity between the two arts, which were therefore often designated as the 'sister arts', found its fullest expression in Horace's (65–8 BC) frequently quoted simile *Ut pictura poesis* ('A poem is like a picture'), which occurs in his earlier mentioned verse essay *Ars Poetica* (1991: 361). This Horatian formula had a very long career and profoundly influenced several theories of poetry, as well as the arts in general, until well into the eighteenth century, when the classical norm that art should be concerned with *mimesis*, that is, the imitation of 'reality', began to give way to the ideal of romantic emotion and individual expression.

The rivalry between word and image

Though the ideas of classical *mimesis* may belong to the past, those of ekphrasis are, in a general sense, still very much alive, in that they continue to feed our constant and irresistible urge to bring about some kind of productive or creative interplay between word and image (Baker-Smith 1990: 1002). It is perhaps what 2000 years ago Quintilian had in mind when he coined the catchphrase 'word picture' (*verbis depingitur*) and insisted that a speech must appeal not only to the hearing but also to the 'eyes of the mind' (*oculis mentis*) (1986: VIII. III.61–72). As a matter of fact, countless writers of shaped poetry, concrete poetry, comic strips and illustrated advertisements and of course, film-makers have satisfied this preoccupation with vision and language. Incidentally, it will be noted that the ekphrastic endeavours of these, what might be called, mixed arts actually produce more or less concrete images, whereas the language of ekphrastic poetry characteristically does not, for if it did, it would have to be called shaped or concrete poetry. Quite the contrary, the language of ekphrastic poetry is expected to call the image to mind, to conjure it up, as it were.[5]

Apart from this prevailing desire for some productive or creative interaction between word and image, there is at the same time a tension and even rivalry between our cognitive abilities of language and vision. For instance, when in classical times, the image was used to jazz up the persuasive powers of the orator, it was still the word that remained in control. By contrast, it seems to me that in recent years in many areas of communication, notably in the mass media and multimedia, it is now the image that dominates the word. In point of fact, if ekphrasis is taken in its broadest sense of an attempt to capture the visual in words, the present-day state of affairs in modern communicative rhetoric may well be seen as an inversion of this classical ideal, in that now 'images are given the task . . . of explaining words, rather than the reverse' (Nunberg 1996: 264).

A brief exposé of cognitive poetics as a spin-off from the cognitive sciences

After the above thumbnail sketch of the cultural history of ekphrasis, and a brief ideological aside, which some people might see as a sign of culture pessimism, I shall make a very short explanatory statement about cognitive poetics, also known as cognitive stylistics.

Given the limited scope of this article, I cannot begin to describe here in detail what cognitive poetics is all about. Therefore, an extremely brief summary must suffice. Cognitive poetics, then, is one of the valuable spin-offs from research into the cognitive sciences in general and cognitive linguistics in particular. It is an interdisciplinary study of how readers process literary texts, or perhaps better still, 'of what happens when a reader reads a literary text' (Stockwell 2002: 5). Probably the main reason why many students of style find fresh inspiration in cognitive linguistics is that this approach does not regard language as a separate and independent cognitive faculty, as it is assumed to be in Chomskyan linguistics. (Compare, for instance, Steven Pinker's fascinating book *The Language Instinct* published in 1994, which is largely inspired by Chomsky's ideas.) On the contrary, cognitive linguists hold that there is a close interactive and meaningful relationship between our linguistic and other cognitive abilities, which include thinking, experience, imagination, learning, memory, perception, attention, emotion, reasoning and problem-solving. All these abilities enable humans to survive and make sense of the world around them. From this it follows that cognitive linguistics is thoroughly experiential from a physical, social, cultural, ideological and emotive point of view. To put it differently, cognitive linguists seek to explain the formal manifestations of language not only in terms of the non-linguistic cognitive abilities which are their plausible providers, but also in terms of the communicative or discursive functions that such empowered language structures perform (Taylor 2002: 8–9).[6] Yet another source of inspiration for stylistics and poetics is that cognitive linguistics was (and still is) developed in relation to other cognitive sciences such as cognitive psychology, anthropology, psycholinguistics and artificial intelligence. This interdisciplinary approach has yielded completely new concepts, theories and ideas which will enable students of style and poetics to analyse, describe and rationalize 'the effects of literary texts on the mind of the reader' (Gavins and Steen 2003: 2). For example, metaphor, metonymy and other figures are no longer seen as an embellishment of language to create a particular stylistic effect, resulting from a process of objective thinking of an independent mind; rather, they are seen as a reflection of how people *construe* their knowledge and experience of the world around them (Lee 2001: 6–7; Taylor 2002: 11; my emphasis).[7] Furthermore, cognitive poetics also draws on other cognitive concepts such as schema theory and frames for research into readers' comprehension of texts (Emmott 1997; Semino 1997), the concept of figure and ground to account for readers' response to foregrounding (Emmott 2002; Stockwell 2002) and some other theoretical concepts from the cognitive sciences that cannot be discussed here because of lack of space. Therefore, I refer to the following recently published collections of articles: Csábi and Zerkowitz (2002), Gavins and Steen (2003), and Semino and Culpeper (2002). They deal with a wide variety of examples of how cognitive poetics can be fruitfully combined with theories and insights from cognitive linguistics and other cognitive disciplines, showing how the cognitive sciences have given fresh impetus to stylistics and poetics.

Cognitive poetics in relation to poetics, stylistics, linguistics and discourse analysis

As its name implies, cognitive poetics is also closely linked with poetics, both in its classical narrower sense of a systematic theory of poetry and in its modern broader sense of 'science' of literature, which includes literary and cultural theory, literary criticism, literary history and aesthetics. Furthermore, it is essential for an effective application of cognitive poetics to keep drawing on the resources of stylistics, linguistics and, last but not least, discourse analysis so as to assess through verbal analysis the validity of readerly intuitions

(Stockwell 2002: 60). This versatility of approach and open-mindedness are called for because in the humanities there are different forms of rationalization, different kinds of arguments and argumentation, and all have strong theoretical foundations, so that any claim of the cognitive sciences to exclusiveness or to having the best methods would lead to a barren exercise.

The nature of literary discourse

I return to my discussion of literary ekphrasis with the important observation that it is in fact concerned with a double representation, namely a verbal representation of a pictorial one (Hamilton 2003: 216). Now, a representation implies not only that it represents *something* but also that it represents this something *to someone* (Jackendoff 2002: 19). Therefore, it may be said that an ekphrastic poem embodies a communicative triangle between the artist, the poet's persona and the reader. In other words, it is very much a discourse, which I define as an interpersonal and context-bound act of communication verbalized in a text, and waiting to be inferred from it. Importantly, context is a matter not simply of physical circumstances but also of the ideas, values, beliefs and emotions inside people's heads. In this sense, all communication is a meeting of minds, and meaning is achieved to the extent that the contexts of the communicating parties come together. With regard to the meanings of *literary* discourses, I hold the view that they are indefinite, undetermined, unstable and indeed often unsettling. So every time readers try to infer a discourse from the same literary text, they are sure to find other meanings, which again and again will refuse to be pinned down (Verdonk 2002: 22). When I wrote this, I was not questioning the basic assumption in most stylistic work that 'the language of literature' does not stand aloof from 'ordinary language'. In fact, I was only trying to formulate tentatively what it is that makes literary discourse different from other types of social discourse. As Simpson has succinctly phrased it, cognitive poetics appears to provide theoretical strategies that allow stylisticians to address precisely this problem in their work, on the basis of the argument that literature is perhaps better conceptualized as a way of reading than as a way of writing (2004: 39).

A stylistic-cum-cognitive poetic reading of William Carlos Williams's 'The Dance'

I will now present a reading of William Carlos Williams's ekphrastic poem 'The Dance', prompted by a linguistic stylistic analysis. (When I say 'a' reading,

I mean of course that it is 'my' reading.) Concurrently with this reading as well as at the end of it, I will suggest what non-linguistic cognitive capacities might be supposed to underlie some of the poem's rhetorical elements or perceived effects, in other words, to what extent they could be rationalized from a cognitive poetic perspective.[8]

When turning my attention to the poem, I am prompted by my real-world experience that all discourse is interpersonal, and therefore I assume instinctively the role of the person being spoken to, and listen to the voice of the speaker in the poem whom I expect to express certain views or sentiments. In poetics, this speaker is usually indicated as the poem's 'persona', which is the Latin word for the mask through which the actors in a classical play spoke their lines. Interestingly, the term persona derives from Latin *per-sonare*, which means to 'sound through'. This verb is most appropriate in this case because by means of a series of highly expressive sound patterns, the persona attempts to make me almost literally hear the bouncing of the dancers in the Brueghel painting, as well as the din of the music to which they dance. For me, these sounds not only are mimetic, in that they add to the poem's lexical meaning by enacting that meaning, but also create meaning by triggering associations between particular sounds and other sensations, memories or images stored in my mind. When saying this, I am well aware that when listening to speech in everyday discourse I tend to disregard the sounds of words and listen only for the meaning. But as a result of social-cultural conditioning and my knowledge of this generic category, I have acquired the cognitive-emotive awareness that in poetic discourse particular individual sounds or patterns of sound tend to reinforce or even add to the poem's lexical sense.

With regard to patterns, I perceive that this poem's discourse makes profitable use of parallelism, that is, it features repetitive patterns on all levels of language organization. It is a well-known fact that humans are invariably charmed by linguistic quirks involving patterned structures of repetition. Most interestingly, cognitive linguists claim that our innate habit to structure things into symmetrical patterns, including patterns of repetition, is in fact a projection of our embodied understanding of symmetry in the world around us. We project this understanding metaphorically on to all our perceptions, actions and imaginings, so as to make sense of the world (Turner 1991: 91). Not surprisingly, this ingrained disposition is stimulated maximally by symmetric structures in art of various forms such as literature, music, painting, sculpture and architecture. Indeed, embodied experience is a key concept in cognitive linguistics. It claims that meaning, understanding, imagination and rationality originate in and are determined by the patterns of our bodily as well as social and cultural experiences, which is diametrically opposed to the abstract, propositional account of meaning in Western philosophy dissociated from any personal experience (Johnson 1987; Lakoff 1987; Lakoff and Johnson 1980, 1999).

In poetry, sound patterns, which include prosodic effects such as metre and rhythm, rhyme, stanza forms and other sound effects like alliteration, assonance and onomatopoeia, are the staple instances of parallelism on the phonological level. Thus in my reading of the metrical structure of 'The Dance', the syllable count per line varies from eight to eleven and the number of stresses from three to four. But when rereading it aloud, I hear (and metaphorically feel!) that its metrical ground plan is not drawn line by line, but ranges right across the poem. Almost bodily, I join in on the beat on the first syllable of 'Brueghel' in the first line and then I feel I am being moved rhythmically round and round from line to line in a waltz-like dance in triple time on the fairly regular dactylic beat of óne, twŏ, thrĕe.[9]

My sense of being swept off my feet by these 'rollicking measures' of a dance is intensified by the syntactic pull of the run-on lines, which carry me breathlessly through to the end. Besides, in a great many of these lines, the pull is particularly strong because the run-on occurs right in the middle of a syntactic constituent. In other words, in the case of enjambement, I get two conflicting prompts: the metrical line-boundary tells me to pause, while the unfinished syntax pulls me into the next line (Verdonk 2002: 61). This syntactic counterpoint to the poem's metre also comes out in the overall grammatical structure of the poem, which consists of only two sentences, with the result that in my reading I am allowed only one brief pause and this comes right at the moment when the dancers turn. Indeed, everything interacts with everything because even the absence of end-rhyme, which would have marked off the line boundaries, speeds up the wild verse-movement of the poem, and to cap it all, many of the lines end with normally weak-stressed function words such as 'and', 'the', 'about', 'those' and 'such', which spur me on to read ever faster in search of words of fuller meaning.

In doing so, I experience yet another sound pattern. This time it is produced by some strings of alliterative consonantal sounds, of which particularly the frequently repeated bilabial plosive /b/, as in 'blare', bagpipes', 'bugle', 'bellies', 'butts' and 'bear up', makes my inner ear aware of the thumping rhythm of the music as well as of the stamping feet of the dancers. By now, I think that the poem's sound structure is its most powerful rhetorical device, because the cacophony of this kermess dance is not only magnified even further by some patterns of assonance, as in the repeated 'go round and around', and in 'squeal' and 'tweedle', but there are also the sound associations evoked by the poem's diction, such as the descriptive nouns of the different noises – the already mentioned 'squeal' and 'tweedle' and 'blare' – and the names of the different musical instruments, 'bagpipes', 'bugle' and 'fiddles'. At this point, I realize that the noises are mentioned first and only then the instruments that produce them. The effect of this syntactic order is that I experience almost physically my search for the producers of this ear-splitting pandemonium.

For this perceptual experience, I refer to my subsequent discussion of the figure–ground principle.

Shifting now to the grammatical level, I become aware of a repetitive pattern of present participles of verbs of motion such as 'tipping', 'kicking', 'rolling' and a few others. I feel that they all converge in sustaining the poem's untiring rhythm because grammatically present participles usually denote continuing action, while here they simultaneously match and reinforce the sense of the motion verbs.

Indeed, it is remarkable that the complexity of the poem's parallelism can still be added to by yet another linguistic element, namely the repeated explicit use of the co-ordinating conjunction 'and', which is traditionally called syndeton from the Greek *syndéton*, meaning 'bound together'. This rhetorical device intensifies for me the listing of all the things to be seen in the painting, and, in terms of vicarious experience, all the things to be 'heard'.

Next, I notice how the speaker in the poem's discourse exploits the use of the present tense, as well as of the definite article, to draw me as it were into the scene of the picture. First, there is the consistent deictic use of the present tense, conveying the dramatic immediacy of the speaker's eye-witness account of the picture and suggesting that his present is my present. Psychologically, it is indeed all self-induced suggestion on my part, because the fact of the matter is that I am unable to check the persona's use of the present tense in relation to real time, as I would have been in a face-to-face conversation. However, guided by my social and cognitive experience to relate a discourse to the context of its occurrence, to take the speaker's viewpoint, and to understand how things would look from his or her time and place, I am able to interpret the persona's use of the present tense as a representation of the time as he experienced it, while describing the picture. At this point, I wish to refer to what I said earlier about ekphrasis being a matter of double representation, namely a verbal representation of a pictorial one. In this context, I also said that the poem actually embodies a triangular discourse between the painter, the poet's persona and the reader. So the conclusion must be that the painter played the same game with the poet's persona as the latter plays with me, the reader. More specifically, the artist has persuaded the poet's persona to assume a presence in the world of the painting through his pictorial rhetoric. In the same way, the latter (i.e. the poet's persona) has persuaded me to imagine myself as participating in the situation described in the poem through his verbal rhetoric.

This leads me to a consideration of the particular use of the definite article in the poem's discourse, which appears to be yet another rhetorical device to engage me, the reader, in the role of addressee. By pretending that virtually all the things he sees are as 'definite' for me as they are for himself, the persona thrusts me, as it were, into the immediate situational context of looking at the painting. In fact, this use of the definite article is in essence 'deictic', too, because it signals that the persona controls the perspective and decides what information in the discourse is rhetorically assumed to be known to the addressee, and by proxy to me, the reader.

Coming to the last line, it strikes me that it repeats literally the first line. I am tempted to interpret this repetition, which appears to frame or enclose the ekphrastic discourse of the poem, as an iconic representation of the framing of the picture.[10] In terms of cognitive perception, I think that texts can suggest spatiality and boundedness. Therefore, this framing of the poem may have the iconic effect of suggesting similarity between the verbal and the visual representations, which, after all, is likely to be the main objective of ekphrasis. This framing, for that matter, may also allude to the fact that paintings and poems are characteristically self-contained so that we have to make a kind of effort to relate them to a relevant context so as to engage them in a discourse.

This last observation brings to mind the theory of figure–ground organization, which is crucial to cognitive linguistics, in particular to the so-called prominence view of language (Ungerer and Schmid 1996: xiii). The figure–ground phenomenon, which was first described by the Danish gestalt psychologist Edgar Rubin in 1915, may be defined as our mental faculty to distinguish a perceived object (the figure) from its background (the ground). Usually, this distinction is relatively easy, but sometimes it is made difficult as, for example, in the case of camouflage, which causes the figure to blend with the ground. As is only to be expected, artists such as the Dutch graphic artist M. C. Escher, may make playful use of this visual mode of perception by designing ambiguous prints or pictures in which the figure could be ground, or the other way round. This basic principle is also applied in cognitive linguistics, for example, for the explication of locative relations and clause patterns (Langacker 1987, 1991; Ungerer and Schmid 1996 serves as an excellent introduction).

Obviously, Brueghel's picture as a self-contained object, with its frame forming clearly defined edges, conspicuously stands out as a figure against its background, in this case a wall of a museum in Vienna. However, when scanning across the scene in the picture, it will be noticed that our figure–ground organization is in essence flexible. By changing our focus on different details of the scene, we can repeatedly create different figure–ground relations. From this it follows that the figure–ground theory is closely linked to the human attentional system, in that our attention is captured by the figure or, the other way round, we create a figure precisely because we concentrate our attention on it. Thus, it is particularly striking that the poet completely ignores the couple in the foreground, who seem to be dashing across purposefully on a diagonal line, rather than being drawn into the dance. In fact, the poet's attention seems to concentrate on about one-third of the area of the picture, that is, the left foreground and right centre.[11]

Now, this is all about visual perception, but in cognitive linguistics, figure–ground alignments also apply to other sensory perceptions (Taylor 2002: 10). Consider, for example, our auditory ability to pick out a particular note from a piece of background music or a particular voice from a babble of voices. Furthermore, the figure–ground theory also relates to our cognitive ability to mentally structure situations and texts in all sorts of ways, for instance, by selecting or omitting specific circumstances, by describing participants in various degrees of detail, by providing different perspectives and by creating conspicuous stylistic features or tendencies that stand out as figures against the background of the rest of the text (Taylor 2002: 11). In point of fact, it may be concluded that, in addition to all the other cognitive motivations I suggested in my analysis, the theory of figure–ground organization provides yet another rational explanation for all the foregrounded patterns of sound, syntax, grammar and diction that captivated my attention when reading this poem, so much so that I really felt drawn into the boisterous world of Brueghel's painting, like Alice who stepped through the looking-glass into Looking-Glass House after many times repeating her favourite phrase 'Let's pretend'.

Acknowledgements

I am grateful to Ron Carter and Peter Stockwell of the University of Nottingham and Mick Short of Lancaster University for inviting me to read earlier versions of this article to staff members and graduate students. The ensuing discussions were most inspiring. I also thank Henry Widdowson, Robert Cockcroft and an anonymous reviewer for their useful comments and suggestions.

Extracted from Verdonk, P. (2005) 'Painting, Poetry, Parallelism: Ekphrasis, Stylistics and Cognitive Poetics', *Language and Literature* 14(3): 231–44.

10

Style

*Thanks to words, we have been able to rise above the brutes;
and thanks to words, we have often sunk to the level of the demons.*
Aldous Huxley, *Adonis and the Alphabet*, 1956
(John Gross 1987: 280).

The etymology of the word 'style'

Etymologically, the word 'style' derives from Latin *stilus*, originally meaning an ancient writing instrument made of metal, wood or bone. It had a sharp-pointed end for scratching letters on a wax tablet and a blunt end for erasing them; in obsolete English, it was 'a style', which was used until well into the nineteenth century. (This spelling with [y] is due to the erroneous notion that it represents the Greek word *stûlos*, meaning 'column'.) In an endearing piece on how children should be taught how to write, Quintilian (c.35-c.95 AD) says:

> As soon as the child has begun to know the shapes of the various letters, it will be no bad thing to have them cut as accurately as possible upon a board, so that the pen (*stilus*) may be guided along the grooves. Thus mistakes such as occur with wax tablets (*ceris*) will be rendered impossible; for the pen will be confined between the edges of the letters and will be prevented from going astray. (*Institutio oratoria*, 1920: I.I.27).

The *Oxford English Dictionary* has this fourteenth-century entry: 'Seinte Barnabe his body was found in a den . . . with Þe gospel of Mathew Þat he hadde i-write wiÞ his owne stile.' (Note the etymologically correct spelling.)

Considering its present-day widespread usage in all kinds of contexts of everyday life, this restricted meaning of 'style' must have gone through a remarkable semantic development. The successive steps in this development are likely to have been the metonymical extension from 'an instrument for writing' to 'a manner of writing', first in the literal sense of 'a writer's characteristic way of shaping letters', and next in the figurative and deeper sense of 'a writer's characteristic mode of expression in terms of effectiveness, clarity, beauty and the like'. Though in the five canons of classical Latin rhetoric (see below), style is termed *elocutio*, the metonym *stilus* is also regularly used in the same sense. For instance, in *Brutus*, Cicero (1939) says about the orations of a certain Gaius Claudius that they are so splendid 'that they would seem almost to have been written by an Attic pen' (*ut paene Attico stilo scriptae esse videantur*) (XLV.167). From the context it is obvious that '*Attico stilo*' means here 'in Attic style'. Of course, the translator's word 'pen' is also a metonym for 'a particular style of writing', as in the well-known saying 'The pen is mightier than the sword'.

The proliferation of style

However, the semantic history of style does not end here, because in later centuries, it was transferred to a great many other contexts. Perhaps this happened because style belongs to the domain of language and its offshoots speaking and writing, and it is a well-known fact that mapping from this domain to other areas of experience is quite common. This is illustrated by examples like 'the *language* of flowers'; '*speaking* colors'; '*telling* figures'; 'their absence *spoke* volumes', etc. It may have been in this way that style gained widespread currency outside the domain of language. Indeed, a particular style may be attributed not only to painting, architecture, music or fashion, but to practically any other mental or physical activity, for example, 'a pen-and-ink sketch in Rembrandtesque style'; 'a revival of the Gothic style'; 'Schubert's *Overture in Italian Style*'; 'a flamboyant style of dress'; 'an autocratic style of management'; 'a country-style dinner'; 'an aggressive style of play', etc.

Furthermore, the term 'style' resulting from this semantic transfer may also be used in a kind of absolute sense to refer to a particular type, make or shape of something, for example, 'these shoes come in all sizes and styles', or to describe a superior quality or manner as such, for example, 'the team has simply been beaten by style'; 'the restaurant is a statement of taste and style in fusion', etc. In sum, a brief questioning of an internet search engine will show that style is omnipresent in practically all domains of human existence.

Some tentative thoughts on the nature of style

Behind the external features of style, as illustrated by the above-mentioned examples, one usually suspects some conscious or unconscious intention and significance. In other words, it is generally assumed that style has a phenomenal as well as a conceptual element, which, though they can be distinguished, are at the same time inseparably interconnected. For instance, Rembrandt's chiaroscuro technique in his painting and Philip Larkin's repeated use of metonyms in his poetry are clearly recognizable phenomenal aspects of their art, which simultaneously convey a deep conceptual significance. In other words, it seems that style is concerned with the mutually creative interplay between perceptible form and intangible content.

All this also implies that in principle, style is associated with humans either as individuals or as a group linked to a specific context of place, time and culture, and that normally the notion of style is not applied to entities or things which are not the result of some human action. Therefore, unless it is a case of personification, it seems odd to speak of the style of, for instance, a gust of wind or a thunderstorm. Significantly, this sense of human consciousness and agency implies that the attribution of a particular style to some artefact, action or performance entails all kinds of underlying social, cultural and ideological implications (Verdonk 2002: 18–21).

Apart from the above tentative ideas about style, it has so far proved to be very difficult to define it as an abstract concept. Again, this is a problem for non-linguistic and linguistic styles alike (Wales 2001: 370–2). Indeed, style as the equivocal interface between form and content, or in stronger terms, style as the confrontation between a perceived outward appearance and some assumed intrinsic value, has never ceased to trouble the human mind. At the same time, it is ironic that style is a creation of that very same mind.

For a possible answer to the question of how style ever came into being as an invaluable asset of the human mind, I will now briefly discuss its relationship with rhetoric.

Rhetoric-cum-style: The earliest beginnings

Because style in language is often related to rhetoric and sometimes even equated with it, I will first give a brief account of the potential effect of what might be called proto- or primary rhetoric on the urge for survival of the human species and their social-cultural evolution. This is followed by a somewhat more detailed discussion of the emergence of classical rhetoric in Western culture and of some of its long-lived intellectual and artistic achievements, interspersed with occasional excursions to present-day views whenever this seems relevant and useful.

Rhetoric, then, may be assumed to be as old as human communication. In a general sense, it may be described as a cognitive and emotive drive in people to use language in such a manner as to impress or emotionalize others and then persuade them to adopt or reject a certain viewpoint, or to undertake or refrain from a particular course of action. The target of this persuasive process may also be one's own self. A famous literary example of self-persuasion is the noble Brutus in Shakespeare's *Julius Caesar,* II.1.10–34, who argues himself into the conviction that Caesar must die.

From an evolutionary perspective, the ultimate source of this basic impulse, and thus of rhetoric, is likely to have been the instinct of self-preservation, and as such rhetoric may be supposed to have contributed to the preservation of the human species (Kennedy 1998: 4). The persuasive force of this primary rhetoric was inevitably conditioned not only by *what* was said, that is, the content, but also by *how* it was said, that is, the form. Now, this formal aspect or manner of expression, which is inseparably interconnected with its content, and at the same time causally related to a relevant social and communicative context, is the natural predecessor of what later evolved into the concept of style.

In the course of human history, the evolution from relatively simple to more complex cultures raised the level of sophistication of this innate rhetorical-cum-stylistic capacity, which also extended to oral forms of literary expression. For instance, centuries before the introduction of rhetoric as a theory, the culture of the ancient Greeks had a long-established tradition of oral poetry on heroic and mythological topics in which forceful eloquence, that is, rhetoric, is a stylistic hallmark. Particularly, in the great Homeric epics the *Iliad* and the *Odyssey* (eighth-century BC), verbal agility is invariably put on a par with physical prowess. For example, in the *Iliad,* when Achilles has resentfully withdrawn from the fighting in the siege of Troy, the old charioteer Phoenix points out to him the two vital qualifications of the Homeric hero: 'It was to teach you all these things, to make *a speaker* of you and *a man of action*. . .' (*Iliad,* Homer 1950: X.443; my emphasis). After Homer's poetry had been written down in the course of the seventh-century BC, the oratorical style of the epic heroes became a favourite object of study in the training schools for rhetoricians and had a strong influence on the conception of the ideal orator in Greek and Roman civilization (Kennedy 1999: 6). For instance, some 800 years later, Cicero recalls the same Homeric tale about Phoenix teaching the young Achilles how to be 'an *orator* and *man of action* too' (*De oratore,* Cicero 1942: III.XV.57).

The rise of classical rhetoric-cum-style in the Greek city-states

Long before the invention of writing, the extraordinary potency of language must have been a constant source of fascination, because after literate cultures had internalized writing, the rhetorical and stylistic uses of language were often the first topics of theoretical study. Indeed, as Ong has put it, 'writing . . . did not reduce orality but enhanced it, making it possible to organize the 'principles . . . of oratory into a scientific art' (1982: 9). This is exactly what happened in major ancient cultures like Mesopotamia, Egypt, Palestine, China, India and Greece (Kennedy 1998: 115–40). In Western culture, the ancient Greeks developed an elaborately structured system aimed at teaching public speech and written composition, which under the name of 'rhetoric' (short for 'the art of rhetoric') was inherited by classical Rome, and became a dominant factor in European culture for more than 2000 years. Obviously, cross-cultural or comparative research-work is needed to establish the correspondences and differences between Western and non-Western rhetoric. See, for example, Kennedy (1998).

The theory and practice of rhetoric-cum-style particularly flourished in the fifth- and fourth-century BC, when new democratic systems of government were introduced in the ancient Greek city-states, of which Athens became the most important. In the political (from Greek *polis* 'city') and judicial institutions of these dawning democracies, vigorous and persuasive self-expression was held to be an essential prerequisite for any position of power and influence. The ensuing social ambition created a booming market not only for itinerant teachers of oratory and rhetoric, known to philosophical history as the Sophists, but also for the establishment of fully fledged schools which provided an education for those who aspired to a place of prominence in public life.

Aristotle's *Art of Rhetoric*

This accumulated practice of oratory brought forth a great many rhetorical handbooks that aimed at developing a theory of eloquence, called in Greek *technē rhētorikē*. Though this phrase is usually rendered as 'the art of rhetoric' (perhaps under the influence of the Latin phrase *ars rhetorica*), Plato, and also Aristotle, had a wider conception of *technē*, which embraced our concepts of art, technique and skill (Lawson-Tancred 1991: 264). Initially, the Sophists had defined rhetoric as 'the art of persuasion', which Aristotle in his seminal treatise *The Art of Rhetoric* (c. 335 BC/1926) subsequently changed into the more theoretical formulation '[the function of rhetoric] is not so much to persuade, as to find out in each case the existing means of persuasion' (I.I.14). This implies that if in a particular case the persuasion is unsuccessful, the theory of rhetoric as a whole remains valid.

In addition to promoting rhetoric to a respectable branch of philosophy, Aristotle also treats the process of persuasion as a human and social reality,

claiming that the use of the body in self-defence is now superseded by the use
of rhetoric because humans are essentially rational beings (I.I.12). Besides, if it
is argued that this verbal capacity can cause a great deal of harm too, it may be
countered that this goes for all good and useful things, if they are badly used
(I.I.13). Therefore, Aristotle's book may be seen as an apologia for rhetoric to
repair the damage to its reputation for which the Sophists were generally held
responsible. Their then leader was Gorgias (c.483-375 BC), who had sceptical
views about the possibility of getting to the truth through reason and about
the validity of traditional ethical notions such as right and wrong. See Wardy
(1996) for an interesting study of Gorgias. These views were ardently propa-
gated by his followers, but unfortunately, the instrument they used for it was
rhetoric. Of course, there were many, as there would be now, who fully realized the dangers of an accomplishment which could argue that what is wrong
is right. It is therefore not unlikely that as a consequence of this realization,
the term 'sophistic', and at least one of the popular senses of 'rhetoric', has
become infected by pejorative overtones ever since.

Gorgias must have been a well-known figure in Athens, because Plato
named his dialogue *Gorgias* (c. 384 BC) after him. It is the earliest example
of a bitter attack on rhetoric, which Plato saw as the source of all corruption.
Socrates, one of the fictional characters in the dialogue, refuses 'to give the
title of art to anything irrational' (465) and voices a number of fierce criticisms:
rhetoric is 'no art at all'; it is 'a sort of knack gained by experience' (462); it is 'a
branch of something which certainly isn't a fine or honorable pursuit' (463); and
it is to be placed 'among the subdivisions of pandering' (463) (Plato 1960). The
question of whether Aristotle wrote his *Rhetoric* in response to Plato's *Gorgias*
will probably always remain unanswered.

Techniques of persuasion: *Ethos/pathos/logos* interconnected by style

Indeed, whereas previous handbooks had focused mainly on the sophistic
persuasive tricks of the oratorical trade, Aristotle's book was the first to provide a theory of public speaking, or civic discourse, founded on psychological,
logical and moral principles. For instance, he divides the means of persuasion
or 'proofs' (*pisteis*) into two types (I.II.2):

1   Non-technical or inartistic proofs such as sworn testimonies, tortures
    (*sic*), contracts and the like, which already exist and need not be
    furnished by the art (*technē*) of the persuader.
2   Technical or artistic proofs which have to be invented by the persuader
    using the principles of the art of rhetoric.

These artistic proofs, in their turn, can be of three kinds (I.II.3–6; repeated in II.I.1–4):

1 The proof derived from the trustworthy character (*ethos*) of the persuader, that is, the ethical and psychological appeal that the speaker makes to the audience by creating a sympathetic image of himself. As Cockcroft observes: . . .'*ethos*: that is, our character, [includes] our goodwill, our morality, our competence and our emotional authenticity, as perceived by the persuadee' (2003: 43–4).

2 The proof derived from the emotions (*pathos*) induced in the audience. It deals with the gamut of sentiments that the persuader must arouse in the listeners to trigger their favourable reactions. In addition, as Nash has aptly put it, during this process of swaying the audience 'There comes a point . . . when the silent partners in the dialogue – the listeners, the readers – are no longer being told; they start to tell themselves, and in doing so help to shape the rhetoric that persuades them' (1989: 197).

3 The proof derived from logical argumentation (*logos*), which is not about establishing the objective general truth as in hard science, but about finding arguments that rest on generally accepted principles and will therefore be acceptable to the audience (I.I.12).

Incidentally, perhaps Aristotle's motivation for his third proof suggests one of the reasons why rhetoric (and, by implication, style) has ever developed in the human mind. Most things in this world cannot be worded unequivocally, nor are they generally agreed on. Persuasion is then a last resort. This, by the way, fits in with modern discourse studies, which have challenged the idea that there is a direct correspondence between language and reality. Besides, this view of words and the world brings rhetoric and literature more closely together (Hesse 1992: 21–2).

Returning to the three techniques of persuasion, it will be noticed that they are closely interrelated. Thus, the *logos* of a speech is only effective if it tunes in with the audience's *pathos*, which, in turn, is to a large extent the outcome of the speaker's *ethos*. In this interconnectedness, a specific use of language, that is, style, plays a crucial role: for example, rhetorical figures like schemes, that is, patterns of conspicuous regularity of form such as parallelism, repetition, antithesis, etc., which intensify meaning without actually changing it; and, tropes, that is, patterns involving a conspicuous change of the standard meaning, such as metaphor, metonymy, irony, etc. All these and other figures may well reinforce the emotional appeal of an argument, which must at the same time adequately reflect the speaker's ethical stance as well as the emotions of the audience.

A modern instance of how *ethos*, *pathos* and *logos* are interconnected by style

The epigraph of this article appears to be a case in point:

> Thanks to words, we have been able to rise above the brutes; and thanks to words, we have often sunk to the level of the demons. (Aldous Huxley)

This is a straightforward piece of rhetoric in which the author's *ethos* [I have the professional and moral experience to speak with authority on this issue], his *logos* or argument [language can be used with good and evil intentions] and the readers' presumed *pathos* [the painful awareness that we are naturally inclined to misuse our gift of language], are closely interconnected and reinforced by specific features of style.

The style is sententious because it relies on antithesis, a classical figure of thought which contrasts certain ideas expressed in contrasting words in a formal parallel structure (Wales 2001: 24). The clash of ideas is set forth by the two metaphorical images 'we have been able to rise above the brutes' and 'we have often sunk to the level of the demons', which effectively refresh our experience that language can be both a blessing and a curse. The formal parallelism is brought about by some conspicuous repetitive patterns such as the lexical phrase 'thanks to words', with the first occurrence properly introducing the beneficial effect of language, while the second occurrence is ironically linked up with its harmful use. There is also marked syntactic repetition. The maxim is made up of one compound sentence consisting of two co-ordinate clauses with basically the same syntactic functions, linked by the conjunction 'and'. One would have expected the antithetical conjunction 'but'. This, however, would not have been compatible with the irony of the repeated phrase 'thanks to words'.

Additionally, the repeated personal pronoun 'we' is rhetorically very effective. It is an instance of its so-called presumptive use implying that the writer assumes that the reader shares the same values. A further implication of this inclusive 'we' may be that it appeals to the collective voice of universal conscience (Wales 1996: 62–3).

And, last but not least, Huxley has chosen a very appropriate text type or genre for his rhetorical lament. It is an aphorism, a classical genre, which is usually defined as a pithily and often authoritatively expressed maxim usually relating to some abstract matter.

The earliest introduction to psychology in a discourse situation

In his *Rhetoric*, Aristotle also provides the earliest introduction to psychology in a discourse situation. By exploring the emotions (*pathos*) that may be awakened in the audience such as anger, calm, friendship, enmity, fear, confidence, shame, pity, jealousy, etc., he allows the persuader a useful insight into the mechanics of human motivation (II.II–XI). This is followed by a discussion of the effects on the human character of the three ages (youth, prime, old age) and of fortune (birth, wealth, power). These potential characteristics of the audience are useful for the persuader to know with a view to adapting his character (*ethos*) accordingly (II.XII–XVII). Interestingly, the pictures Aristotle presents of youth, prime and old age appear to be a reflection of the common stereotypical characters of antiquity that can also be seen in the comedies of Menander and his Roman imitators, Plautus and Terence (Kennedy 1991: 163). The tradition they represented is responsible for the form and style taken by English comedy up to the nineteenth century and perhaps even by many present-day sitcoms.

Genre and style

Because deploying arguments is not only a matter of logic but also of the objective of the persuasion, Aristotle divides rhetoric into three genres or areas of activity in relation to the type of audience: deliberative (political), forensic (judicial) and epideictic (concerned with praise or blame) (I.II.22–III.4). These three genres of oratory became canonical and persisted throughout the long history of rhetoric and even beyond.

The concept of genre, in the sense of a culturally specific type of discourse, like these three kinds of rhetorical speeches or, for that matter, a newspaper article, a business letter, an aphorism, a poem, etc. is highly relevant to style. This is because speakers and writers tend to adapt their language, that is, their style, in a particular type of discourse to the conventions imposed on it by its social role and setting. This, however, is a reciprocal process because listeners and readers normally are also tuned in to these socialized stylistic conventions. Thus, once they have made themselves familiar with a particular genre, they have usually also developed a sense of what kind of style they can expect, and therefore they adjust their listening or reading accordingly.

On the other hand, both producers and consumers of texts also know that there is not always a one-to-one correspondence between genre and style. For example, novels, advertisements, newspapers, mock epics, etc. may feature an overlapping of different styles. Now, looking at genre from this broad stylistic perspective, some scholars of stylistics have adopted the view that the conventional distinction between 'literary' and 'non-literary' texts is in fact unnecessary (Fowler 1996: 94). For an interesting and plausible cognitive linguistic approach to the role of genre in language and style, see Steen (2002a: 183–209).

Aristotle's ambivalent view on style

In the very last sentence of Book II of his *Rhetoric*, Aristotle writes: 'It only remains to speak of style and arrangement' (II.XXVI.5). Up to this point, Aristotle has not yet said a word about style (*lexis*, in his terminology), though it must have been uppermost in his mind when he was devising his theory of the three modes of persuasion. But he delays a discussion of style to the last, only coming to it in chapters 1–12 of Book III. In fact, there is a theory that Books I–II and Book III may originally have been separate works, and that the final sentence of Book II was added later as a linkage when the three books were made a single treatise (Kennedy 1991: 302). Anyway, Aristotle, somewhat surprisingly, begins by saying that he has so far ignored the matter of style because in rhetoric, the emphasis must be first of all on the logical invention of the most effective arguments and also because 'it is thought vulgar' (III.I.5). Here his old teacher, Plato, must have been looking over his shoulder, prompting him that all that should matter is evidence and logic, while style is just empty words. However, then Aristotle goes on to say that since the whole business of rhetoric is to sway opinion, he must pay attention to style, not because it is right but necessary and also because 'it is of great importance owing to the corruption of the hearer' (III.I.5–6). At this moment, it seems that the Sophists have taken Plato's place as his guide, because from here on he discusses style at great length.

Some highlights from Aristotle's stylistic precepts

The main virtues of style are clarity and appropriateness (III.II.2; the latter is repeated in III.VII.2–11). To be clear, the speaker or writer should steer a middle course between ordinary and poetic language as appropriate to the subject and the occasion. On the other hand, it is permissible and even recommendable to give one's language a certain strangeness 'for men admire what is remote, and that which excites admiration is pleasant' (III.II.3). In poetry, this often occurs and there it is appropriate. If this artifice is used in prose, it must be concealed, because one must avoid speaking artificially instead of naturally; 'for that which is natural persuades, but the artificial does not' (III.II.4–5).

It will be noted that more than 2000 years later, Aristotle's observation that the language of poetry is characteristically 'strange' was to be literally repeated by the Russian formalists with the phrase *ostranenie* 'making strange'. See Wales (2001: 135) for 'estrangement' and Short (1996: 10–79) for a detailed discussion of the related stylistic concept of foregrounding.

Consequently, the orator must also make proper use of metaphors because they provide clarity, pleasure and unfamiliarity. '[They] should therefore be derived from what is beautiful either in sound or in signification, or to sight, or to some other sense' (III.II.6–13). Simile, for that matter, is like metaphor. It belongs to poetry, but is also useful in prose, though with restraint (III.IV.2–3).

In later chapters of his book, Aristotle adds, among others, the requirements of purity or grammatical correctness (III.V.5–7), rhythm (III.VIII) and ornamentation (III.X–XI). With regard to the latter, he returns again to his favourite figure, the metaphor (III.XI), putting a special emphasis on visual metaphors 'which set things before the eyes'. Such metaphors signify activity (*energeia*) as, for instance, in 'The spear-point sped eagerly through his breast' from Homer's *Iliad*.

Finally, the last chapter (III.XII) on style contains a discussion on its suitability to the genres he discussed in Book I: political, judicial and epideictic. Political oratory resembles a rough sketch and needs little precision because the larger the crowd, the less is the attention. The style of judicial oratory should be much more meticulous and involves the smallest degree of rhetoric. Finally, the epideictic style is most like that of written composition.

In subsequent sections of this essay, Aristotle's stylistic precepts of clarity, appropriateness, purity and ornamentation will be discussed in the light of speech act theory and cognitive linguistics.

The audience factor in classical rhetoric and beyond

In spite of Aristotle's earlier-mentioned scepticism about the moral integrity of his listeners, his rhetoric and style are definitely audience-directed, in that he evaluates every rhetorical and stylistic device not only in terms of what it *is* but also of what it *does* to the listener. This audience factor and, by extension, the reader factor, completes a threefold communicative framework in classical rhetoric comprising the interaction between a speaker (or writer), a text and an audience (reader). This communicative triangle fits in with some relatively recent developments in literary theory, stylistics, education, composition, textual studies and discourse studies. However, it should be noted that the huge theoretical apparatus of rhetoric does not mention a single word about the possibility of an active role of the audience (reader) in the process of meaning production. The audience was only the passive object of the intended persuasive effects of the text. This situation remained unaltered when the Renaissance humanists rediscovered Aristotle, Cicero and Quintilian, and also throughout the following centuries, things remained as they had always been. Even the most influential literary theories formulated in the first three decades of the twentieth century perpetuated this passivity of the reader. In Russian Formalism, the Prague Linguistic Circle, Practical Criticism and New Criticism, the formal autonomy of the text was fully maintained and there was no role for the reader in the activation of meaning. This situation was to last until the 1970s and 1980s when post-formalist theories were advanced, in which a text was no longer seen as an autonomous object but as a discourse, that is, as a contextualized socio-cognitive interaction in which meaning is not unidirectional but rather a matter of negotiation between speakers or writers on the one hand and listeners or readers on the other. See Widdowson (1975 and 1992), Fowler (1981) and Carter and Simpson (1989).

The decline of Greek rhetoric as a practice

In 338 BC, the Greek city-states were subjected to Macedonian rule, which put an end to the democratic institutions in Athens and therewith to the practice of political and forensic rhetoric. Only epideictic oratory could survive; but this tended to degenerate into tedious panegyrics on the Macedonian kings. Paradoxically, though the practice of rhetoric had virtually come to an end, its theory was considerably expanded in the following 250 years of what is now called the Hellenistic period. One of the leading figures in this development was Theophrastus (c.370-c.285 BC), who had been a pupil of Aristotle and had succeeded him as head of Aristotle's Lyceum. Though his writings have not survived, it is known from other sources that he developed some of Aristotle's ideas considerably and, as the works of some later Roman writers show, his influence on rhetoric was greatest in the areas of style and delivery.

In parallel with this growth in theory, rhetorical training in hypothetical situations became firmly established in the educational system, that is, in the elite establishments for the sons (*sic*) of the well-to-do. Obviously, in the absence of a professional practice, this instruction in rhetoric became entirely formal and, in fact, an end in itself.

The Roman takeover

Ironically, the history of the rise of rhetoric as a system during the budding democracy of the Greek city-states repeated itself, under broadly similar circumstances, in the Roman Republic in the middle of the second century BC. During the political deliberations in the Senate and the legal actions in the law courts, the spoken word was predominant and eloquence became an indispensable weapon. So it was an ideal opportunity for the appropriation of the well-tried devices of persuasion provided by the theory of rhetoric and style as devised by the Greeks, and *technē rhētorikē* was Latinized as *ars rhetorica*.

The ranking of style in Roman rhetoric

The Roman rhetoricians regarded style as the most difficult task for the orator (Quintilian 1921: VIII.13). Thinking up what to say and arranging it is one thing, but finding the most effective words for it is another! It was again Quintilian who was most outspoken, maintaining that without the power of style 'all the preliminary accomplishments of oratory are as useless as a sword that is kept permanently concealed within its sheath' (1921: VIII.15).

Whereas Aristotle, for reasons of his own, relegated the treatment of style to the last part of his *Rhetoric*, the Latin rhetoricians unambivalently rank style (*elocutio* in their terminology) as the third of the five canons or divisions of rhetoric: (1) invention, (2) arrangement, (3) style, (4) memory and (5) delivery. There is no attempt, though, to integrate these elements into a coherent whole. In his most influential work, *De oratore* (55 BC), Cicero comes up with a refreshing formulation of these five components of oratory:

> And, since all the activity and ability of an orator falls into five divisions, I learned that he must first hit upon what to say [*inventio*]; then manage and marshal his discoveries, not merely in orderly fashion, but with a discriminating eye for the exact weight, as it were, of each argument [*dispositio*]; next go on to array them in the adornments of style [*elocutio*]; after that keep them guarded in his memory [*memoria*]; and in the end deliver them with effect and charm [*actio*]. (The Latin interpolations are mine.) (Cicero 1942: I.xxxi.142–143)

The troubled relationship between content and form (style)

The metaphorical phrase 'to array them in the adornments (*vestire atque ornare*) of style' raises again the ever recurrent issue of the divide between content (*ratio rerum*) and form or style (*ratio verborum*). It is a mechanical metaphor suggesting that style is something added. Similar metaphors include 'clothing', 'dress', 'coat' and 'colors', which have been fashionable for many centuries. For instance, after more than 1600 years, in 1666, in his *Preface to Annus Mirabilis*, John Dryden still gives a full Ciceronian account of the five divisions of rhetoric, describing style as follows: '. . . the third is Elocution, or the Art of clothing and adorning that thought so found . . . in apt, significant and sounding words.'

On the other hand, in direct contradiction to his 'dress and ornament' metaphor, the very same Cicero, elsewhere in his *De oratore* (III.XVI.61), dubs a separation between form and content as an 'undoubtedly absurd and unprofitable and reprehensible severance between the tongue and the brain'. In point of fact, in Greek and Roman rhetoric, the divide between the *what* and the *how* was conditional and artificial. It probably originated in rhetorical pedagogy requiring students to analyse texts in terms of content and form. This, too, turned out to become a long-standing tradition. Thus, in 1512, Erasmus of Rotterdam wrote a textbook entitled *De copia verborum ac rerum* ('On the abundance of verbal expressions and ideas'), in which he asked his students to produce as many formal variations as possible of all kinds of sentences. He himself sets the example by coming up with 150 different stylistic versions of the Latin sentence '*Tuae literae me magnopere delectarunt*' ('Your letter has pleased me very much'). Obviously, some of the resulting versions will be silly and unusable, but this kind of teaching experiment will increase the student's awareness of the stylistic flexibility of language (Corbett 1990: 461–2).

Style as motivated choice

It will be noted, by the way, that Erasmus's exercise might be seen as a kind of forerunner of one of the present-day popular definitions of style, namely, style as choice. In this view, style is seen as the making of conscious and unconscious choices of certain linguistic forms and structures in preference to others that could have been chosen but which were not. Obviously, every linguistic choice that is made is co-determined by a wide variety of contextual considerations, such as the genre of text, time, place, the nature of the communicative context, etc. See Wales (2001: 370–2) and Verdonk (2002: 5–6).

These choices, which may also be regarded as stylistic markers, are assumed to be made on particular levels of the structure of language (the text) in relation to the contextual and communicative situation (pragmatics and discourse). Though there are various models distinguishing different numbers of levels, here I will make use of the following six-level model of linguistic structure and discourse. It will be understood that in reality, language and discourse are not so neatly organized as they are represented in this diagram, which therefore only serves as a basic groundwork for analysis and discussion. For a detailed account of style in relation to the levels of language and discourse, see Simpson (2004: 5–8).

1 Graphology (typographical features: typeface, punctuation, etc.)
2 Phonology (sounds, rhythm, rhyme, etc.)
3 Lexis (vocabulary)
4 Syntax; grammar (sentence structure, use of tenses, etc.)
5 Semantics (considerations of textual meaning)
6 Pragmatics; discourse (features of external context; communicative situation).

In fact, all these levels are interconnected and interdependent. For example, Charles Dickens's apparently simple choice to put quotation marks, from the level of graphology, around the opening lines of his novel *Hard Times* (1854/1988: 47), has far-reaching consequences on the level of pragmatics and discourse:

'Now, what I want is, Facts. Teach these boys and girls nothing but Facts. Facts alone are wanted in life. Plant nothing else, and root out everything else. You can only form the minds of reasoning animals upon Facts: nothing else will ever be of any service to them. This is the principle on which I bring up my own children, and this is the principle on which I bring up these children. Stick to Facts, sir!'

Though it is a brief example, it features a great many stylistic markers of which, given the scope of this article, I can only point out a few. To begin on the level of discourse, it is a representation of free direct speech of one of the characters. It is called 'free' because the only evidence of the narrator's presence are the quotation marks. Thus, there is no clause in which the narrator reports the speech (as 'He said'), which on the level of discourse would indicate that the character is held in leash by the narrator. On the contrary, by choosing free direct speech, the narrator delegates the point of view to the character, leaving him (assuming for the moment it concerns a man) to speak for himself. This furthermore implies that the narrator does not describe the character but lets him describe himself.

At various points in the text, reference is made to persons, places and time by means of grammatical and lexical words or phrases like 'I', 'you', 'sir', 'these boys and girls' and the present tenses of verbs, for example, 'want', 'is', 'bring up', etc. Now, prompted by their experience of the real world and their knowledge of the stylistic conventions of fiction, readers will understand these linguistic expressions as representations of the people, place, and time in the story and will act on them as cues to imagine themselves as participating in the situation of the fictional world of the discourse. By persuading readers to assume a presence in the world of the novel, these textual cues or deictics (from Greek 'pointing'), as they are technically called, prompt the following important questions: Who is telling the story? Who is the narrator or character talking to? Where and when do the events take place? And, importantly, from whose point of view is the story told? The deictics in a text may answer this last question, because human beings are cognitively primed to relate space, time and persons in the world around them to their own subjective position, that is, to view them from their own point of view. A quick look again at the deictics in the above text will show that so far everything in the story world is experienced from the character's perspective, which was already confirmed by the representation of the character's words in free direct speech.

Shifting again to the levels of syntax, lexis and graphology in relation to other relevant levels, the reader will be struck by the strident shortness of the sentences, and the insistent and monotonous repetition of the word 'Facts', each time written with a capital, probably to mark the character's emphatic pronunciation of the word. This emphasis becomes even stronger through the repetitive use of the excluding phrases 'nothing but', 'alone' and 'nothing else' used in relation to the speaker's cherished 'Facts'.

On the interconnected levels of lexis, semantics, pragmatics and discourse, when the speaker talks insensitively about the boys and girls as 'reasoning animals', using the degrading metaphoric images 'plant nothing else, and root out everything else', as if their minds were the fertile soil in which his facts could be sown, he dehumanizes the children depriving them of their imagination and emotions.

Finally, back to the level of pragmatics and discourse: the reader may notice the irony in the speaker's insistent reference to *facts* in the opening passage of a work of *fiction*. Anyway, a long time ago, the above stylistic choices held enough fascination for this reader to be persuaded by the character's awful rhetoric to enter this fictional world and to read and reread this great novel.

The content/style issue has become a critical tool and a literary game

As is only to be expected, the content/style issue has never ceased to haunt people's minds. For while content and style are definitely assumed to be one, they are still frequently being discussed in terms of two separate entities, which creates the paradox of simultaneously postulating a oneness and a 'twoness'. As it is, this paradoxical thinking has provided considerable scope for creativity in that it has become an evaluative tool in the hands of literary critics as well as a source of inspiration for poets and writers. The following is a perfect illustration of this. In the introduction to her book *The Breaking of Style*, the American critic Helen Vendler writes:

> To represent style, I use the word 'body' (rather than the perhaps more customary image of dress) because I want to emphasize the inextricable relation of style to theme. Yeats's bravado in 'A Coat' with respect to doffing his 'old embroideries' – 'There's more enterprise / In walking naked' (*Collected Poems*, 125) – suggests, misleadingly, that one *can*, in poetry, walk naked – and that one can easily slough off a style. Nothing could be further from the truth' (1995: 2).

This is the poem referred to:

> A Coat
> I made my song a coat
> Covered with embroideries
> Out of old mythologies
> From heel to throat;
> But the fools caught it,
> Wore it in the world's eyes
> As though they'd wrought it.
> Song, let them take it,
> For there's more enterprise
> In walking naked.
>
> (W. B. Yeats, *Collected poems* 1956: 125)

The poet playfully states his intention that he will remove all stylistic ornamentation from his poetry and allow the content to 'walk naked'. With this metaphor of divestment, Yeats jocularly announces a shift in his earlier style, while at the same time upbraiding certain fellow poets for imitating it. It is evident from the 'coat' metaphor that the poet is making artistic use of the classical style/content divide, and by giving a free rein to his imagination, he creates from it his own literary world.

It may be true that Vendler's 'body' metaphor emphasizes less strongly than the classical 'dress' metaphor that style is an additional element, but she does not escape from the inherent paradox mentioned earlier. In fact, the confusion is complete when she appears to miss the ironical point of Yeats's literary game and criticizes him for doing something she has just done herself.

Besides, this poem has become an autonomous literary event, which Vendler cannot use to tackle Yeats on a difference of opinion she has with him in the 'real' world.

The three levels or types of style (*genera dicendi*)

Though the long lists of precepts in their handbooks may give a different impression, the classical rhetoricians did not aim at a general normative model of style. Thus, in his *Institutio oratoria*, Quintilian writes that the reading of poets, historians and philosophers is of great service to the orator, though he must not follow these writers in everything because of the obvious differences between the various genres (1922: X.I.27–36). Besides, in oratory, too, there are three different genres to be observed and therewith three different styles: judicial, political and epideictic. And even within the same genre, the orator must be able to vary his style: '. . . some things require a gentle and others a violent style, some require an impetuous and others a calm diction, while in some cases it is necessary to instruct and in others to move the audience, in all these instances dissimilar and different methods being necessary' (X.II.23).

However, in spite of the fact that the rhetorical theorists gave the practising orator a lot of leeway to choose a particular style, they still felt the need to establish a broad framework of three different levels or types of oratorical style:

1 The grand style (*genus grave or grande*) features a smooth and ornate arrangement of impressive words. It is an artful style, with figures of speech, and suited to the conclusion of an important oration.
2 The middle style (*genus medium*) is somewhat more relaxed without descending to the most ordinary prose. It is suited to descriptive passages in an oration, its effect being mainly aesthetic.
3 The low or plain style (*genus humile*) is brought down to the most ordinary speech of every day. It is suitable for the narrative part in an oration.

This three-part division had already been devised by the Greek Theophrastus, in a work now lost, and was later adopted by the anonymous author of *Rhetorica Ad Herennium*, dating from the first-century BC and wrongly attributed to Cicero until the fifteenth century (Cicero 1954: IV.VIII–XI), and by Cicero in *Orator* (1939: VI.20–XIII.42).

In literature, the grand style was regarded suitable for epic and tragedy, the middle style for didactic poetry and the low style for comedy and pastoral poetry. Virgil's works are often used as an illustration of the three styles: the epic *Aeneid*, the didactic *Georgics* and the pastoral *Eclogues*. It is striking that this theory is concerned with particular types of style, on the one hand, and with a division into three social classes on the other hand: warriors (*Aeneid*), peasants (*Georgics*) and shepherds (*Eclogues*). In European literature, this tradition continued at least until the Romantic period.

The four virtues of style (*virtutes dicendi*)

In addition, there are four virtues of style that are common to all three types. (Compare Aristotle's stylistic precepts discussed earlier). These, too, were first classified by Theophrastus and later developed in the anonymous *Rhetorica ad Herennium* (Cicero 1954: IV.XII.17–LV.69), by Cicero in *De oratore* (1942: III.IX.37–LV.212) and Quintilian in *Institutio oratoria* (1921 and 1922: VIII–XI). These stylistic qualities may be briefly summarized as follows:

1 Correctness or purity (*Latinitas*) is mainly concerned with the correct use of language and is therefore on the borderline between grammar and rhetoric. The language must be clear, elegant and well-adapted to produce the desired effect.

2 Clarity (*perspicuitas*) is of course closely allied to correctness. There must be propriety in our words, their order must be straightforward and the sentences must not be too long. The language will be approved by the learned and clear to the uneducated. There must be no obscurities or ambiguities.

3 Decorum (*aptum*) or the quality of appropriateness is not only a matter of style but of every aspect of an oration. Our style must be adapted to every condition in life, to every social rank, position or age, and a similar distinction must be made in respect of place, time and audience. Quintilian also adds a moral dimension: it is becoming 'to all men at all times and in all places . . . to act and speak as a man of honor', *Institutio oratoria*, 1922:XI.I.14), which seems to be an early precursor to Buffon's celebrated eighteenth-century dictum 'Le style, c'est l'homme même'.

4 Ornament (*ornatus*) is concerned with the decorative aspects of style, in particular the figures, which are aimed at adding force to the intended effect and affect. 'Figures' is a general term for any linguistic device or pattern as a result of which meaning is either changed or intensified. The rhetorical figures are traditionally divided into the following:

 1 Figures of speech, which, in turn, are subdivided into the following:

    1.1 Tropes (Greek *tropos* 'turn') in which words or phrases are used in such a way that their ordinary meaning is conspicuously changed. Examples include simile, metaphor, metonymy, oxymoron and also figures like hyperbole, irony and litotes owing to which meaning cannot be taken literally. Leech (1969: 74) defines tropes as foregrounded irregularities of content.

    1.2 Schemes (Greek *skhēma* 'form, figure') are figures in which words are arranged into particular lexical, syntactic or phonetic patterns which intensify or enhance meaning without actually changing it. Examples include repetition, chiasmus, antithesis and zeugma. Schematic patterns of sound include alliteration and assonance. Leech (1969: 74) defines schemes as foregrounded repetitions of expression.

 2 Figures of thought are often loosely associated with the figures of speech, though they are different in their form and function. They have a pragmatic function at sentence or text level in the presentation of the argument or theme to the listener or reader, for example, rhetorical questions, apostrophe, amplification and antithesis (Wales 2001: 152–4). For an example of antithesis, see the analysis of Huxley's aphorism.

The virtues of style in terms of speech act theory

One might argue that rhetoric is concerned with speech in action, so that the virtues of style, which are clearly audience oriented, could provide an interesting point of comparison with speech act theory (Austin 1962; Searle 1969). Thus, the stylistic qualities of correctness and clarity are obviously required for a meaningful locutionary act, that is, the act of uttering a meaningful linguistic expression. The quality of decorum corresponds with the appropriate context, or the so-called felicity conditions, on which the success of the illocutionary act, that is, the act of conveying some communicative purpose, depends. This is in the present case the rhetorical act of persuasion (Fahnestock, forthcoming).

However, speech act theory is less suited to deal with the stylistic quality of ornament involving figurative language, because it perpetuates the traditional view that such language is deviant and that understanding such language is different from ordinary linguistic processing. Now, recent research in cognitive linguistics has shown that not only is a lot of our language figuratively structured, but so also is much of our cognitive processing. So people understand, that is, conceptualize their everyday experiences in figurative terms through metaphor, metonymy, irony, oxymoron, etc., and these codes underlie the way we think, reason and imagine (Gibbs 1994: 5). Therefore, it is more profitable to consider the stylistic quality of ornament from the perspective of cognitive linguistics.

The rhetorical figures considered from the point of view of cognitive linguistics

In various writings, Aristotle, Cicero and Quintilian make some casual remarks about the ordinariness of metaphor in everyday language. For instance, Aristotle observes that 'we all use metaphors in conversation' (*Rhetoric* 1926: III.II.3–6), while Cicero writes that they 'were brought into common use for the sake of entertainment, for even country folk (*sic*) speak of "jeweled vines"' (*De oratore* 1942: III.XXXVIII.155). And, finally, Quintilian notices that metaphor is 'often employed unconsciously or by uneducated persons (*sic*)' (*Institutio oratoria* 1921: VIII.VI.4–5). Now, if they had taken this view more seriously with regard to all genres of discourse, they would have been much closer to the present-day view that metaphor, and by implication all figurative language, is an omnipresent phenomenon that forms an integral part of our way of thinking and all uses of language. But, as we know, the ancient rhetoricians rejected the idea of figurative language being 'ordinary' when used for decorative and affective stylistic purposes in rhetoric and literary discourse. To put it differently, the above wording of the stylistic virtue of 'ornament' means that figuration is mainly a matter of embellishing literal language to create a particular stylistic effect.

For instance, the rhetoricians would see the antithetical metaphors 'we have been able to rise above the brutes' and 'we have often sunk to the level of the demons' in Huxley's aphorism as a creative and ornamental way of expressing literal equivalents, like, for instance, 'we have been able to live as civilized human beings' and 'we have often been cruel and destructive'. In such a view, language and mind are independent of each other and both intrinsically literal. This traditional approach to figurative language has been dominant in the humanities in Western culture for thousands of years.

However, in cognitive linguistics, things are just the other way round: tropes and schemes, and figures of thought, are no rhetorical by-products of a process of objective thinking of an independent mind; rather, they are a reflection of how people *construe* their knowledge and experience of the world around them (Lee 2001: 6–7; my emphasis).

For example, a metaphor (from Greek, literally meaning 'transference') is essentially a device that involves conceptualizing one domain of experience in terms of another, which implies that every metaphor is founded on a source domain and a target domain. Thus, in the metaphoric images 'we have been able to rise above the brutes' and 'we have often sunk to the level of the demons', the source domain is people's everyday physical experience of all kinds of spatial orientations, in this case UP-DOWN. The target domains are abstract concepts like VIRTUE ('living a decent life') and DEPRAVITY ('being cruel and destructive'). (Note that it has become a convention to use small capitals for the concepts that underlie a metaphorical expression.) It will be observed that the former concept gets an 'upward' orientation and the latter a 'downward' orientation. This example also shows that source domains tend to be relatively concrete areas of experience and target domains to be more abstract (Lee 2001: 6).

Note that in Western culture, this type of metaphors is quite common. They are based on a mundane source domain related to a particular spatial orientation of the human body and a target domain referring to some abstract concept. For example, HAPPY IS UP; SAD IS DOWN ('My spirits *rose*.' 'He *fell into* a depression.'); HEALTH AND LIFE ARE UP; SICKNESS AND DEATH ARE DOWN ('He is in *top* shape.' 'He is *sinking* fast.' 'He *dropped* dead.'); GOOD IS UP; BAD IS DOWN ('Things are looking *up*.' 'Things are at an all-time *low*.'). (Lakoff and Johnson 1980: 14–21; Kövecses 2002: 35–6).

This cognitive process of using a simpler concept to get to grips with a more difficult one yields what is called a 'conceptual metaphor', such as HAPPY IS UP. Here is another example: RELATIONSHIPS ARE BUILDINGS ('They have *built* a solid relationship'). Conceptual metaphors must be distinguished from linguistic metaphors, which consist of linguistic elements such as 'built' that derive from the language used for the simpler conceptual source domain such as BUILDINGS in the foregoing example. In this connection, Heywood et al. (2002: 35–54) and Steen (2002b: 17–33) make interesting reading.

Of course, the language of writers and poets may be expected to be more creative on this score, but in essence they make use of the same figures and schemes as the non-professionals. As the above examples show, metaphors are so common in everyday talk that we hardly seem to notice them. Consider how we ordinarily speak or write about time: 'We are *wasting* time'; 'We have no time *to lose*'; 'We are *running out of* time'. These are all metaphorical expressions or, more precisely, they reveal how in our everyday experience we conceive of time as something that is in short supply, which may result in a conceptual metaphor like TIME IS A LIMITED RESOURCE. When Andrew Marvell writes:

> But at my back I always hear
> Time's winged chariot hurrying near.
> And yonder all before us lie
> Deserts of vast eternity. ('To His Coy Mistress')

he is using the same experiential conceptual metaphor, be it, of course in a much more creative fashion. It is equally important to realize that we, in turn, use the same conceptual metaphor TIME IS A LIMITED RESOURCE in making sense of Marvell's poem (Gibbs 1994: 6–8). For an interesting cognitive linguistic approach to metaphor in literary prose, see Weber (1995: 32–44) discussing Doris Lessing's short story 'To Room Nineteen'.

Another important figure of speech, or in cognitive linguistic terms, a figurative mode of thought, is metonymy (Greek 'name change'; the Latin term is *denominatio*). Metonymy occurs when the name of one thing is given to another thing with which it is closely associated, within one and the same conceptual domain. Consider, for instance, the sentence 'I heard the *piano*'. Obviously, only sounds can be heard, not objects. What is conveyed is that I heard, not the piano as such, but a sound coming from the piano (Taylor 2002: 112). In cognitive linguistic terms, a metonym involves a process in which one conceptual entity provides mental access to another conceptual entity, within the same domain, in this case THE INSTRUMENT FOR THE PRODUCT (Kövecses 2002: 145). Some more examples include 'He's got a *Picasso* in his den' (PRODUCER FOR PRODUCT), 'The *sax* has the flu today' (OBJECT USED FOR USER) and '*Exxon* has raised its prices again' (INSTITUTION FOR PEOPLE RESPONSIBLE) (Lakoff and Johnson 1980: 38).

In cognitive linguistics, the rhetorical figure synecdoche (Greek 'taking together') is regarded as a special case of metonymy. In synecdoche, a part of something is used to refer to the whole, or (more rarely) the whole is used to signify a part. Metonymic concepts like THE PART FOR THE WHOLE are so common in everyday speech that we hardly notice them. Consider, for example, 'All *hands* on deck!' for 'sailors', 'The *White House* has plans for the economy' for 'the whole system of the US government', etc. Advertising frequently uses this type of metonymy, for example, 'Drink your *Heineken* now!' (PRODUCER FOR PRODUCT).

Furthermore, like metaphors, metonyms are the mainstays of novelists and poets. Consider how the poet Philip Larkin uses a string of synecdochic images to evoke the depressingly huge supermarket catering for the trivial needs in the humdrum lives of the working-classes:

> The large cool store selling cheap clothes
> Set out in simple sizes plainly
> (Knitwear, Summer Casuals, Hose,
> In browns and greys, maroon and navy)
> Conjures the weekday world of those
>
> Who leave at dawn low terraced houses
> Timed for factory, yard and site.
> (Philip Larkin, 'The Large Cool Store')

After the enormous amount of attention that has been paid to metaphor in cognitive linguistic research, it appears that now metonymy has come into focus. Interestingly, the hypothesis has been put forward that metonymy is even more fundamental to cognitive and linguistic processes than metaphor, to the extent that many conceptual metaphors are founded on metonymic stimuli. See Panther and Radden (1999) and Steen (2004).

Cognitive stylistics (also called cognitive poetics)

One of the valuable spin-offs from cognitive linguistic research is cognitive stylistics, also called cognitive poetics. It is an interdisciplinary study of how readers process literary texts, or perhaps better still, 'of what happens when a reader reads a literary text' (Stockwell 2002: 5). Probably the main reason why many students of style find fresh inspiration in cognitive linguistics is that this approach does not regard language as a separate and independent cognitive faculty, as it is assumed to be in Chomskyan linguistics. On the contrary, cognitive linguists hold that there is a close interactive and meaningful relationship between linguistic and other cognitive abilities, which include thinking, imagination, learning, memory, perception, attention, emotion, reasoning and problem-solving. All these abilities enable humans to survive and make sense of the world around them. From this it follows that cognitive linguistics is thoroughly experiential from a physical, social, cultural, ideological and emotive point of view.

To put it differently, cognitive linguists seek to explain the formal manifestations of language not only in terms of the cognitive abilities that are their plausible providers, but also in terms of the communicative or discursive functions that such empowered language structures perform (Taylor 2002: 8–9). Yet another source of inspiration for stylistics and poetics is that cognitive linguistics was (and still is) developed in relation to other cognitive sciences, such as cognitive anthropology, psychology, psycholinguistics and artificial intelligence. This interdisciplinary approach has yielded completely new concepts, theories and ideas that will enable students of style and poetics to analyse, describe and rationalize 'the effects of literary texts on the mind of the reader'. See Gavins and Steen (2003: 2).

In addition to the foregoing cognitive analyses and interpretations of metaphor, metonymy and other rhetorical figures, cognitive stylistics and poetics also draw on other cognitive concepts, such as schema theory and frames for research into readers' comprehension of texts (Semino 1997; Emmott 1997), the concept of figure and ground to account for readers' response to foregrounding (Emmott 2002; Stockwell 2002) and a lot of other theoretical concepts from the cognitive sciences that cannot be discussed here because of lack of space. The following collections of essays deal with a wide variety of examples of how cognitive stylistics and poetics can be fruitfully combined with theories and insights from cognitive linguistics and other cognitive disciplines: Csábi and Zerkowitz (2002), Gavins and Steen (2003), and Semino and Culpeper (2002), which all show how the cognitive sciences have breathed new life into stylistics and poetics.

Rebirth of rhetoric-cum-style?

To go by the title of an interesting book published nearly 15 years ago (Andrews 1992), rhetoric appears to have been reborn. However, in its blurb text, this idea of a 'rebirth' is somewhat qualified by the statement that 'the book does not aim to resurrect classical or Renaissance rhetoric, but to remake rhetoric within a contemporary context'.

I think that this very process of adaptation to the needs of the times has shaped the attitude towards rhetoric in all periods of history, dependent on the ongoing changes in government, politics, law, education, the production and reception of the arts–in brief, the changes in the overall social, ideological, and cultural situation. Surely, without this continuous practice of adjustment, classical rhetoric would have faded into oblivion a long time ago. Indeed, there is every reason to believe that the practice and theory of rhetoric-cum-style, in one form or another, will forever be a vital factor in human existence because, as said earlier, 'persuasion' is a cognitive and psychological symptom of human communication.

Extracted from Verdonk, P. (2006) 'Style', in Brown, K, (Editor-in-Chief) *Encyclopedia of Language and Linguistics, Second Edition*, volume 12, pp. 196–210. Oxford: Elsevier.

11

A cognitive stylistic reading of rhetorical patterns in Ted Hughes's 'Hawk Roosting': A possible role for stylistics in a literary critical controversy

The meaning of style does not primarily reside in its linguistic form

Rhetoric, in its most basic sense of effective and persuasive communication, may be assumed to be as old as human speech. This is all the more likely because rhetoric has turned out to be a cognitive and emotive drive in people to use language in such a manner as to impress or emotionalize others and then persuade them to adopt or reject a certain viewpoint. Therefore, in this day and age of cognitive science, I tend to accept the hypothesis that from an evolutionary perspective, the ultimate source of this basic impulse is likely to have been the instinct of self-preservation. As such, rhetoric in its primary sense may be supposed to have contributed to the preservation of the human species and its subsequent social-cultural evolution (Kennedy 1998: 4). Indeed, in these days, the word rhetoric is on everyone's lips, with President Barack Obama being hailed as the new Cicero (Higgins 2008).

But to pick up the thread of my argument, the persuasive force of this primary or proto rhetoric was inevitably produced not only by *what* was said, that is, the content, but also by *how* it was said, that is, the form. Now, this formal aspect or manner of expression is the natural predecessor of what via classical Greek and Roman rhetoric subsequently evolved into the present-day notion of style, which, unsurprisingly, has so far proved to be very difficult to define as an abstract concept. All the same, one might say that behind the external features of style, one usually suspects some conscious or unconscious intention and significance. Putting it differently, it is generally assumed that style has a phenomenal as well as a conceptual element, which, though they can be distinguished, are at the same time inseparably interconnected. For instance, the dominant rhetorical pattern of present-tense forms in Ted Hughes's 'Hawk Roosting' is a clearly recognizable phenomenal aspect of the poem, which, as we shall see, simultaneously conveys a deep conceptual significance. It is precisely with regard to this process of signification that in the last two decades or so, most stylisticians, I think, inspired by the so-called cognitive revolution in the 1970s, have parted company with the ancient rhetoricians about the role of language in meaning making. Cognitive stylisticians now hold the view that the meaning of style does not primarily reside in its linguistic manifestations on the page but in the conceptual or mental representations of some earlier relevant experience evoked in the mind of the reader. At the same time, it should not be overlooked that these mental representations are also structured and affected by a relevant socio-cultural and historical context, with the important reservation, though, that it is not this context as such that influences the language of discourse but rather how it is subjectively interpreted by the participants in a discourse (Van Dijk 2008: 16). Summing up, it may be said that as form language serves the purpose of conveying our conceptualized and contextualized knowledge of the world and therewith facilitates the communication of meaning (Kövecses 2006: 11).

A cognitive stylistic-cum-rhetorical analysis of Ted Hughes's 'Hawk Roosting'

After these preliminaries, I will propose a cognitive stylistic-cum-rhetorical analysis of the poem 'Hawk Roosting' by the late poet laureate Ted Hughes. Here I am using the term rhetorical rather loosely, namely, in the sense that my stylistic focus will be on features of language which in my view carry literary persuasion (Cockcroft and Cockcroft 2005: 5).

HAWK ROOSTING
I sit in the top of the wood, my eyes closed.
Inaction, no falsifying dream →
Between my hooked head and hooked feet:
Or in sleep rehearse perfect kills and eat.

    5   The convenience of the high trees!
The air's buoyancy and the sun's ray→
Are of advantage to me;
And the earth's face upward for my inspection.

My feet are locked upon the rough bark.
    10   It took the whole of Creation→
To produce my foot, my each feather:
Now I hold Creation in my foot→

Or fly up, and revolve it all slowly–
I kill where I please because it is all mine.
    15   There is no sophistry in my body:
My manners are tearing off heads– →

The allotment of death.
For the one path of my flight is direct →
Through the bones of the living.
    20   No arguments assert my right:

The sun is behind me.
Nothing has changed since I began.
My eye has permitted no change.
    24   I am going to keep things like this.
Ted Hughes (1960) (To Sylvia Plath)

Note: The arrows at the end of several lines of the poem indicate enjambement or run-on lines.

Before suggesting a possible interpretation of the poem, I wish to emphasize that when using the term 'the reader' or 'readers', I definitely include the readers of this essay as well as myself in that category. At the same time, I am of course well aware that the poem may trigger a lot of different reactions in all kinds of readers, which may all be equally defensible (Lindauer 2009: 54–5). Because of this wide variety of possible readings of the poem, I am highly interested to know what the outcome would be of an empirically based reading. In a recent article on the subject, it is stated that not enough empirical research has been conducted on poetry reading to present a fully worked out and empirically based description of poetry reading (Hanauer 2001: 116). Therefore, I hope that the following stylistic analysis, and those by other stylisticians, will provide positive encouragement to continue this enterprise with renewed energy.

The discourse situation in the poem

With these provisos in mind, I think that what will probably strike many readers first of all is that in the discourse situation of the poem, it is the hawk who thinks and speaks throughout. (Therefore, I use the personal relative pronoun 'who' instead of 'which'.) The poet, or rather his persona, is conspicuous by his absence from a scene he has obviously created himself. There is nothing in the text that gives away the poet's own voice, except, it seems, in the poem's title 'Hawk Roosting', which is remarkably, perhaps ironically, peaceful compared with the violence expressed in the poem itself. Indeed, apart from this single indication of the poet's presence, there is no hint at all of his perspective on the hawk's megalomaniac claims. In other words, no distinction is made between the observing, human intelligence and the creature observed (Walder 1987: 40). I wish to add here that in my view, the poet has deliberately hidden behind a mask for rhetorical reasons, leaving readers entirely to their own devices to come up with an emotional and/or moral response to the hawk's self-revelatory monologue. Yet another effect of the poet's absence as an omniscient commentator appears to be that the hawk's total lack of self-irony and lack of a sense of perspective are in no way held up to ridicule or subjected to irony.

Actually, this mask that the poet has put on is a typical example of personification, with the hawk being represented as if it had human qualities. In the persuasive toolbox of the classical rhetorician, it is a figure of speech or trope known as *prosopopoeia*, which originates from a Greek word literally meaning 'to make a face or a mask'. Generally speaking, this figure of speech enabled the orator to shift the responsibility for an unpleasant event or situation onto some personified abstraction or animal. Just like the hawk in our poem, who is saddled, unduly I think, with all kinds of nasty streaks of human behaviour!

However, as I said earlier, the meaning of style, in this case in the form of personification, does not reside in its linguistic manifestation, but in the mental representation of some earlier relevant experience stored in our mind. Therefore, most readers will not be too much surprised by this anthropomorphic hawk because in our early childhood, we played with toy animals which often had humanlike faces, arms and legs, etc., and we listened to, and later on read ourselves, fables, fairy-tales and allegories, and, not to forget, saw films featuring speaking and thinking animals. All these memories were stored as highly adaptable images in the knowledge structures of our minds, which in different branches of cognitive science are referred to as schemata, frames, domains or idealized cognitive models. Anyway, it is adjustable experiential knowledge which enables us to grasp the idea of a hawk vested with human qualities. Actually, this is also the reason why in cognitive metaphor theory, personification is primarily treated as a type of ontological metaphor, in which non-human creatures are talked about, or more formally are constructed, in terms of human knowledge and experience (Semino 2008: 38, 101). In this case, it seems that the battleground of human life is considered to be not unlike that of the hawk.

Various linguistic patterns of foregrounded regularity

I will now look at the poem's main formal structure, which appears to be built up by various linguistic patterns of foregrounded regularity. Such patterns were the favourite persuasive tools of the ancient rhetoricians and are traditionally referred to as schemes, which should not be confused with the earlier-mentioned mental schemata. In cognitive psychology, it has been hypothesized that the intuitive ease with which we recognize symmetries of all kinds and our inclination to structure things symmetrically are a projection of our embodied understanding of the symmetries and repetitive patterns of all kinds of categories, that is, mental representations for objects and events, in the world around us (Turner 1991: 68–98). Not surprisingly, this ingrained disposition is also maximally stimulated by symmetric structures in various art forms such as film, music, dance, painting and, of course, architecture. Interestingly, in a very recent publication, the case has been made that art-making and art-appreciation are an integral part of our evolutionary-biological heritage (Lindauer 2009: 34).

The cognitive theory of figure–ground organization

The earlier-mentioned phenomenon of foregrounding also brings to mind the theory of figure–ground organization, which is crucial to cognitive linguistics. The figure–ground phenomenon may be defined as our mental faculty to distinguish a perceived object (the figure or trajector) from its background (the ground or landmark). For the purpose of this analysis of Ted Hughes's poem, it is interesting to know that the figure–ground theory also relates to our cognitive ability to mentally structure or 'construe' situations and texts in all sorts of ways, for instance, by selecting or omitting specific circumstances, by describing participants in various degrees of detail, by providing different perspectives and by creating conspicuous stylistic features that stand out as figures against the background of the rest of the text (Taylor 2002: 11). In point of fact, it may be concluded that, in addition to all the other cognitive motivations I suggested, or will suggest further on, the theory of figure–ground organization provides yet another rational explanation for all the foregrounded patterns of sound, syntax, grammar and diction that captivated my attention when reading this poem. By the way, our hawk also makes use of the very same faculty when, in full flight, it targets its prey (the figure) in a large open field (the ground).

While working on this essay, I read in a recent research report on sensory physiology, that is, the study of the normal functions of living things, the following information, which may throw an interesting light on the theories of foregrounding and figure–ground organization. Our eyes collect an enormous amount of information about our visual environment, but much of it is not transmitted to the brain. The retina, a very compact network of neurons lining the inside of our eyes, selects which information is important and which is not. But the underlying selection principles and the neuronal mechanisms responsible for this selection are poorly understood. However, there appears to be one general principle in this process of selection, namely, unpredictable information is transmitted to the brain more readily than predictable information. This is as it should be, because if we were not able to perceive the unexpected, evolution would have got rid of us long ago (Kamermans 2009: 5).

The foregrounded pattern of the first-person pronoun and its related forms

The first foregrounded pattern, then, that is likely to grab the reader's attention is formed by the pronoun 'I', and its related forms 'my', 'mine' and 'me', occurring in nearly every line. Having concluded that the anthropomorphized hawk is the only speaker in the discourse-world of the poem, we look for somebody being spoken to. We do so because prompted by our cognitively stored real-world experience, we know that written and spoken discourses are, in principle, interpersonal, that is, if there is an 'I', there must be a 'you'. Guided by the same experience, we also know that in ordinary conversation, people usually take turns in their roles of speaker and addressee and, as a result, become sometimes 'I' and sometimes 'you'. Obviously, together with this deictic shift, the point of view changes as well. It is therefore quite significant that this turn-taking does not happen in the poem because the 'you' does not show up. Prompted by this rhetorical manipulation of the text and our socio-cognitive consciousness, we are drawn into the discourse world of the poem and intuitively fill this vacuum, though, counter-intuitively the perspective remains all the time with the speaker, that is, the hawk, holding us spellbound. The hawk keeps referring to himself rather obsessively by means of the pronouns 'I', 'my', 'me' and 'mine', which actually occur no less than 21 times and stand out as a conspicuous rhetorical pattern, with the first-person 'I' opening the first and the last lines. To top it all, the reader may spot the phonetic pun in the last line 'My eye has permitted no change'.

The foregrounded pattern of present tenses

The second rhetorical pattern that is likely to affect the reader is an extensive series of present tenses. It is a well-known fact that in English, the present tense as a grammatical category does not always signify present time in the strict sense of the word (Quirk et al. 1985: 175). This semantic discrepancy also occurs in the poem, in which the present-tense forms do not primarily signify present time. Let us look at the hawk's abrupt statements, which give the reader a pretty good idea of what metal our hawk is made:

> (1) 'I sit in the top of the wood'
> (4) 'Or in sleep rehearse perfect kills and eat'
> (6/7) 'The air's buoyancy and the sun's ray/Are of advantage to me'
> (9) 'My feet are locked upon the rough bark'
> (12/13) 'Now I hold Creation in my foot/Or fly up, and revolve it all slowly'
> (14) 'I kill where I please because it is all mine'
> (15) 'There is no sophistry in my body'
> (16) 'My manners are tearing off heads'
> (18/19) 'For the one path of my flight is direct/Through the bones
>   of the living'
> (20) 'No arguments assert my right'
> (21) 'The sun is behind me'.

In all these brusque utterances, the dominant present tenses can be construed as signifying a state or a habit without reference to a specific time. The present tenses in the poem often sound like a kind of conceited self-focused commentary, which even seem to imply a rejection of time. It is as if time stands still. There is not really a sense of the passing of time in human terms. Therefore, there also seems to be no real sense of the past with its potential for personal reflection, repentance and self-improvement.

As a result, the single past tense in lines 10/11 'It took the whole of Creation/To produce my foot, my each feather' appears to denote an event cut off from now. It refers to a one-off action of Creation ending in total submission to the hawk, who triumphantly claims in lines 12/13 'Now I hold Creation in my foot/Or fly up, and revolve it all slowly–', like the earth revolving around the sun! The reader is made to believe that the hawk has in fact created his own universe.

Nor will there be a future time with its potential for change: (22–4) 'Nothing has changed since I began./My eye has permitted no change./I am going to keep things like this'. At this point, the reader might notice that there is bitter irony involved here. It is even dramatic irony because the hawk's words carry an implied extra meaning that the reader is aware of but he himself is not. If indeed the hawk is 'going to keep things like this', and sees nature as a cycle only servicing himself, that cycle inevitably also includes his own death, which ironically will then be nature's last service to him.

None of the normally free agents of nature are independent

The first line of the poem is the beginning of the third rhetorical pattern in which nature is represented as completely subservient to the hawk. His bold statement 'I sit in the top of the wood' does not only refer to his natural habitat, but may also be read as a metaphor for his position of absolute power. He can even afford to be off his guard and close his eyes! Nature serves merely as a convenient context for him. The high trees offer him comfort (5), the air's buoyancy, that is, the upward current of warm air, keeps him afloat (6), the sun is always behind him while blinding his victim when he attacks (6/7 and 21) and the face of the earth turns itself upwards for his inspection, no doubt revealing at the same time the hiding places of potential prey (8). This graphic account of the submissive attitude of nature, with the hawk being its permanent focus of attention, is reinforced by the obsessive pattern of the earlier discussed self-directed personal referents 'I', 'my' and 'me'. Indeed, it is extremely striking that none of the normally free elements of nature are independent (Cluysenaar 1982: 304).

As to the hawk's relation to other creatures around him, there can be no doubt about his utter ruthlessness. Even in his sleep, he practises his hunting and swallowing other animals: (4) 'Or in sleep rehearse perfect kills and eat'. He kills where and when he pleases because he thinks the existence of other animals as his prey is part of the purpose of Creation: (14) 'I kill where I please because it is all mine'. Jokingly one might say that the hawk is a kind of secret agent like 007 having a licence to kill, as it is put bluntly in ll. 16–17: 'My manners are tearing off heads–/The allotment of death'. The allotment of death is his prerogative, he and only he decides who is going to die. Considering that in the world of humans, the word 'manners' is usually described as 'behaviour that is considered to be polite', readers may feel that the phrase 'My manners' in line 16 in relation to its complement 'tearing off heads' is deliciously ironic, particularly so if the word 'table manners' comes to mind.

From the boastful statements in ll. 10/13: 'It took the whole of Creation/To produce my foot, my each feather:/Now I hold Creation in my foot/Or fly up, and revolve it all slowly–', it may well be concluded that the hawk thinks he has turned the tables on Creation, in that he now takes the position of strength and advantage that was formerly held by Creation. The reader may well wonder whether this is a classical case of hubris, of excessive self-confidence and pride, which will be followed by its appropriate nemesis, that is, divine revenge and punishment. Perhaps it is significant that the proud boast in line 12: 'Now I hold Creation in my foot' occurs conspicuously right in the middle of the poem.

The meaningful contrast between Latinate and Anglo-Saxon lexical items

The fourth rhetorical pattern stands out because of its contrasting lexical make-up. Native speakers of English intuitively know that their language has almost a double lexicon, in which, ever since the Norman Conquest in 1066, words from the original Germanic/Anglo-Saxon word stock are often paired with words from Norman French, a Latinate language spoken by the power elite after the invasion of England. Latinate words are generally associated with greater formality, abstraction and emotional neutrality, whereas English words of Anglo-Saxon origin are generally associated with things which are fundamental, familiar, concrete or emotional in our lives. Taking this distinction into account, it is remarkable that within his relatively short monologue, the hawk uses such a high proportion of Latinate words. Examples include 'inaction' (2), 'falsifying' (2), 'rehearse' (4), 'perfect' (4) 'convenience' (5) 'buoyancy' (6), 'advantage' (7), 'inspection' (8), 'Creation' (10) (12), 'revolve' (13), 'allotment' (17), 'arguments' (20), 'assert' (20), 'permitted' (23) and a few others. This Latinate affectation makes the style of the hawk's speech cold, self-possessed, distanced and abstract. Notice in this connection also the pattern of negatives: (2) 'no falsifying dream', (15) 'There is no sophistry in my body', (20), 'No arguments assert my right', (22) 'Nothing has changed since I began' and (23) 'My eye has permitted no change'. These negative phrases appear to reinforce the complete domination that the hawk maintains.

On the other hand, there are the no-nonsense words of Anglo-Saxon stock, which the hawk prefers with regard to his weaponry, plumage and predatory killings: 'my hooked head and hooked feet' (3), 'kills and eat' (4), 'My feet are locked upon the rough bark' (9), 'my foot', my each feather' (11), 'body'(15), 'tearing off heads' (15), 'death'(17), 'the one path of my flight' (18), 'through the bones of the living' (19), 'my right' (20) and the ominous, all-out Anglo-Saxon, statement in the last line 'I am going to keep things like this'. Considering his varied vocabulary, we may perhaps conclude that there is more than one side to the hawk's character. It is intriguing that both words in the poem's title are of Germanic, that is, Anglo-Saxon stock. Dutch speakers will recognize in them the words 'havik' and 'rusten'. In his monologue, the hawk prefers the Latinate 'inaction' to 'roosting'. As I said earlier, the title is the only locus where the reader might sense the presence of the poet's persona.

The poem's versification: The relation between its metre, sound and syntactic structure

Lastly, we have to look at the poem's versification, that is, its metre and its sound and syntactic structure, which may well reinforce the rhetorical patterns we have discussed just now. The verse pattern is regular (six verses of four lines), though the rhyme and metre are free (3 to 6 stresses and 6 to 11 syllables per line), which only befits a bird of prey on the wing. Readers scanning the poem's metre will find, or rather hear, that at the end of several lines, there are two successive heavy stresses, which appear to reinforce the sense. For example: (1) 'eyes closed', (3) 'hooked feet', (5) 'high trees', (6) 'sun's ray', (9) 'rough bark', (14) 'all mine' and (23) 'no change'.

Most verse lines are made up of relatively short sentences reinforcing the hawk's syntax of unshakeable conviction, culminating in the last stanza in which each of the four lines is made up of one full sentence so that metre and syntax run parallel. Furthermore, there are relatively few instances of enjambement or run-on lines, in which the syntax goes beyond the metrical boundary at the end of the line. I have marked these with an arrow in lines 2, 6, 10, 12, 16 and 18. It is at these places that the effects of the interplay between syntax and metre may have a marked semantic impact. We might say that in the case of enjambement, readers get two conflicting prompts: the metrical line-boundary tells them to pause, be it ever so shortly, while the unfinished syntax pulls them into the next line. Therefore, however brief it may be, the resulting wavering is bound to cause some tension, which, on the one hand, heightens our awareness of the last word in the run-on line and, on the other, causes us to wonder about the first word in the next line. Any interpretation of enjambement is highly speculative, but I think that poetry readers cannot resist having a try. Thus, the enjambement or leap from line 2 to 3 seems to emphasize that the hawk does not allow any ambivalent thought to come between his killer instinct and his deadly weapons. Perhaps the hawk is mocking at our squeamishness or at human conscience in general, which is supposed to distinguish us from the beasts. The enjambement in line 6 may be felt to emphasize the total subservience of nature to the hawk's existential needs. Perhaps the rush of enjambements in lines 10, 12 and 16, of which those in lines 12 and 16 even run over the verse boundaries, are perhaps a reflection of the hawk's fierce excitement about having gained control over Creation (Cluysenaar 1982: 305). Finally, the enjambement in line 18 appears to catch the reader unprepared for the horrible image in the next line in the image 'through the bones of the living'.

While still on the matter of syntax, it may strike the reader that there are only three subordinate clauses: 'where I please' (14), 'because it is all mine' (14) and 'since I began' (22). Particularly, in relation to the hawk's fierce statement 'No arguments assert my right' (20), these sub-clauses must have escaped from the hawk's 'hooked head' unintentionally because they seem to come near to a grudging argumentation for his absolute authority (Cluysenaar 1982: 305).

Stylistics brings literary critical appreciation into clearer focus

So far my attempt at a stylistic analysis, which cannot do justice, of course, to a poem which has gained great admiration for its verbal artistry, and justly so, I think. At the same time, it has aroused considerable controversy between two fundamentally different readings. Because this dispute is spread across a great many books and articles, it is impossible to discuss all its ins and outs within the scope of this essay. Therefore, I must limit myself to a few heavily summarized points ranging from the allegation that the hawk's state of mind is that of a ruthless dictator to the enlightened point of view that it is the hawk's natural function that defines his violent nature.

First some points of adverse criticism:

1   Because the absurdity of this single-minded concern with violence is not challenged from within the poem, the consciousness of violence comes to us unmediated (Lucas 1986: 193–7).
2   It is a disturbing thought that Hughes appears to recommend the hawk's violent behaviour to his human readers (Williams 1985: 68–71).
3   The whole world in the poem is defined in ruthlessly egocentric terms (Smith 1982: 155–69).

Then a moderate view:

4 The hawk's natural function defines its nature and the poem reveals it
glorying in what it is. The crucial question is: are we, too, invited to glory
in what it is? Critics have taken this as the essential meaning of the
poem, extending it to include a glorification of totalitarianism (Walder
1987: 39–41).

And, finally, the view that the violence is in the mind of the reader:

5 The wit of the poem is that no hawk has the self-realization here
described. Only human beings have this moral awareness of their place
in the world and their actions. The hawk does not need to be absolved
from behaving as it must (Spurr 1997: 283–90).

Considering this wide and perhaps even unbridgeable gap between these
two literary critical views, the question arises whether stylistics can help
readers, especially student readers, in taking up an academically defensible
stance in this matter. I really think it can, for the following reasons. But first,
I wish to make the obvious point that the way in which stylistics and literary criticism each approach a literary text exemplifies a particular perspective,
namely, a perspective on the study of literature. Thus, very generally speaking,
literary criticism directs attention to the larger-scale significance of what is
represented by a product of verbal art. On the other hand, stylistics tends to
focus on how this significance can be related to specific features of language,
that is, to the linguistic texture of a literary work. Following this argument,
I think the literary critical and stylistic perspectives are complementary, or
perhaps the poles of a dialectical process. Obviously, this complementarity
does not provide the means of arriving at a definitive interpretation, which, of
course, does not exist anyway. But a stylistic analysis does enable readers,
especially student readers, to obtain textual evidence for a particular literary
critical view of a poem and, not least, to heighten their own sense of what a
literary text means to themselves (Rubik and Widdowson 2000: 6). In sum,
stylistics brings literary critical appreciation into clearer focus (McIntyre and
Busse 2010: 84–94).

Extracted from Verdonk, P. (2010) 'A cognitive stylistic reading of rhetorical
patterns in Ted Hughes's 'Hawk Roosting': A possible role for stylistics in a
literary critical controversy', in McIntyre, D. and Busse, B. (eds) *Language and
Style: In honour of Mick Short,* pp. 84–94. Houndmills, Basingstoke: Palgrave
Macmillan.

Notes

Chapter 2

1 This paper was presented at a one-day symposium on linguistics and the study of literature at the University of Utrecht in November 1983. The occasion was the twenty-fifth anniversary of the Institute of English Language and Literature of this university. Other speakers included Roger Fowler, Guido Latré, Geoffrey Leech, Mick Short and Willie van Peer.

2 PALA is an acronym for Poetics and Linguistics Association, which is an international academic association for those who work in stylistics, poetics and associated fields of language and linguistics.

3 This article has recently been reprinted in Leech, G. *Language in Literature: Style and Foregrounding.* Harlow: Pearson/Longman.

4 The term 'the New Stylistics', as Fowler (1975) points out, should not be taken as a common denominator of a particular school of stylistics, but as a pragmatic designation of the output of writings produced by scholars mainly in Britain and the United States during the 15 years or so after the publication of Sebeok's *Style in Language* in 1960.

5 On the theory of foregrounding, see Mukařovsky (1964) and Leech (1969: 56–9). For discussions of problems connected with foregrounding, see Short (1973) and Cluysenaar (1976: 59–62).

6 Believing in the interaction between research and teaching, I have made profitable use of the results of a stylistic analysis carried out in a working group of advanced literature students in the English Department of the University of Amsterdam, three of whom deserve a special mention: Bev Jackson, Alexander Peters and Loes Visser.

7 I am most grateful to Emma Darbyshire, Image Library Assistant, Fitzwilliam Museum, Cambridge, for all her help in procuring this JPEG image.

8 Relief etching is a method of etching in which the parts of the design that take the ink are raised above the surface of the plate rather than incised into the plate (as in conventional etching). The method was used by William Blake, who called it 'woodcut on copper'.

9 The external thematic statement given here is mainly based on S. Foster Damon (1965: 244–5). See also S. Foster Damon (1969: 283) and E. D. Hirsh Jr. (1964: 93–5 and 262–5).

10 The *OED* gives 1806 as the first evidence for the use of 'to charter' = 'to hire (a ship) by charter party'. Therefore, we cannot be certain of the extent to which this meaning was available to Blake in the 1790s.

11 It is obvious that the two coordinated clauses 'How the Chimney-sweepers cry/Every blackning Church appalls' and 'And the hapless Soldiers sigh/Runs in blood down Palace walls', which make up the entire third stanza, can only function as direct object of the verb 'hear' occurring at the end of line 8 in the second stanza, if there is no full stop after this verb. There is no such punctuation mark in the text of the poem as it appears in Ostriker (1977), Erdman (1969: 275–6), Erdman (1981:144), and the *Oxford Anthology of English Literature* (eds, Bloom and Trilling). Nor does a period occur on Blake's colour plate of 'London' (Keynes 1970: plate 46, see note 7). It is remarkable, however, that in other editions of the poem, we find a variety of punctuation marks after the verb 'hear' in line 8. For example, in the *Norton Anthology of English Literature* (eds, Abrams et al.) and in the Oxford Standard Authors edition of the *Complete Writings* (ed., Keynes) (cf. Keynes 1970: plate 46), there is a full stop, in Stevenson (1971: 213–14), we find a dash, while the text in Brooks and Warren (1976: 129) shows a colon. Evidently, this is only a very small selection from the much larger number of editions available.

Chapter 3

1 This essay is based on the text of guest lectures I have given in Birmingham, Norwich and Louvain, and I wish to thank Elizabeth Newman, the late Roger Fowler, Herman Servotte and Guido Latré for their instructive comments, but most of all I acknowledge my great indebtedness to Walter Nash, who was kind enough to scrutinize the draft of this essay and to come up with many invaluable suggestions.

2 On the internet, there are many reproductions of the three paintings Auden's poem appears to allude to.

3 *The Massacre of the Innocents* must have been on loan to the Musée des Beaux Arts in Brussels at the time of Auden's visit because this painting belongs to the permanent collection of the Kunsthistorisches Museum in Vienna.

4 I am grateful to Professor Peter de Voogd of the University of Utrecht for his insightful comment on the poem's rhyme scheme.

5 Grammetrics refers to the relationship between grammatical structure and metrical organization. For example, the grammatical units of a poem may synchronize with metrical units, which may result in a tightly structured encasement of a particular line of thought. For example, the two opening lines of Pope's *An Essay on Man*: Know then thyself, presume not God to scan;/The proper study of Mankind is Man. Or, conversely, run-on lines or enjambements may interrupt the grammatical structure in the middle of a constituent. See, for example, the analysis of Owen's 'Anthem for Doomed Youth' in this book. Evidently, grammetrics may be a strong rhetorical weapon.

6 Graphology (not to be confused with the study of handwriting) is concerned with such things as punctuation, use of capitals, lay-out, typeface, etc.

7 The only non-deictic use of the definite article occurs in the phrase 'at the edge of the wood' in which the first article is used with cataphoric reference to the modifier 'of the wood'.

8 For this conception of metonymy, see Wellek and Warren 1966: 186–211 and Lodge 1977: 73–111.

9 The term 'ideology' is used here in the sense of 'the system of beliefs, values, and categories by reference to which a person or a society comprehends the world' (Fowler 1986: 130).

Chapter 4

1 This paper is based on an earlier version presented at the annual Conference of the Poetics and Linguistics Association (PALA) at the University of Lancaster in April 1987. I am grateful to Professor Walter Nash of the University of Nottingham for his detailed and constructive criticisms.

2 One poem was 'The Next War' and the other 'Anthem for Doomed Youth' (Bell 1985: Letter 549).

3 For that matter, the texts of the Second and the Third Collects, praying for Peace and for Grace, respectively, make an interesting juxtaposition with Owen's theme. Significantly, the Collect for Peace contains the words 'Defend us thy humble servants in all assaults of our enemies, that we, surely trusting in thy defence, may not fear the power of any adversaries'; and the Collect for Grace prays 'Lord our heavenly Father, Almighty and everlasting God, who has safely brought us to the beginning of this day: Defend us in the same with thy mighty power'.

4 The phrase 'The Two Nations' refers to Benjamin Disraeli's political novel *Sybil or The Two Nations* (1845), which is concerned with the miserable conditions of the urban and rural poor. It was particularly successful and certain attitudes expressed in it foreshadowed future social legislation.

5 This refers to the former custom of closing the blinds whenever there was a death in the house for as long as the corpse lay within doors. The purpose of drawing the blinds was to advise outsiders of one's bereavement, and so forestall intrusions. However, once the funeral was over, the blinds were opened again, to signal the resumption of 'normal' life. Presumably, Owen's point is that for the war-bereaved at home, the blinds are always drawn, because they can never bury their dead in the ordinary way.

6 About the 'passing bell', or (death) knell, Walter Nash sent me this touching note: 'For me, the significance of this is the human scale, the relationship to an *individual*. The passing bell is a single bell, tolling at regular intervals, or sometimes in sequences divided by pauses In my native parish, it was the custom to ring the passing bell once for every year of the dead individual's life Some parishes would ring different bells for men and women – a bell of lower tone for a man, of higher tone for a woman. I have also heard of churches ringing different sequences (e.g. groups of three, or four, or six) to announce that the woman being 'brought home' was married or unmarried.

Anyone taking careful note of this very orderly and quiet phenomenon could therefore tell at least the age, perhaps the sex, even the marital status of the person concerned. The passing bell is the last tribute to *individuality* – but the troops in Owen's poem are dying in droves: no individuality for them, no precisely tolling bell – only the monstrous anger of the guns.

It had never occurred to me until now that there is a strange echo here of the opening of' Gray's 'Elegy Written in a Country Churchyard':

> The curfew tolls the knell of parting day,
> The lowing herd winds slowly o'er the lea . . . etc.

The text of Owen's second draft, beginning 'What passing-bells for you who die in herds?' suggested this to me. (See Hibberd 1973, for the text of this draft.)

7 See, for example, Blunden (1930), Sassoon (1945), Welland (1960), Hibberd (1973), Bäckman (1979) and Lucas (1986).

8 As a result of this mixture of the two sonnet techniques, England and the Continent are relevantly linked. I thank Professor Peter de Voogd of the University of Utrecht for this interesting observation.

9 In connection with 'these who', consider the accent patterns of the poem, and in particular the linkage – which has been suggested in the discussion of the third-person references – of *these* (line 1), *their* (line 4) and *them* (line 5). If *these* were a 'determinative' in the noun phrase, it would be unaccented. When we accent it, it implies, as I have already suggested, exophoric reference, that is, extra-linguistic reference to the situational world of the text. A comma would clarify this grammatical interpretation:

> 'What passing-bells for these, who die as cattle?'

This, of course, will raise the question of why, if Owen intended this meaning, he omitted the comma? It is conceivable that – consciously or unconsciously – he wanted the best of two constructions.

10 Though it does not affect the main line of my argument, it is perhaps an important point that *without* the definite article the plural nouns are fully generic (e.g. the noun phrases beginning with a negative or restrictive expression, i.e. 'only', 'no', 'nor', 'nor any'), whereas *with* the definite article, their genericness is deictically restricted by the text (Werth 1980: 250–89).

11 One might also recall Shakespeare's 'bare ruin'd choirs, where late the sweet birds sang' (Sonnet 73), and also, perhaps, the Prayer Book phrase mentioned before, 'In Quires and Places where they sing. . .'

Chapter 5

1 I would like to thank Mick Short for his valuable comments on an earlier version of this paper and Katie Wales for her stimulating response. As usual, the responsibility for whatever flaws that still exist is entirely mine.

2 It will be understood that this was the situation near the end of the 1980s.

3 This essay has recently been reprinted in Geoffrey Leech (2008), *Language in Literature: Style and Foregrounding*. Pearson Longman Education, Harlow.

4 Interestingly, some 20 years after my analysis, Peter Stockwell explores the same poem in his great book *Texture: A Cognitive Aesthetics of Reading* (2009).

5 The name of Ariel is full of allusions such as:

a) A Hebrew name signifying 'lion of God';

b) In *Isaiah* XXIX, 1–7, it is applied to Jerusalem;

c) In astronomy it refers to a satellite of Uranus;

d) In demonology and literature, it is the name of a spirit. Thus, Ariel is one of the rebel angels in Milton's *Paradise Lost*; a sylph, the guardian of Belinda, in Pope's 'Rape of the Lock'; but best known as an 'ayrie spirit' in Shakespeare's *The Tempest*. (See *Brewer's Dictionary of Phrase & Fable* (1963). Cassel & Co. Ltd.)

Chapter 6

1 I thank Roger D. Sell for his valuable comments.

2 For an interesting collection of various kinds of literary pragmatic case studies, see Sell (1991).

3 See for a detailed treatment of literature as a mode of discourse, Herrnstein Smith (1983); Fowler (1981, 1986); Leech and Short (1981); and Sell (1986, 1987).

4 See also Barthes's 'From work to text' (1980: 73–81).

5 I thank Elena Semino (1997: 50) for her critical comment on the original version of this passage.

6 Interestingly, on his recording of *The Whitsun Weddings*, Larkin himself reads 'more and more' as an adjective (Larkin 1965).

Chapter 7

1 For this view of poetry as contextualized discourse, I am deeply indebted to Roger Fowler (1986: 85–101).

2 It is important to distinguish between the notion of *situational context* and that of *linguistic context*. In the case of deictic reference, as we have seen, the identification of the element to which the deictic refers is made on the basis of the *situational context*, which, for that matter, may be quite narrow or extremely wide. For example, in 'He put *the* milk back in *the* fridge', 'the milk' and 'the fridge' are identified in a domestic situation, whereas in 'We all sat in *the* sun', the definite article 'the' refers to something in our general experience of the world. However, in the case of non-deictic reference, it is the *linguistic context* that makes identification possible. For instance, in

'I hear you disliked his latest novel. I read his first novel, and *that* was boring, too', the demonstrative 'that' refers to 'his first novel' mentioned earlier in the text. In 'He told the story like *this*: 'Once upon a time. . .', the demonstrative 'this' refers to the phrase 'Once upon a time' following later in the linguistic context. Similarly, in 'Punishment', the identification of 'the nape' in line 2 is based on the following semantic link with the modifying phrase 'of her neck'.

Note that in the case of backward reference, we speak of *anaphoric reference*, while forward reference is called *cataphoric reference* (see *A Dictionary of Stylistics* by Katie Wales (1990; 2nd edition 2001) for a systematic and clear overview).

Interestingly, we may also distinguish *indirect anaphoric reference*, which occurs when a reference becomes part of the listener's/reader's knowledge indirectly, that is, by inference from what has already been mentioned in the discourse, for example, 'John bought *a bicycle*, but when he rode it one of *the wheels* came off'. The definite reference to 'wheels' is possible because a bicycle has been mentioned, and we know that bicycles have wheels. Other examples of indirect anaphoric reference often occur when a particular topic has been introduced. For instance, once the topic of an *orchestral concert* has been introduced in the discourse, we may expect definite references like *the programme*, *the audience*, *the conductor*, etc. (Quirk et al. 1985: 267–8).

Furthermore, it is noteworthy that the type of reference may be ambiguous. For example, in a sentence like 'Travel books like *this* do not tell the truth', the pronoun 'this' can perhaps be interpreted as either deictic (with situational reference) or non-deictic (with linguistic reference). It is non-deictic and anaphoric if it refers to 'travel books' mentioned earlier in the sentence. However, if the speaker actually points to a particular specimen of the travel books s/he is talking about, 'this' is used deictically (with situational reference).

Finally, it should be noted that not all present- and past-tense forms of verbs are deictic. In our foregoing example 'Travel books like this do not tell the truth', the present-tensed verbal group 'do not tell' is not deictic because it is not oriented to the speaker's or writer's temporal situation; clearly, it is a general statement.

Chapter 8

1   For this brief outline of the relation between rhetoric, poetics and stylistics, I benefited from Leeman and Braet (1987), Nash (1989) and Preminger (1975: 702–5).

2   The following handbooks provide a fascinating overview of the extremely high standards set for the classical training as a rhetorician: *Ad Herennium* (anon: 1954); *De Oratore*, Books I-III (Cicero 1942a, 1942b); *Institutio Oratoria*, Books I-XII (Quintilian 1920, 1921a, 1921b, 1922).

3   Through the centuries, the concept of *inventio* in poetics has been interpreted in many different ways. See Preminger (1975: 401–2) for an overview.

4 For a discussion of the *memoria technica*, the pigeon-hole method, see Cicero, *De Oratora*, Book II.1xxxvi. 350–67, pp. 465–79. For a detailed description of the ideal delivery of an oration, see Quintillian, *Institutio Oratoria*, Book XI.iii. 40–184, pp. 265–349.

5 For a clear overview of the development of the role of the reader, see Fowler 1996, pp. 233–55.

6 For this brief summary of schema theory, I have greatly benefited from Cook (1994), Forrester (1996), Fowler ([1986] 1996) and Semino (1995).

7 It has become common practice to write schemata in small capital letters.

8 My reading of the poem corresponds to a large extent with that of Petch 1981: 90–1.

Chapter 9

1 See http://www.khm.at for a reproduction and brief description of Brueghel's picture 'The Kermess', also called 'Peasant Dance', at the Kunsthistorisches Museum in Vienna. In the Low Countries, the Kermess used to be a local popular feast day and fair, originally to mark the anniversary of the consecration of the local church; cf. modern Dutch 'kermis' (funfair) derived from 'kerk' (church) and 'mis' (mass) via the older forms 'kercmisse' and 'kermiss(e)'.

2 For a very long time, *Rhetorica ad Herennium* was attributed to Cicero, and his name, though in square brackets, still features on the cover of the English edition in the prestigious Loeb Classical Library. However, in the meantime, all recent editors have agreed that this attribution must be erroneous (Kennedy 1999: 108).

3 Henry Widdowson, who was so kind as to read a draft of this article, questions the usefulness of Hollander's distinction between actual and notional ekphrasis for stylistics. Does it matter, he wonders, whether a poet has the object in sight or in mind? Or whether, if in mind, it is imperfectly recalled, deliberately modified or even entirely imagined? For even when there are deictic signals in the text that suggest a particular picture, we cannot be sure that this is not a device for creating a vacuum effect to draw the reader in. My response to this query is that when I say that Hollander's distinction between actual and notional ekphrasis might be useful, I am only thinking of ekphrases from an art-historical point of view. So I entirely agree with him that the distinction is of little use to a stylistic or rhetorical analysis of an ekphrastic poem.

4 Though we know he made a drawing of a particular vase and was impressed by other Greek vases in the British Museum and that he relied on various literary resources, Andrew Motion has argued convincingly that Keats's urn is his own invention (1997: 389–91).

5 For further details on the theory and practice of ekphrasis, see Aisenberg (1995); Heffernan (1991, 1994); Lessing (1984 [1766]); Mitchell (1980, 1986); Steiner (1982).

6 Given the vast number of publications on cognitive linguistics, I can only suggest a limited selection for further reading. Useful introductions include Dirven and Verspoor (2004), Lakoff (1987), Lee (2001), Taylor (2002) and Ungerer and Schmid (1996). Suitable for more advanced study are Janssen and Redeker (1999) and Langacker (1999), as are the two seminal books, Langacker (1987) and (1991).

7 The cognitive approach to metaphor, metonymy and other rhetorical figures has grown into an extensive field of research, which has yielded a huge number of publications. A small selection includes Freeman (1993), Gibbs (1994), Gibbs and Steen (1999), Goatly (1997), Kövecses (2002), Lakoff (1987), Lakoff and Johnson (1980), Lakoff and Turner (1989), Panther and Radden (1999), Steen (1994) and (1999), Weber (1995).

8 In doing this exercise, I act on a suggestion made by Peter Stockwell in his inspirational book Cognitive Poetics (2002: 7).

9 For this sense of being moved almost bodily as a result of the poem's rhythms, I found support in Raymond Gibbs's plenary paper at the PALA Conference 2001 in Budapest (2002).

10 For further reading on iconicity in language and literature, see the edited volumes of Nänny and Fischer (1999) and Fischer and Nänny (2001) as well as Nänny and Fischer (2006). These two researchers have also developed a highly interesting website on iconicity: http://home.hum.uva.nl/iconicity/.

11 For this keen observation, I am indebted to Robert Cockcroft.

References

Ad Herennium (formerly attributed to Cicero) (1954), Caplan, H. (trans). Cambridge, MA: Harvard University Press.

Aisenberg, K. (1995), *Ravishing Images: Ekphrasis in the Poetry and Prose of William Wordsworth, W. H. Auden and Philip Larkin.* New York: P. Lang.

Allott, K. (ed.) (1950), *The Penguin Book of Contemporary Verse.* London: Harmondsworth.

Andrews, R. (ed.) (1992), *Rebirth of Rhetoric.* London and New York: Routledge.

Aristotle (1926), *Art of Rhetoric.* Freese, J. H. (trans). Cambridge, MA: Harvard University Press.

—(1983), *Classical Literary Criticism.* Aristotle: *On the Art of Poetry.* Horace: *On the Art of Poetry.* Longinus: *On the Sublime.* Dorsch, T. S. (trans). Harmondsworth: Penguin Books.

Auden, W. H. (1938), *Another Time.* London: Faber & Faber.

—(1948), *The Dyer's Hand and Other Essays.* London: Faber & Faber.

—(1966), *Collected Shorter Poems 1927–1957.* London: Faber & Faber.

Austin, J. L. (1962), *How to Do Things with Words.* Oxford: Oxford University Press.

Bäckman, S. (1979), *Tradition Transformed: Studies in the Poetry of Wilfred Owen.* Lund: C.W.K. Gleerup.

Baker-Smith, D. (1990), 'Literature and the visual arts', in Coyle, M., Garside, P., Kelsall, M. and Peck, J. (eds), *Encyclopedia of Literature and Criticism.* London: Routledge, pp. 991–1003.

Barthes, R. (1976), *The Pleasure of the Text.* London: Cape.

—(1980), 'From work to text', in Harari, J. V. (ed.), *Textual Strategies: Perspectives in Post-Structuralist Criticism.* London: Methuen, pp. 73–81.

Bauschatz, C. M. (1980), 'Montaigne's conception of reading in the context of Renaissance poetics and modern criticism', in Suleiman, S. R. and Crosman, I. (eds), *The Reader in the Text.* Princeton, NJ: Princeton University Press, pp. 264–91.

Beach, J. W. (1957), *The Making of the Auden Canon.* Minneapolis: University of Minnesota Press.

Bell, J. (ed.) (1985), *Wilfred Owen: Selected Letters.* Oxford: Oxford University Press.

Bergonzi, B. (1975), 'Auden and the Audenesque', *Encounter.* 44: 65–75.

Blunden, E. (ed.) (1931), *The Poems of Wilfred Owen.* London: Chatto & Windus.

Blunden, F. (1930), 'The soldier poets of 1914–1918', in Brereton, F. (ed.), *An Anthology of War Poems.* London: Collins Sons & Co.

Bolinger, D. (1980), *Language: The Loaded Weapon.* London: Longman.

Booth, S. (ed.) (1977), *Shakespeare's Sonnets.* New Haven: Yale University Press.

Brooks, C. (1975[1947]), *The Well Wrought Urn*. New York: Harcourt Brace Jovanovich.

Brooks, C. and Warren, R. P. (1976), *Understanding Poetry*. 4th edition. New York: Holt, Rinehart and Winston.

Brown, G. and Yule, G. (1983), *Discourse Analysis*. Cambridge: Cambridge University Press.

Caesar, A. (1987), 'The 'human problem' in Wilfred Owen's poetry', *Critical Quarterly* 29(2): 67–84.

Carpenter, H. (1981), *W.H. Auden: A Biography*. London: Allen & Unwin.

Carter, R. and Simpson, P. (1989), *Language, Discourse and Literature*. London: Unwin Hyman.

Chafe, W. L. (1970), *Meaning and the Structure of Language*. Chicago, IL: University of Chicago Press.

Chesnokova, A. and Yakuba, V. (2011), 'Using stylistics to teach literature to non-native speakers', in Jeffries, L. and McIntyre, D. (eds), *Teaching Stylistics*. Basingstoke: Palgrave/English Subject Centre, pp. 95–108.

Ching, M. K .L., Haley, M. C., Lunsford, R. F. (eds) (1980), *Linguistic Perspectives on Literature*. London: Routledge and Kegan Paul, pp. 235–41.

Cicero (1939), *Brutus*. Hendrickson, G. L. (trans). *Orator*. Hubbell, H. M. (trans). Cambridge, MA: Harvard University Press.

—(1942a/1988), *De Oratore*, Books I and II. Sutton, E. W. & Rackham, H. (trans). Cambridge, MA: Harvard University Press & London.

—(1942b), *De Oratore*, Book III, Rackham, H. (trans). Cambridge, MA: Harvard University Press.

—(1954/1989), *Rhetorica ad Herennium*, Caplan, H. (trans). London: Heinemann.

Clark, K. (1992), 'The linguistics of blame: representations of women in the *Sun*'s reporting of crimes of sexual violence', in Toolan, M. (ed.), *Language, Text and Context: Essays in Stylistics*. London: Routledge, pp. 208–24.

Close, R. A. (1975), *A Reference Grammar for Students of English*. London: Longman.

Cluysenaar, A. (1976), *Introduction to Literary Stylistics*. London: Batsford.

—(1982), 'Formal meanings in three modern poems', *Dutch Quarterly Review of Anglo-American Letters* 12(4): 302–20.

Cockcroft, R. (2003), *Rhetorical Affect in Early Modern Writing: Renaissance Passions Reconsidered*. Basingstoke: Palgrave Macmillan.

Cockcroft, R. and Cockcroft, S. (2005), *Persuading People: An Introduction to Rhetoric*. Second edition. Basingstoke and New York: Palgrave Macmillan.

Cook, G. (1994), *Discourse and Literature*. Oxford: Oxford University Press.

Corbett, E. P. J. (1990), *Classical Rhetoric for the Modern Student*. Oxford: Oxford University Press.

Corcoran, N. (1986), *Seamus Heaney*. London: Faber & Faber.

Corder, S. P. and Allen, J. P. B. (eds) (1974), *The Edinburgh Course in Applied Linguistics*, III. Oxford: Oxford University Press.

Csábi, S. and Zerkowitz, J. (eds) (2002), *Textual Secrets: The Message of the Medium*. Budapest: School of English and American Studies, Eötvös Loránd University.

Culler, J. (1975), *Structuralist Poetics: Structuralism, Linguistics and the Study of Literature*. London: Routledge & Kegan Paul.

Culpeper, J., Short, M. and Verdonk, P. (eds) (1998), *Exploring the Language of Drama: From Text to Context*. London: Routledge.

D'haen, Th. (ed.) (1986), *Linguistics and the Study of Literature*. Amsterdam: Rodopi.

Davie, D. V. (1955), *Articulate Energy*. London: Routledge and Kegan Paul.

Day Lewis, C. (ed.) (1963), *The Collected Poems of Wilfred Owen*. London: Chatto & Windus.

van Deel, T. (1982), 'Over Brueghels *De Val van Icarus*'. *De Revisor*1:50.

Dickens, C. (1988), *Hard times*. London: Penguin Group.

van Dijk, T. A. (2008), *Discourse and Context: A Sociocognitive Approach*. Cambridge: Cambridge University Press.

Dirven, R. and Verspoor, M. (2004), *Cognitive Exploration of Language and Linguistics*. Amsterdam: John Benjamins.

Dorsch, T. S. (trans) (1983), *Classical Literary Criticism*. Aristotle: *On the Art of Poetry*. Horace: *On the Art of Poetry*. Longinus: *On the Sublime*. Harmondsworth: Penguin Books.

Eliot, T. S. (1951), *Selected Essays*. London: Faber & Faber.

Emmott, C. (1997), *Narrative Comprehension*. Oxford: Clarendon Press.

—(2002), 'Responding to style: cohesion, foregrounding and thematic interpretation.' In Louwerse, M. and van Peer, W. (eds), *Thematics: Interdisciplinary Studies*. Amsterdam: Benjamins, pp. 91–117.

Epstein, E. L. (1981), 'The self-reflexive artefact: the function of mimesis in an approach to a theory of value for literature', in Freeman, D. C. (ed.), *Essays in Modern Stylistics*. London and New York: Methuen, pp. 166–99.

Erdman, D. V. (ed.) (1981), *The Selected Poetry of Blake*. New York: First Meridian Printing Press.

Erdman, D. V. (1969), *Blake: Prophet Against Empire*. Princeton New Jersey: Princeton University Press.

Evans, I. H. (1978), *Brewer's Dictionary of Phrase and Fable*. London: Cassell Ltd.

Fahnestock, J. (2005), 'Rhetorical stylistics', in Hamilton, C. A. (ed.) 'Rhetoric and Beyond.' *Language and Literature*, 14(3): 215–30.

Firth, J. R. (1957), *Papers in Linguistics 1934–1951*. Oxford: Oxford University Press.

Fischer, O. and Nänny, M. (eds) (2001), *The Motivated Sign: Iconicity in Language and Literature*, vol. 2. Amsterdam: John Benjamins.

Forrester, M. A. (1996), *Psychology of Language*. London: Sage.

Forrest-Thomson, V. (1978), *Poetic Artifice: A Theory of Twentieth-Century Poetry*. Manchester: Manchester University Press.

Foster Damon, S. (1965), *A Blake Dictionary. The Ideas and Symbols of William Blake*. Providence, Rhode Island: Brown University Press.

—(1969), *William Blake. His Philosophy and Symbols*. London: Dawsons of Pall Mall.

Fowler, R. (1971), *The Languages of Literature: Some Linguistic Contributions to Criticism*. London: Routledge & Kegan Paul.

—(1977), *Linguistics and the Novel*. London: Methuen.

—(1981), *Literature as Social Discourse: The Practice of Linguistic Criticism*. London: Batsford.

—(1986), *Linguistic Criticism*. Oxford: Oxford University Press.

—(1996), *Linguistic Criticism* (2nd ed.). Oxford: Oxford University Press.

—(ed.) (1973), *A Dictionary of Modern Critical Terms*. London: Routledge and Kegan Paul.

—(ed.) (1975), *Style and Structure in Literature: Essays in the New Stylistics*. Oxford: Basil Blackwell.

Freeman, D. C. (ed.) (1981), *Essays in Modern Stylistics*. London: Methuen.

—(1993), 'According to my bond: *King Lear* and re-cognition', *Language and Literature* 2(1): 1–18.

—(ed.) (1970), *Linguistics and Literary Style*. New York: Holt, Reinhart and Winston.

Garvin, P. L. (ed. and trans.) (1964), *A Prague School Reader on Esthetics, Literary Structure and Style*. Washington D.C.: Georgetown University Press.

Gavins, J. and Steen, G. (eds) (2003), *Cognitive Poetics in Practice*. London: Routledge.

Gibbs, R. W. (1994), *The Poetics of Mind: Figurative Thought, Language, and Understanding*. Cambridge: Cambridge University Press.

—(2002), 'Feeling moved by metaphor', in Csábi, S. and Zerkowitz, J. (eds), *Textual Secrets: The Message of the Medium*. Budapest: School of English and American Studies, Eötvös Loránd University, pp. 13–28.

Gibbs, R. W. and Steen, G. (eds) (1999), *Metaphor in Cognitive Linguistics*. Amsterdam: John Benjamins.

Glob, P. V. (1969), *The Bog People: Iron Age Man Preserved*. London: Faber & Faber.

Goatly, A. (1997), *The Language of Metaphors*. London: Routledge.

Grice, H. P. (1975), 'Logic and conversation', in Cole, P. and Morgan, J. L. (eds), *Syntax and Semantics 3: Speech Acts*. New York: Academic, pp. 41–58.

Gross, J. (ed.) (1987), *The Oxford Book of Aphorisms*. Oxford: Oxford University Press.

Haffenden, J. (1981), *Viewpoints: Poets in Conversation with John Haffenden*. London: Faber and Faber.

Halliday, M. A. K. (1966), 'Descriptive linguistics in literary studies', in McIntosch, A. and Halliday, M. A. K. (eds), *Patterns of Language: Papers in General, Descriptive and Applied Linguistics*. London: Longman.

—(1971), 'Linguistic function and literary style: An inquiry into the language of William Golding's 'The Inheritors', in Freeman, D. C. (ed.), (1981) *Essays in Modern Stylistics*. London: Methuen.

—(1976), 'Types of process', in Kress, G. (ed.), *Halliday: System and Function in Language*. Oxford: Oxford University Press.

—(1978), *Language as Social Semiotic: The Social Interpretation of Language and Meaning*. London: Edward Arnold.

Halliday, M. A. K., McIntosh, A. and Strevens, P. (1964), *The Linguistic Sciences and Language Teaching*, London: Longman.

Hamilton, C. A. (2003), 'Ekphrasis, repetition and Ezra Pound's "Yeux Glauques"', *Imaginaires* 3: 215–23.

Hanauer, D. I. (2001), 'What we know about reading poetry: Theoretical positions and empirical research', in Schram, D. and Steen, G. (eds), *The Psychology and Sociology of Literature*. Amsterdam and Philadelphia: John Benjamins Publishing Company, pp. 107–28.

Heaney, S. (1972), *Wintering Out*. London: Faber and Faber.

—(1975a), *Bog Poems*. London: Rainbow Press. (Limited edition.)

—(1975b), *North*. London: Faber & Faber.

—(1980), *Preoccupations: Selected Prose 1968–1978*. London: Faber and Faber.

—(1984), *Station Island*. London: Faber and Faber.

—(1987), *The Haw Lantern*. London: Faber and Faber.

—(1988), *The Government of the Tongue*. London: Faber and Faber.

—(1990), *The Redress of Poetry: An Inaugural Lecture Delivered before the University of Oxford on 24 October 1989*. Oxford: Oxford University Press.

Heffernan, J. (1991), 'Ekphrasis and Representation', *New Literary History* 22(2): 297–316.

—(1994), *The Museum of Words: The Poetics of Ekphrasis from Homer to Ashberry*. Chicago, IL: University of Chicago Press.

Herrnstein Smith, B. (1983), *On the Margins of Discourse: The Relation of Literature to Language*. Chicago, IL: University of Chicago Press.

Hesse, D. D. (1992), 'Aristotle's *Poetics and Rhetoric*: Narrative as Rhetoric's Fourth Mode', in Andrews, R. (ed.), *Rebirth of rhetoric*. London and New York: Routledge, pp. 19–38.

Heywood, J., Semino, E. and Short, M. (2002), 'Linguistic metaphor identification in two extracts from novels', *Language and Literature* 11(1), 35–54.

Hibberd, D. (ed.) (1973), *Wilfred Owen: War Poems and Others*. London: Chatto & Windus.

—(1981), *Poetry of the First World War*. London: Macmillan.

Higgins, C. H. (2008), 'The new Cicero', *The Guardian*, 26.11.2008.

Hirsch Jr., E. D. (1964), *Innocence and Experience: An Introduction to Blake*. New Haven and London: Yale University Press.

Hoggart, R. (1961), *Auden: An Introductory Essay*. London: Chatto and Windus.

Hollander, J. (1995), *The Gazer's Spirit: Poems Speaking to Silent Works of Art*. Chicago, IL: University of Chicago Press.

Homer ([1950]1974), *The Iliad*, E. V. Rieu (trans). Harmondsworth: Penguin Books.

Horace ([1929]1991), *Satires, Epistles and Ars Poetica*, Fairclough, H. R. (trans)., Cambridge, MA: Harvard University Press.

Hughes, T. (1960), *Lupercal*. London: Faber and Faber.

Innes, M. M. (trans.) (1955), *Ovid's Metamorphoses*. London: Penguin Books.

Jackendoff, R. (2002), *Foundations of Language: Brain, Meaning, Grammar, Evolution*. Oxford: Oxford University Press.

Jakobson, R. (1960), 'Closing statement: linguistics and poetics', in Sebeok, T. A. (ed.) *Style in Language*. Cambridge, MA: MIT Press, pp. 350–77.

Janssen, T. and Redeker, G. (eds) (1999), *Cognitive Linguistics: Foundations, Scope and Methodology*. Berlin: Mouton.

Jeffries, L. (2001), 'Schema theory and White Asparagus: readers of literature as culturally multilingual', *Language and Literature* 10(4): 325–43.

—(2008), 'The role of style in reader-involvement: deictic shifting in contemporary poems', *Journal of Literary Semantics* 37(1): 69–85.

Johnson, M. (1987), *The Body in the Mind: The Bodily Basis of Meaning, Imagination and Reason*. Chicago, IL: University of Chicago Press.

Johnston, J. H. (1964), *English Poetry of the First World War: A Study in the Evolution of Lyric and Narrative Form*. Princeton, NJ: Princeton University.

Jones, E. D. (1965[1916]), *English Critical Essays (Nineteenth Century)*. Oxford: Oxford University Press.

Kamermans, M. (2009), *Het Zien van het Onvoorspelde – Het Onvoorspelde van hetZien (Seeing the Unpredicted – The Unpredicted of Seeing)*. Amsterdam: Vossiuspers UvA.

Kennedy, G. A. (1991), *Aristotle on Rhetoric: A Theory of Civic Discourse*. New York and Oxford: Oxford University Press.

—(1998), *Comparative Rhetoric*. New York and Oxford: Oxford University Press.

—(1999), *Classical Rhetoric and its Christian and Secular Tradition from Ancient to Modern Times*, 2nd ed. Chapel Hill: University of North Carolina Press.

Keynes, G. (ed.) (1970), *William Blake. Songs of Innocence and of Experience*. London and New York: Oxford University Press.

Kövecses, Z. (2002), *Metaphor*. Oxford: Oxford University Press.

—(2006), *Language, Mind, and Culture*. Oxford: Oxford University Press.

Kranz, G. (1975), *Gedichte auf Bilder: Anthologie und Galerie*. Munich: Deutscher Taschenbuch Verlag.

Kuby, L. (1974), *An Uncommon Poet for the Common Man: A Study of Philip Larkin's Poetry*. The Hague: Mouton.

Lakoff, G. (1987), *Women, Fire, and Dangerous Things: What Categories Reveal about the Mind*. Chicago, IL: University of Chicago Press.

Lakoff, G. and Johnson, M. (1980), *Metaphors We Live By*. Chicago, IL: University of Chicago Press.

—(1999), *Philosophy in the Flesh: The Embodied Mind and its Challenge to Western Thought*. New York: Basic Books.

Lakoff, G. and Turner, M. (1989), *More Than Cool Reason: A Field Guide to Poetic Metaphor*. Chicago, IL: University of Chicago Press.

Langacker, R. W. (1987), *Foundations of Cognitive Grammar*. vol. 1, *Theoretical Prerequisites*. Stanford, CA: Stanford University Press.

—(1991), *Foundations of Cognitive Grammar*. vol. 2, *Descriptive Applications*. Stanford, CA: Stanford University Press.

—(1999), 'Assessing the cognitive linguistic enterprise', in Janssen, T. and Redeker, G. (eds), *Cognitive Linguistics: Foundations, Scope and Methodology*. Berlin: Mouton, pp. 13–60.

Larkin, P. (1955), *The Less Deceived*. London. The Marvell Press.

—(1957), 'The pleasure principle', *Listen* II. London: Marvell Press.

—(1964), *The Whitsun Weddings*. London: Faber & Faber.

—(1965), *Philip Larkin reads The Whitsun Weddings*. London: The Marvell Press.

—(1983), *Required Writing: Miscellaneous Pieces 1955–1982*. London: Faber & Faber.

—[1974] (1979), *High Windows*. London: Faber & Faber.

Lawrence, D. H. (1985), *The Shades of Spring* in *The Prussian Officer and Other Stories*. London: Granada Publishing Ltd.

Lawson-Tancred, H. C. (trans). (1991), *Aristotle: The Art of Rhetoric*. Harmondsworth: Penguin.

Le Page, P. V. (1973), 'Some reasons for rhyme in Musée des Beaux Arts', *The Yearbook of English Studies* 3.

Lee, D. (2001), *Cognitive Linguistics*. Oxford: Oxford University Press.

Leech, G. N. (1965), '"This bread I break": language and interpretation', *Review of English Literature* 6: 66–75. Reprinted in Freeman, D. C. (ed.), (1970), pp. 119–28.

—(1966), 'Linguistics and the figures of rhetoric', in Fowler, R. (ed.), *Essays on Style and Language*. London: Routledge & Kegan Paul, pp. 135–56.

—(1969), *A Linguistic Guide to English Poetry*. London: Longman.

—(1971), *Meaning and the English Verb*. London: Longman.

—(1977), 'Literary criticism and linguistic description', *The Dutch Quarterly Review* 7: 2–22.

—(1983), *Principles of Pragmatics*. London: Longman.

—(1985), 'Stylistics', in Dijk, T. A. van (ed.) *Discourse and Literature*. Amsterdam: Benjamins, pp. 39–57.

—(1987), 'Stylistics and functionalism', in Fabb, N., Attridge, D., Durant, A. and MacCabe, C. (eds), *The Linguistics of Writing: Arguments between Language and Literature*. Manchester: Manchester University Press, pp. 76–88.

—(2008), *Language in Literature: Style and Foregrounding*. London: Longman.

Leech, G. N. and Short, M. H. (1981), *Style in Fiction: A Linguistic Introduction to English Fictional Prose*. London: Longman.

—(2007), *Style in Fiction: A Linguistic Introduction to English Fictional Prose*, Second Edition. Harlow: Pearson.

Leeman, A. D. and Braet, A. C. (1987), *Klassieke Retorica*. Groningen: Wolters-Noordhoff/Forsten.

Lessing, G. E. (1984 [1766]), *Laocoön*, McCormick, E. A. (trans). Baltimore, MD: Johns Hopkins University Press.

Levin, S. R. (1965), 'Internal and external deviation in poetry', *Word* 21: 225–37.

Levinson, S. C. (1983), *Pragmatics*. Cambridge: Cambridge University Press.

Lindauer, M. A. (2009), *Psyche and the Literary Muses*. Amsterdam and Philadelphia: John Benjamins.

Lodge, D. (1977), *The Modes of Modern Writing*. London: Arnold.

Lucas, J. (1986), *Modern English Poetry from Hardy to Hughes*. London: Batsford.

Lyons, J. (1977), *Semantics*, Cambridge: Cambridge University Press.

MacGibbon, J. (ed.) (1978), *Stevie Smith: Selected Poems*. Harmondsworth: Penguin.

MacLeish, A. (1935), *Poems*. London: Borriswood.

Man, P. de (1980), 'Semiology and rhetoric', in Harari, J. V. (ed.) *Textual Strategies: Perspectives in Post-Structuralist Criticism*. London: Methuen, pp. 121–40.

Martin, G. (1984), *Bruegel*. London: Bracken Books.

McIntyre, D. (2006), *Point of View in Plays: A Cognitive Stylistics Approach to Viewpoint in Drama and Other Text-types*. Amsterdam: John Benjamims.

McIntyre, D. and Busse, B. (eds) (2010), *Language and Style: In honour of Mick Short*. Houndmills, Basingstoke: Palgrave Macmillan, pp. 84–94.

Melia, D. F. (1974), 'Review of Essays on Style and Language edited by Roger Fowler', *Foundations of Language* 11: 591–4.

Mendelson, E. (1981), *Early Auden*. New York: The Viking Press.

Mills, S. (1992), 'Knowing your place: A Marxist feminist stylistic analysis', in Toolan, M. (ed.), *Language, Text and Context: Essays in Stylistics*. London: Routledge, pp.182–205.

Mitchell, W. J. T. (1986), *Iconology: Image, Text, Ideology*. Chicago, IL: University of Chicago Press.

—(ed.) (1980), *The Language of Images*. Chicago, IL: University of Chicago Press.

Morrison, B. (1980), *British Poetry Since 1970*. Manchester: Carcanet.

Morrison, B. and Motion, A. (eds) (1982), *The Penguin Book of Contemporary British Poetry*. Harmondsworth: Penguin.

Motion, A. (1993), *Philip Larkin: A Writer's Life*. London: Faber & Faber.

—(1997), *Keats*. London: Faber and Faber.

Mukařovsky, J. (1964), 'Standard language and poetic language', in Garvin, P. L. (trans. and ed.), *A Prague School Reader on Esthetics, Literary Structure, and Style*, pp. 17–34. Washington, D.C.: Georgetown University Press. Reprinted in Freeman, D. C. (ed.), (1970), pp. 40–56.

Nänny, M. and Fischer, O. (2006), 'Iconicity in Literary Texts', in K. Brown (ed.), *The Encyclopedia of Language and Linguistics*, 2nd ed., vol. 5. Oxford: Elsevier, pp. 462–72.

—(eds) (1999), *Form Miming Meaning: Iconicity in Language and Literature*, vol. 1. Amsterdam: John Benjamins.

Nash, W. (1989), *Rhetoric: The Wit of Persuasion*. Oxford: Blackwell.

Nørgaard, N., Busse, B. and Montoro, R. (2010), *Key Terms in Stylistics*. London: Continuum.

Norris, C. (1983), 'Perpetuum Mobile', *PN Review* 32: 61–2.

Nowottny, W. (1962), *The Language Poets Use*. London: The Athlone Press.

Nunberg, G. (ed.) (1996), *The Future of the Book*. Berkeley: University of California Press.

O'Brien, C. C. (1975), 'A Slow North-east Wind', *Listener*, (25 September): 404–5.

Ohmann, R. (1971), 'Speech acts and the definition of literature', *Philosophy and Rhetoric* 4: 1–19.

Ong, W. J. (1982), *Orality and Literacy: The Technologizing of the Word*. London: Routledge.

Osborne, C. (1980), *W.H. Auden: The Life of a Poet*. London: Eyre Methuen.

Ostriker, A. (ed.) (1977), *William Blake. The Complete Poems*. London: Penguin Books.

Panther, K. U. and Radden, G. (eds) (1999), *Metonymy in Language and Thought*. Amsterdam: John Benjamins.

Paul, A. (1997) 'Gesprek met Graham Swift: Een mens is alle dingen die hij of zij ooit is geweest.' My translation: 'Interview with Graham Swift: A human being is all those things he or she has ever been.'], Vrij Nederland, 15th February 1997, pp. 67–8.

van Peer, W. (1984), 'Between stylistics and pragmatics: the theory of foregrounding', in Peer, W. van and Renkema, J. (eds), *Pragmatics and Stylistics*. Leuven: Acco, pp. 291–315.

—(1986), *Stylistics and Psychology: Investigations of Foregrounding*. London: Croom Helm.

Perkins, D. (1976), *A History of Modern Poetry*. Cambridge, MA: Harvard University Press.

Petch, S. (1981), *The Art of Philip Larkin*. Sydney: Sydney University Press.

Pinker, S. (1994), *The Language Instinct*. London: Penguin Books.

Plath, S. (1965), *Ariel*. London: Faber and Faber.

Plato (1960), *Gorgias*. Hamilton. W. (trans). London: Penguin Group.

Pope, Alexander. ([1711]1965), *An Essay on Criticism*, in: Butt, J. (ed.), *The Poems of Alexander Pope*. London: Methuen, pp. 143–68.

Porter, P. (1978), 'Peter Porter writes. . .', *The Poetry Book Society Bulletin* 96.

Potter, D. (1987), 'Dennis Potter en de controverse': een interview met H. Bouman. ['Dennis Potter and controversy: an interview with H. Bouman (my translation). *De Tijd*, 2 October 1987, 44–7.

Poutsma, H. (1916), *A Grammar of Late Modern English, Part II, Section I, B, Pronouns and Numerals*. Groningen: Noordhoff.

Preminger, A. (ed.) (1975), *Princeton Encyclopedia of Poetry and Poetics*. London: Macmillan.

Press, J. (1969), *A Map of Modern English Verse*. Oxford: Oxford University Press.

Quintilian (1920), *Institutio Oratoria*, Books I–III, Butler, H.E. (trans). Cambridge, MA: Harvard University Press.

—(1921a), *Institutio Oratoria*, Books IV–VI, Butler, H.E. (trans). Cambridge, MA: Harvard University Press.

—(1921b), *Institutio Oratoria*, Books VII–IX, Butler, H.E. (trans). Cambridge, MA: Harvard University Press.

—(1922), *Institutio Oratoria*, Books X–XII, Butler, H.E. (trans). Cambridge, MA: Harvard University Press.

Quirk, R., Greenbaum, S., Leech, G. and Svartvik, J. (1985), *A Comprehensive Grammar of the English Language*. London: Longman.

—(1972), *A Grammar of Contemporary English*. London: Longman.

Richards, I. A. (1976 [1924]), *Principles of Literary Criticism*. London: Routledge & Kegan Paul.

Rubik, R. and Widdowson, H. (2000), 'The stylistic intersection: On an integrated course in language and literature', *Arbeiten aus Anglistik und Amerikanistik* 25(1): 5–28.

Rubin, E. (1921 [1915]), *Visuell Wahrgenommene Figuren*, trans. P. Collett. Copenhagen: Gyldenalske Boghandel.

Sassoon, S. (1945), *Siegfried's Journey: 1916–1920*. London: Faber & Faber.

—(1964), 'Wilfred Owen – a personal appreciation', in Walsh, T. J. (ed.) *A Tribute to Wilfred Owen*. Birkenhead: Birkenhead Institute.

Searle, J. R. (1969), *Speech Acts: An Essay in the Philosophy of Language*. Cambridge: Cambridge University Press.

Sebeok, T. A. (ed.) (1960), *Style in Language*. Cambridge, MA: MIT Press.

Sell, R. D. (1986), 'The drama of fictionalized author and reader: a formalist obstacle to literary pragmatics', *REAL: The Yearbook of Research in English and American Literature* 4: 291–316.

—(1987), 'The unstable discourse of Henry Vaughan: a literary-pragmatic account', in Rudrum, A. (ed.), *Essential Articles for the Study of Henry Vaughan*. Hartford, Conn.: Archon Books, pp. 311–31.

—(ed.) (1991), *Literary Pragmatics*. London: Routledge.

Semino, E. (1995), 'Schema theory and the analysis of text worlds in poetry', *Language and Literature* 4(2): 79–108.

—(1997), *Language and World Creation in Poems and Other Texts*. London: Longman.

—(2008), *Metaphor in Discourse*. Cambridge: Cambridge University Press.

Semino, E. and Culpeper, J. (eds) (2002), *Cognitive Stylistics: Language and Cognition in Text Analysis*. Amsterdam and Philadelphia, PA: John Benjamins.

Servotte, H. (1980), *Language into Meaning*. Louvain: Acco.

Short, M. (1973), 'Some thoughts on foregrounding and interpretation', *Language and Style* 6: 97–108.

—(1986), 'Literature and language teaching and the nature of language', in D'Haen, T. (ed.), *Linguistics and the Study of Literature*. Amsterdam: Rodopi, pp. 152–86.

—(ed.) (1989), *Reading, Analysing and Teaching Literature*. London: Longman.

—(1996), *Exploring the Language of Poems, Plays and Prose*. Harlow, Essex: Addison Wesley Longman Limited.

—(2011), 'A teaching career in three chapters and three examples: Why I teach stylistics, how I teach it, and why I enjoy it, in Jeffries, L. and McIntyre, D. (eds), *Teaching Stylistics*. London: Palgrave Macmillan, pp. 30–50.

Short, M., McIntyre, D., Jeffries, L. and Bousfield, D. (2011), 'Processes of interpretation: using meta-analysis to inform pedagogic practice', in Jeffries, L. and McIntyre, D. (eds), *Teaching Stylistics*. Basingstoke: Palgrave/English Subject Centre, pp. 69–94.

Silkin, J. (ed.) (1979), *The Penguin Book of First World War Poetry*. 2nd edition. Harmondsworth: Penguin.

—(ed.) (1985), *Wilfred Owen: The Poems*. Harmondsworth: Penguin.

Simpson, P. (1993), *Language, Ideology and Point of View*. London: Routledge.

—(2004), *Stylistics: A Resource Book for Students*. London: Routledge.

Sinclair, J. (1966), 'Taking a poem to pieces', in Fowler, R. (ed.) *Essays on Style and Language*. London: Routledge, pp. 68–81.

Smith, S. (1982), *Inviolable Voice: History and Twentieth-century Poetry*. Dublin: Gill and Macmillan Humanities Press.

Spurr, B. (1997), *Studying Poetry*. London: Macmillan Press.

Stallworthy, J. (1974), *Wilfred Owen*. Oxford: Oxford University Press.

Steen, G. (1994), *Understanding Metaphor in Literature*. Harlow: Longman.

—(1999), 'From linguistic to conceptual metaphor in five steps', in Gibbs, R. W. and Steen, G. (eds), *Metaphor in Cognitive Linguistics*. Amsterdam: John Benjamins, pp. 57–77.

—(2002a), 'Metaphor in Bob Dylan's "Hurricane": genre, language, and style', in Semino, E. and Culpeper, J. (eds), *Cognitive stylistics*. Amsterdam: John Benjamins, pp. 183–209.

—(2002b), 'Towards a procedure for metaphor identification.' *Language and Literature* 11(1), 17–33.

—(ed.) (2004), 'Metonymy'. *Style* 38(2), special issue.

Steiner, W. (1982), *The Colors of Rhetoric*. Chicago, IL: University of Chicago Press.

Stevenson, W. H. (ed.) (1971), *The Poems of William Blake*. London: Longman.

Stockwell, P. (2002), *Cognitive Poetics*. London: Routledge.

—(2009), *Texture: A Cognitive Aesthetics of Reading*. Edinburgh: Edinburgh University Press.

Taylor, J. R. (2002), *Cognitive Grammar*. Oxford: Oxford University Press.

Thurley, G. (1983), *Counter-Modernism in Current Critical Theory*. London: Macmillan.

Thwaite, A. (1973/4), 'The poetry of Philip Larkin', *Phoenix* 11/12: 41–58.

—(1978), *Twentieth-Century English Poetry*. London: Heinemann.

Traugott, E. C. and Pratt, M. L. (1980), *Linguistics for Students of Literature*. New York: Harcourt Brace Jovanovich.

Turner, M. (1991), *Reading Minds: The Study of English in the Age of Cognitive Science*. Princeton, NJ: Princeton University Press.

Ungerer, F. and Schmid, H. J. (1996), *An Introduction to Cognitive Linguistics*. Harlow: Addison Wesley Longman.

Vendler, H. (1966), 'Review of Essays on Style and Language edited by Roger Fowler', *Essays in Criticism* XVI(4): 457–63.

—(1995), *The Breaking of Style*. Cambridge, MA: Harvard University Press.

Verdonk, P. (1984), 'Poetic artifice and literary stylistics', *Dutch Quarterly Review of Anglo-American Letters* 3: 215–28. Reprinted in D'haen, T. (ed.) (1986), *Linguistics and the Study of Literature*. Amsterdam: Rodopi, pp. 42–55.

—(1987), 'We have art in order that we may not perish from truth': The universe of discourse in Auden's "Musée des Beaux Arts", *Dutch Quarterly Review of Anglo-American Letters* 17(2): 77–96.

—(1988), 'Who are the performers of Owen's "Anthem for Doomed Youth"?', *Parlance. The Journal of the Poetics and Linguistics Association* 2: 203–22.

—(1989), 'The language of poetry: the application of literary stylistic theory in university teaching', in Short, M. (ed.), *Reading, Analysing and Teaching Literature*. London: Longman, pp. 241–66.

—(1991), 'Poems as text and discourse: the poetics of Philip Larkin', in Sell, R. D. (ed.), *Literary Pragmatics*. London: Routledge, pp. 94–109.

—(1999), 'The liberation of the icon: a brief survey from classical rhetoric to cognitive stylistics', *Journal of Literary Studies* 15(3–4): 291–304.

—(2002), *Stylistics*. Oxford: Oxford University Press.

—(2005), 'Painting, poetry, parallelism: ekphrasis, stylistics and cognitive poetics', *Language and Literature* 14(3): 231–44.

—(2006), 'Style', in Brown, K. (ed.), *Encyclopedia of Language and Linguistics, Second Edition*, Volume 12. Oxford: Elsevier, pp. 196–210.

—(2010), 'A cognitive stylistic reading of rhetorical patterns in Ted Hughes's "Hawk Roosting": a possible role for stylistics in a literary critical controversy', in McIntyre, D. and Busse, B. (eds), *Language and Style: In Honour of Mick Short*. Basingstoke: Palgrave, pp. 84–94.

—(ed.) (1993), *Twentieth Century Poetry: From Text to Context*. London: Routledge.

Verdonk, P. and Weber, J. J. (ed.) (1995), *Twentieth Century Fiction: From Text to Context*. London: Routledge.

Virgil (1974), *The Aeneid*, Jackson Knight, W. F. (trans). Harmondsworth: Penguin Books.

Vivas, E. (1944), 'The objective correlative of T. S. Eliot', *The American Bookman*, 1: 7–18.

Walder, D. (1987), *Ted Hughes*. Milton Keynes and Philadelphia: Open University Press.

Wales, K. (1989), *A Dictionary of Stylistics*. London: Longman.

—(1996), *Personal Pronouns in Present-day English*. Cambridge: Cambridge University Press.

—(2001), *A Dictionary of Stylistics* (2nd edn). Harlow, Essex: Pearson Education Limited.

—(2006), 'Stylistics', in Brown, K. (ed.), *Encyclopedia of Language & Linguistics, Second Edition*, Volume 12. Oxford: Elsevier, pp. 213–17.

—(2011), *A Dictionary of Stylistics* (3rd edn). Harlow, Essex: Pearson Education Limited.

Walsh, T. J. (1964), *A Tribute to Wilfred Owen*. Birkenhead: Birkenhead Institute.

Wardy, R. (1996), *The Birth of Rhetoric: Gorgias, Plato and their Successors*. London: Routledge.

Weber, J. J. (1995), 'How metaphor leads Susan Rawlings into suicide: a cognitive linguistic analysis of Doris Lessing's "To room nineteen"', in Verdonk, P. and Weber, J. J. (eds), *Twentieth-Century Fiction: From Text to Context*. London: Routledge, pp. 32–44.

Welland, D. S. R. (1960), *Wilfred Owen: A Critical Study.* London: Chatto & Windus.

Werth, P. (1976), 'Roman Jakobson's verbal analysis of poetry', *Journal of Linguistics.* 12: 21–73.

—(1980), 'Articles of association: determiners and context', in Van der Auwera, J. (ed.), *The Semantics of Determiners.* London: Croom Helm.

—(1999), *Text Worlds: Representing Conceptual Space in Discourse.* Harlow, Essex: Pearson Education Limited.

Widdowson H. G. (1992), *Practical Stylistics.* Oxford: Oxford University Press.

—(1974), 'Stylistics', in Corder, S. P. and Allen, J. P. B. (eds), *The Edinburgh Course in Applied Linguistics.* Oxford: Oxford University Press, pp. 202–31.

—(1975), *Stylistics and the Teaching of Literature.* London: Longman.

—(1980), 'Stylistic analysis and literary interpretation', in Ching, M. K. L., Haley, M. C. and Lunsford, R. F. (eds), *Linguistic Persectives on Literature.* London: Routledge & Kegan Paul, pp. 235–41.

Williams, J. (1985), *Reading Poetry: A Contextual Introduction.* London: Edward Arnold.

Williams, W. C. (1944), *The Wedge.* Cummington, MA: Cummington Press.

—(1962), *Pictures from Brueghel and Other Poems.* New York: New Directions.

—(1985), *Selected Poems.* New York: New Directions.

Wimsatt, W. K. ([1954]1967), *The Verbal Icon: Studies in the Meaning of Poetry.* Lexington: University of Kentucky Press.

Yeats, W. B. (1956), *Collected Poems.* New York: Macmillan.

Zandvoort, R. W. (1975), *A Handbook of English Grammar.* (7th edn). Groningen: Wolters-Noordhoff.

Index